Two Shores of the Ocean was
trilogy conceived while the author was travelling across ....
and Sahara in 1985. The first part, *The Reflected Face of Africa*, was published in
1988 in the United Kingdom and South Africa in two editions; and republished
in 2006 in a revised edition.

Two Shores of the Ocean, first published in 1992, chronicles the author's
journeys in Mozambique to Sofala and Moçambique Island while the
Portuguese colonial empire still reigned in 1971; in India along the Malabar
and Coromandel Coasts; in East Africa on the Kenya Coast, Lamu and
Zanzibar Islands and in South Africa in 1987-88. These journeys seem to be
unconnected, but there was a purpose : to further the author's knowledge of
particular historical places associated with the early history of the Indian
Ocean rim, and the ancient Indian Ocean trading system with its powerful
impacts on Africa. Denis Montgomery had learned that it is impossible to
understand historical events without studying the places where they occurred
on the ground.

Two Shores of the Ocean was the gateway for the author's study of the
Seashore Hypothesis for the evolution of humankind, and the pre-history of
Africa after the migration of modern people out-of-Africa about 80,000 years
ago. Above all, it is also the story of lighthearted adventure in the company of
an old travelling companion in India and his young nephew in Kenya.

✠

The cover photograph is Vasco da Gama's *padrão* at Malindi, Kenya,
marking his visit en route to India in 1498.

Revised edition.

TWO SHORES OF THE OCEAN

Denis Montgomery

By the same author
The Reflected Face of Africa 1988
revised edition 2006

Crest of a Wave 2007
Seashore Man & African Eve 2007
Mud, Sands & Seas 2007
A Beautiful Ivory Bangle 2008

Two Shores of the Ocean was first published in 1992 by The Malvern Publishing Company, ISBN : 0-947993-61-4

This is a revised edition.

Composed with WordPerfect v 14 in Palatino Linotype. Photographs from the author's collection.

African Insight
41 Majors Close
Chedburgh, Suffolk, England
www.sondela.co.uk

Published by Lulu in the United States of America
www.lulu.com
Lulu registration : 979546

ISBN : 978-0-557-01624-2

Semper aliquid novi Africam adferre.
Africa always brings (to us) something new.

- Gaius Plinius Secundus, (AD23-79)

And these are the last marts of Azania on the right hand from the land of Bernike. For after these places the unexplored ocean curves round to the west, and extending southwards in the opposite direction from Aithiopia and Libya and Africa, mingles with the western sea.

- *The Periplus of the Erythraean Sea* (c100 AD), Anonymous.

The king of China had sent valuable gifts to the sultan, including a hundred slaves of both sexes, five hundred pieces of velvet and silk cloth, musk, jewelled garments and weapons, with a request that the sultan would permit him to rebuild the idol-temple which is near the mountains called Qarájíl [Himalaya].

- Shaykh Abú Abdalláh Muhammad ibn Battúta, (1304-1368)

This little isle (a barren healthless Nook)
Of all these Parts is the most noted *Scale*
For such as at QUILOA'S Traffick look,
Or to MOMBASSA, and SOFALA, sayle.
Which makes Us here some inconvenience brook,
To gather, for a mortal life, and frayle:
And (to inform you in one word of All)
This little Isle Men MOZAMBIQUE call.

- *Os Lusiadas.* Luis Vaz de Camões, (1524-1580)

The Author in Tsavo National Park, Kenya
(see Chapter Twenty one)

CHAPTER INDEX

INTRODUCTION

In 1965 I travelled 25,000 kilometres in a Landrover with a companion from London to Durban in Natal, South Africa, along the coast of North Africa to Egypt and down the eastern and central regions of the continent. It was immediate post-colonial Africa. Algeria was still ravaged by civil war and Nasser was the youth-hero of the Arab world. From Uganda to the Zambesi River, overland travellers were rare and the machinery of the British Empire was still largely operating. Rhodesia was on the brink of UDI. In South Africa, the theoretical Verwoedian concepts of Apartheid were still being rigorously applied.

The historiography of Black Africa was then dominated by the European colonial period. The role of Arabs, Persians and Indians in eastern Africa was a footnote. In twenty years the pendulum had often swung to a predominantly African viewpoint. This had not always been healthy and it had been fashionable for some academics to write popular books and produce television programmes which were either biased through inaccurate statements, selection of material or speculations presented as sound theory. This bias was usually anti-European and the influences of Middle-Eastern and Indian Civilisations remained a footnote, or were presented as African developments. Particularly with regard to East Africa, Europeans were portrayed as barbaric and alien colonists contributing nothing but destruction, whereas Arab-Indian influence was presented as a benign and peripheral stimulus to the emergence of an indigenous Swahili Civilisation.

I was increasingly fascinated by the pre-European period in Africa from the two opposite ends of the time spectrum. I particularly studied the 16th and early 17th century history of Mozambique and the beginning of interaction between European, Arab and African peoples in southern Africa. Coincidentally, popular books were being published which gave new insights into the evolution of mankind millions of years ago in Africa and our close relationship to animal cousins. I was excited by all this.

I learned that the Indian Ocean was routinely navigated for about 2,000 years before Columbus crossed the Atlantic, but the scale of this human activity eluded me. I wished to read about it but found nothing to read. The academic pendulum was busy swinging and brush-strokes were being applied heavily: it was an 'impressionistic' period in African historiography. I realised that the catalyst of the Indian Ocean in African and world affairs was neglected because nobody was very interested. Too much intellectual effort was being devoted to the Black-and-White paintings of Africa, creating stereotypes of vicious European plunderers and noble native defenders and thus drawing caricatures.

In the 1970s, sandwiched between my commercial career activities, I researched an illustrated history of South Africa for a Cape Town publisher. I travelled to Great Zimbabwe and other ruined medieval stone towns in southern Africa. I wandered over the land, photographed historic buildings and stood on hilltops looking into African distance where almost-forgotten events lurked psychically. I visited legendary Sofala and Mozambique Island where few tourists had gone. In 1985, I traversed the continent again, overland, visiting fourteen countries in six months and published *The Reflected Face of Africa*. In 1987-88 I journeyed further to see places that contributed to the story of Indian Ocean trade and to pursue understanding of some of its history. This book of a traveller's tales resulted.

I started this book in Mozambique, because that country is a historical vortex and had places of personal psychic power and importance.

Thereafter, it inevitably falls into distinct parts: India, East and South Africa. My travels in India were dominated by the unknown and the immense inertia of inherited culture, and I was overwhelmed by the sheer volume of its people and history. I sank into India and bobbed on its vast flood, only able to grasp briefly at the places I passed by and sniff tentatively at its rich and spicy perfumes. Geographically, I am an African and the visit to Kenya and Zanzibar was a new look within a milieu that was familiar. I was at home and relaxed. I was also travelling with my young nephew and, apart from the influence of his lively character, I deliberately looked through his eyes from time to time. That part of the travelling became more lighthearted. The tales ended in South Africa, disastrously isolated then by contemporary politics, but integrated with all Africa both in the past and in the future. Actions of short-lived politicians are fleeting in the long roll of history however painfully they affect ordinary masses in their day.

Always, I was seeking an understanding of the peoples around the shores of the western Indian Ocean. In my heart and mind I was always aware of the extraordinary *presence* of that benign sea. And what it has contributed to the existence of all humankind today.

*

This book was published in 1992 when this Introduction was written and is now long out of print although a few copies surface in secondhand bookstores. Here it is re-published without changing the general text, apart from correcting a few printing errors and adding notes where appropriate. My original thoughts and impressions have been preserved intact. Most are still relevant today.

After publishing my book on the origins of human evolution and the pre-history of Africa, inextricably entwined with the Indian Ocean, *Seashore Man & African Eve*, I wished to maintain the publishing continuity of my original concept. *Two Shores of the Ocean* was the gateway to my serious pursuit of a grander scholarship of Africa's past.

Denis Montgomery
September 2008.

MOZAMBIQUE - 1971

CHAPTER ONE : SOFALA AND MOÇAMBIQUE ISLAND

A full moon rose out of the ocean as the sun set behind the little beach resort near Sofala. After a simple dinner, my companion and I sat on worn rocks of the ancient coral reef, listening to the wash of waves far down the beach where the springtide had taken the sea.

The lighthouse at Macuti Point, north of Beira, flashed distantly to remind us that we were still in the 20th century. We talked quietly and drank a bottle of rough red wine, feeling wonderfully at ease in the soft floodlight of the moon and the warmth of the aromatic land breeze, scented with woodsmoke from the distant Swahili village. Suddenly, I sensed a rhythmic thudding and heard an occasional splash. As it grew louder, it sounded like a group of men running along the beach in perfect time, and we were alarmed for the Mozambique War of Independence was at its height, although I told myself that we were many miles from any conflict. We stood and stared along the silvered sand to the south where the mouth of Sofala Bay lay. The black silhouettes of uncovered reef and dark patches of water confused the picture, but a dark moving shape came into focus.

"What is it?" my companion breathed.

I stared, my mind not understanding what my eyes had concluded. The thudding noise was louder and there was a bright flash of spray as the shape ploughed through a pool. "My God!" I said, my voice strangled by excitement. "My God! It's a hippo!"

We stood and watched the hippo run by, not slackening its pace, running like a steam locomotive, occasionally grunting, until it passed between the mangrove trees and the ocean to the north. "I don't believe it!" I cried. "I just don't believe it. It's some weird omen."

At dawn I still could not believe it and I wandered on the beach looking for any trace of its track that the next tide had not washed away. I had given up and was walking back when I saw a mark on dry sand where the animal had swerved round an outcrop of rocks. It was a hippo's footstep. What full-moon madness had sent it pounding along the beach so that I cannot ever forget Sofala?

In the late 1960s and early 1970s I travelled often in Mozambique on commercial business, that large eastern African country which spreads along the coast from Tanzania to South Africa. Whereas the Omani Arabs dislodged the Portuguese from the littoral towns of Kenya and Tanzania and took over their precarious political and commercial control in the late 17th century, Mozambique remained a Portuguese colony until revolution in Lisbon finally resulted in independence in 1974. Apart from a particularly good friend, Tito, I knew many Mozambicans well at that time when I was engaged in a large eco-tourism project which involved frequent visits to Inhambane, a sleepy town on the shores of a large and beautiful bay in southern Mozambique. Inhambane was a Somerset Maugham town surrounded by holiday-brochure tropical seascapes.

14

I learned that Inhambane was historically interesting for two reasons. Firstly, there was a low promontory on the nearby coast almost exactly on the Tropic of Capricorn which was called Cape Corrientes, (Cape of the Currents). This was the traditional southern limit of navigation in the Indian Ocean prescribed by Arab navigators, because beyond that point the weather deteriorated, the regular wind systems became unreliable and the strong south-going ocean current carried ships away to oblivion. Secondly, the Portuguese name for the district was *Terra da Boa Gente* - "The Land of Good People". This name appealed to me enormously; what a marvellous name for a place to have! I was told that the great Portuguese explorer of the ocean-route to India, Vasco da Gama, had given the name because of the amicable and helpful people his men had met there in 1498. They were the first Bantu-speaking Black people whom the Portuguese had met in eastern Africa and the story of that meeting, lasting several days, is a model of respectful and friendly intercourse.

I discovered over the next couple of years that Inhambane had an atmosphere of relaxed harmony that I have seldom encountered elsewhere. I was in love with Inhambane and became fascinated by Indian Ocean history. The exact location of the happy meeting between Vasco da Gama's Portuguese and Bantu people on the shores of *Terra do Boa Gente* became an obsession and I knew I had found the place. I engaged in a correspondence with Professor Eric Axelson of Cape Town University, an expert, and read voraciously about African, Portuguese and Arab in eastern Africa. It was this fascination stimulated by Inhambane that prompted my journeys to Sofala and Mozambique Island in those years.

Sofala lies 150 miles south of the main mouth of the Zambezi River and 25 miles as the gull flies across the Pungue estuary from Beira, the modern port city whose railways efficiently served central Africa before the Mozambique civil wars began. From Sofala, before the 15th century, Arabs, Indians and Swahilis traded up the Zambezi, Save and Limpopo River valleys with the old Zimbabwean Empire and the stone-building peoples of South Africa and Botswana. The gold of southern Africa has always been fabulous. It fuelled trade in the western Indian Ocean for at least 500 years before the European explorers arrived there. Gold from southern Africa helped the expansion of the great Mediterranean trading states during the Middle Ages. In the 16th century the Portuguese recorded that there were seven hundred Moslem 'Moors' and Indians living at Tete, the main inland trading town 300 miles upriver on the Zambezi. Sofala was

15

occupied by the Portuguese in 1505 and in 1511 Antonio Fernandes was sent to explore the Zambezi River and Zimbabwe, 350 years before David Livingstone followed. Portuguese maybe visited Great Zimbabwe itself a century or more after the stone-built imperial town had been abandoned and they built trading posts on the middle Zambezi in the 17th century.

In July 1973 I had flown with a companion to Beira, hired an Avis car at the airport and asked about roads and accommodation at Sofala. The pretty girl at the counter laughed and said I must find my way from my own small scale map which she studied with interest. "Ah, so that is where is Sofala," she said. "I do not know anyone who has travelled there."

The road was very rough, too rough really for the hired saloon car, but we reached Sofala in the late afternoon. At first, when we turned off the main tarred road to Rhodesia and Malawi with some trepidation, we travelled across an empty flood-plain. Pale, dry-season grass stretched to a horizon where columns of smoke rose vertically in the still air. It was hot and the rumblings and lurchings of the car accentuated the stillness and wilderness we had entered. The mysterious faraway smoke columns were Biblical. We were being led into enchantment.

The land rose gradually above the level of the flood-plain and the smoke columns were passed on either side of us. There were sugar and cotton plantations and we met some snorting tractors hauling battered trailers piled high with cut cane and roughly bagged cotton on their way to the mill or packing stations. The drivers waved to us and called cheerfully. At a river, we crossed on a simple ferry hauled across with chains by singing men. On the other side there were no more plantations and, as we approached the coast, I had the feeling that we were moving back in time. The road became a soft track of white sand tunnelling through coastal dune-forest of tall richly green trees cobwebbed by creepers and monkey ropes. Still in the forest we drove through a village of square, well-built white-washed houses with blue decorations and palm thatch or tiled roofs. The people did not have Negro features and it suddenly struck me that they looked exactly like the Arab-Indian-Negro mix of the Swahili of the Kenya coast. Some of the older men wore long white gowns and embroidered Moslem caps and the wrap-around *kangas* of the women were brightly coloured. They were Swahili people!

Further on, approaching the river, I followed a faded international camping sign and drove down a track to a collection of palm-thatched rondavels, standing on ancient decaying coral beneath a grove of coconut palms and casuarina pines on the edge of the ocean. A larger rondavel on a little promontory housed a bar-restaurant and there was a ruined building in the trees. We were the only visitors and that night the hippo pounded along the beach and was deeply branded on my memory.

The next day we explored. It was a forlorn and strange experience because the old town was a washed away ruin in the sands of the Bay. I will always remember the particular feeling of dismay that I felt as we climbed over the brow of a sand dune to see a great low-tide plain of yellow sand before us with a small pyramid of dark stone in its centre, surrounded by black specks and pimples, like a rash. A brilliant kingfisher alighted nearby as I took photographs with my telephoto lens. We walked out on the drying sand, thankful that fate had made the tides suit us, and came to the pyramid of jumbled stone blocks that was all that was left of the Fortress of São Caetano, built in 1505. When the tide forced us to return, I searched the rubble of the destroyed town and in the sand I found part of an old square bottle of thick greenish glass, roughly moulded, with bubbles in it. It is my souvenir.

Back at the bar-restaurant in the evening I asked about the ruined fortress and the lost town.

"Ah, yes. That is old Sofala," the elderly Indian proprietor told me. "The new town is on the river, further along."

"Yes, we visited it later, but it has no character of course. What happened to the old town, do you know?"

"Oh, yes! Of course I know. My father came from Goa with my grandfather and he actually went to school in the fort which was still used as a government building when he was a boy, just arrived. There was a terrible cyclone storm, about 1905 I think, and the whole town disappeared when the sea changed the entrance to the Bay."

"It was there for 400 years, then suddenly went?" I said, awed. "I expect it happened with an exceptional spring-tide with the cyclone blowing in from the sea."

"Something like that," he agreed. "My father used to talk about it a lot when he was old."

"I bet he did," I murmured.

Later he and his wife talked about themselves and their fears. They had done well in the 1960s when Rhodesians who knew about their little resort would come regularly to fish, swim and relax in the quiet by the sea. But war had stopped all that. They did not know

17

what was to happen because they could not carry on much longer and the Black Marxist government would be sure to take over their simple property.

"Perhaps we can go to South Africa," said his plump little wife, dressed in a bright sari. "It is the only hope for our children. I have in-laws in Swaziland and in Durban and they would help us."

"What will you do there?" I asked.

"Who knows?" She shrugged. "We will be like refugees. And anyway we will never find a place like this again. ..."

That evening, by the sea again, watching the moon and listening to small, regular waves swishing on the coral sand, we were silent thinking of the dreadful insecurity and ruin for ordinary people that follows modern political revolution. The agony of Mozambique was about to begin. I could feel the ominous dark hand of it in the black night behind me as we faced the silver sea and felt the gentle caress of warm salt-laden air on our naked skin. I felt strong emotion thinking of the pyramid of ruined stone in the sand of the bay: stone carried there in the bilges of Portuguese ships to this sandy land to build a little European fortress to guard against the Arabs from the north. But, whether the masters of old Sofala were Arab or Portuguese, their rule had directly touched the tribal people for a thousand years and the trade that had passed through had created the great medieval Zimbabwean Empire. I guessed that trade was going to cease and a new era was coming with greater destructive power on everyday life than a dozen cyclones. Inevitably, in that place I thought much about history and to break our melancholy I talked about the Portuguese, sitting quietly beneath the softly rustling leaves of the coconut palms.

The Indian Ocean was secret to Europeans until the end of the 15th century. This was because the Arab and Turkish rulers of the Middle-East were protecting their near-monopoly of trade between East and West, a monopoly that had been fiercely contended in the massive and long-running confrontations of the Wars of the Crusades. The human barrier in the Levant to European penetration of the Indian Ocean was supported by the apparently impossibly task in those days of sailing there around the southern end of Africa. All the intelligence that Europeans could gather from jealous Arab and Indian sources told that below the latitude of the Tropic of Capricorn, the ocean was unnavigable; which was true for the dhows of the Arab seafarers which were designed for the gentler tropical seas and the predictable seasons of the monsoon.

For a number of reasons, ambitious leaders of little Portugal rose to this challenge and it was decided that their shipbuilders and seamen would find ways. In a story of courage and determination, over a period of seventy years, they succeeded.

In the 13th and 14th centuries Portugal, with the occasional help of the French and the English, had thrown off the rule of Arabic Moors in a drawn-out struggle and they knew quite a lot about the Indian Ocean from association with their colonial masters. Arrangements were concluded to pool intelligence with Genoa, the rivals to Venice in the spice and silk cloth trade via the Middle East. In 1487, a Portuguese spy, Pedro do Covilhão, was sent off with Genoese help to Cairo, Mecca, India and south-east Africa disguised as a Levantine merchant and he successfully sent reports home. He visited Sofala. Resistance to European entry around the southern Cape was expected from the Middle-Eastern nations, but they also knew enough to believe that there should be no antagonism from Indian trading princes. The Portuguese went out as peaceful traders, but knowing that they had to contend with Arabs, who were the race that had oppressed them for so long, their ships were armed. They were determined to penetrate the Levantine monopoly and their commercial zeal was fuelled by Christian fervour to break the Islamic hegemony in the Mediterranean. It was a renewal of the Crusades.

The pyramid of jumbled stone in the sand of Sofala Bay brought the history of that time close, especially perhaps because it was a ruin neglected by archaeologists and historians, never mentioned in tourist brochures or popular travel articles. Viewing museums and finely restored and intimately described great buildings cannot begin to be so poignant to me. The undisturbed ethers of all the old people were there to provide a psychic atmosphere to breath at Sofala. Perhaps the war in Mozambique must be respected for keeping tourist ballyhoo away from Sofala for a while; there is a balance to everything in life.

The next day we left, and I particularly felt the leaving when we passed through the Swahili village again and returned the grave salutes of the old men sitting in front of their blue and white houses. One day I hope I can return. I have a photograph which I treasure, taken at sunset across the dunes at Sofala with pitch-black silhouettes of coconut palms and baobab trees against a blood coloured sky.

Because of apathy in the past and war in recent years, little archaeological research has been done at Sofala and on the Mozambique coast. In a way this is extraordinary, since Sofala was the entrepôt between the Arab civilisation that settled on the eastern coast and the powerful indigenous African gold-trading empire in the interior of southern Africa. Sofala is romantically linked in legend with Ophir, the Queen of Sheba and King Solomon. Poetry has been written about it. Yet it lies ruined and lost, ravaged by tropical weather systems, quiet under the sun.

Old 16th century maps show that the Dondo River estuary, which provided Sofala with a port, was sheltered by a large island with trees on it that lay off the river mouth and that there were two channels to the open sea. The Portuguese fort was built on the north bank of this wide estuary. To-day the island has long gone and the stones of the fort lie a quarter of a mile from highwater mark. Paul Sinclair is the only professional archaeologist I know of to have carried out a modern survey of Sofala. He investigated local folk-memory and carried out a small dig on land up one of the creeks feeding the estuary where evidence of a bygone Swahili chief's house was found. He was also impressed by the impermanence of the sandy coastland in a cyclone zone and wondered whether the 15th century Sofala that the Portuguese occupied was the original town from where the first Arab contact with Iron-Age society in southern Africa was launched. Sinclair examined the mouth of the Save River, 50 nautical miles southwards, and was intrigued by the possibilities. Apart from anything else, wherever the oldest Sofala was situated, traders would have had to follow the Save River down from the South African-Zimbabwean highveld, through the mountains, to the sea. Silting and changes of the Save River delta could have overwhelmed any older Sofala, forcing a move. There was another possible site at the mouth of the nearby Dura River where there was a small modern colonial settlement on the Ilha de Chiloane. Chiloane was known to Arab navigators and was shown on a Turkish admiral's maps in 1554, two degrees of latitude south of Sofala. Sagara [Delagoa Bay] was also recorded then and there is no knowing how much of the South African coastline was penetrated by Arabs.

It is interesting that the Portuguese were disappointed with Sofala when they reached it after finding magnificent Swahili towns further north. There was nothing except a typical African village occupied by a community of Swahili traders. The village I found there in 1973 would not have been much different. They did not understand how such an insignificant settlement could have been the channel for the gold wealth which was one of the main stimulants of the Arab colonies of East Africa. It is a puzzle for anybody to-day. I would like to think, like Sinclair, that there is another older Sofala buried in the sands of that coast: a Sofala of coral-stone palaces and fine mosques. Inevitably, my imagination is also drawn to consider ancient Rhapta, described by an Alexandrine Greek in the 1st century AD, which maybe lies lost in the Rufiji Delta of Tanzania. They are the twin lost ports of ancient Indian Ocean trade in Africa.

*   *

Moçambique Island is a low-lying coral island just off the coast in the easternmost position of southern Africa, almost equidistant between Sofala and Zanzibar. I do not know when it was first occupied by seatraders, but it is certainly a convenient, safe and secure port on the route from Kilwa, the city which ruled the southern African trade, and Sofala, the base for contact with the gold of Zimbabwe. As a town it was probably founded in the 11th century but it must have been known and explored much earlier, maybe as early as the 1st century AD and before.

To visit Moçambique Island, I drove from Johannesburg to Harare in June 1970 and then to Tete on the Zambezi. Tete was interesting since it had been an important Arab-Swahili and early Portuguese town, but the only old building I saw was the fort of Luis I which had been converted to a prison. From Tete I entered Malawi for a week's relaxation and then drove for three days down a little used road due east to the Moçambique coast. The sea suddenly came into sight through coconut palm plantations; a watery azure plain stretching away from brilliantly white coral sand beaches, the dark pencil shapes of dugout canoes moved about ridden by the black blobs of people. I was excited to see the graceful white triangles of lateen sails against the horizon proving that Arab civilisation had dominated this coast. From the abandoned buildings which had been used as a British passenger flying boat depot after World War II, a long bridge on piles ran out to the island which lay shimmering in the haze. It was exhilarating to smell the salty breeze after days of dusty roads. The people were Swahili, the women shrouded in bright purple and yellow cloth and some covering their heads with black veils. They watched with interested dignity, their eyes boldly following mine.

I asked at the cafe-restaurant in the town centre where I might get accommodation and was directed to a simple boarding house on the ocean side where the fresh monsoon breeze blew every day. I was given a plain room and there was a hole-in-the-floor toilet and shower.

Two pleasant Swahili girls seemed to run the place and looked after me courteously and chatted about local customs and life on the island in a mixture of Portuguese and English. They put on thick rice-flour paste masks every morning to stop sunburn from making their skin dark and in the evening they spent a long time in the shower together splashing and giggling before emerging in clean clothes and spicily scented with sandalwood. One night I was awoken about 3.0 a.m., by an argument which seemed to involve two couples and penetrated the thin walls. There was long wrangling disagreement and angry talk in Portuguese and just as I was going back to sleep, I heard the crash of a bottle and the sound of coins being flung on the floor followed by shrill female abuse from a voice that I recognised. Ah! I was staying in a brothel, the pretty girls were prostitutes. Next morning, everything was normal, the girls greeted me with cheerful politeness as usual. I felt that I was living with history: Moçambique Island had been a resort for sailors for a thousand years and more.

The whole island was a living museum. Only one peripheral road was open to traffic, no advertising signs were permitted, the several churches were freshly whitewashed, the streets were clean and tidy, no new buildings out of character had been allowed. The several thousand inhabitants went about busily and proudly. Each part of the island seemed devoted to long settled traditional activities: there was the fishing village, the market, the port, the Swahili residential area, the Portuguese town houses, the warehouses, a fine mosque, the grand parade with mosaic chips in elaborate design and a brooding bronze statue of Vasco da Gama.

The Palace of the Portuguese 'Captain-General of the Indian Ocean' was in perfect order, painted ochre to compliment the warmly weathered pantiles of its roof. At the northern end the great 400 year old fortress stood firm on its coral rock foundation. I had stepped back in time. I could not get enough of it all. Luis de Camões, epic poet, and St.Francis Xavier, first Catholic missionary to India and China, sojourned there in the 16th century. I was exulted.

I explored everywhere: the several chapels, a convent, the naval base, the fish and vegetable markets full of the abundance of ocean and land. The island was small enough to walk easily from end to end, but I also rode in rikshas pulled by cheerful talkative men. I sat in the one cafe in the central square and drank strongly roasted coffee with Borges brandy in the evening. There were no other tourists, no beggars or peddlers. A man came one morning with coral and shells to sell because he had heard I was there. Most of my time was spent in the great fortress of São Sebastião and in the Captain-General's Palace where the curator showed me around. The Portuguese government had commissioned an architect to restore the Palace and this was done with care and sensitivity. Period furniture was bought, repaired and transported there from Lisbon, Goa and Bombay in India: elaborately carved ebony settees and chairs, ivory inlaid tables, original paintings, maps and wall hangings. Porcelain from India and China, local pottery and glass from Europe and Persia was displayed. In the basement servants' quarters I found old graffiti that had been preserved: scrawled names, caricatured faces and a well executed drawing of a 19th century three-masted barquentine.

The fortress contained an historical gem. Below its north-east bastion stood a perfectly preserved chapel with 16th century graves in its floor, dedicated to 'Our Lady of the Bulwark'. As far as I know, it is the oldest surviving Christian church in the whole Southern Hemisphere.

In the great fortress it was easy to be transported in time as I wandered the battlements or penetrated the cool barrack-rooms and stores smelling of old dust and fresh limewash. Turkish pirates and Omani Arabs had threatened the Island but the latent power of the fortress always dissuaded them from serious attacks. In the 17th century, the Dutch had recently fought for independence from the Hapsburg Empire and they saw the conquest of Spanish and Portuguese colonies as a legitimate continuation of that struggle. It was the Dutch who gave the fortress at Moçambique Island its test. On 17 June 1604 an exploring Dutch East India Company fleet of twelve ships arrived and made a sally at the fortress, which was fiercely defended, so they pillaged the town and retreated.

In March 1607 another Dutch fleet arrived, nine ships and a thousand soldiers, which had the specific task of taking the island. The Portuguese Captain had sent most of his garrison up the Zambezi to support an African tribal ally and a desperate siege followed. The Dutch mined the walls but a wild night counter-attack disillusioned them and they retreated after burning the Swahili town and cutting down coconut palms. The following year a fleet of thirteen ships with 1800 soldiers arrived who were confident of success this time. The Dutch soldiers paraded the town with bands playing and became drunk on the contents of the wine stores before landing siege guns. A portion of the walls was demolished but the Portuguese and Swahili defenders fought like demons, and eventually the Dutch gave up after hanging hostages in a row before the gates of the fortress and razing the town again.

I was told an amusing story about the fortress of São Sebastião by the purser of a trading steamer at the Island. Prince Bernhard of the Netherlands, when President of the World Wildlife Fund, visited Mocambique Island on a tour of East Africa in a Naval cruiser. The visit was non-official, therefore he was somewhat surprised when his arrival was greeted by a full twenty-one gun salute from the old cannons of the fortress. Prince Bernhard, dressed in shorts, was met by the Port Captain in full uniform with his highly polished official car, and driven to the castle. As he stood at the gate to receive an honour guard, he told the Port Captain how much he appreciated these honours, but that they were really not necessary. He was told: "The honours are not without meaning. At last, the Dutch have entered our castle!"

The failure of the Dutch to seize Mocambique had two dramatic results in terms of world history. Firstly, they sailed to the eastern side of the Indian Ocean to find more economical ways of reaching Indonesia, and Abel Tasman discovered Australia. Secondly, they founded a colony at the Cape of Good Hope in 1652 to establish a base and half-way house refreshment station for their fleets.

In 1973, just before Independence, I went back to Mocambique Island. The guerilla war against the Portuguese was at its height and the fortress was being used as a convalescent barracks for dreadfully wounded young soldiers. The sight of these battered young men struggling about on crutches or waving bandaged stumps of arms upset me badly at first, but I saw them as part of the long roll of history in that place always bearing the heavy burden of a strategic position on an old crossroads of the Indian Ocean. At dusk, a military band paraded the town. There was a file of six drummers and two files of fife players; the leader was a tall, smart Black warrant officer and the band were mostly walking wounded. They marched to slow time and the drums sounded military, but the tunes they played were sad and plaintive, hymns some of them, adapted Portuguese *fado* tunes or local African songs and there was a haunting slow march that had the goose-pimples out on my arms every evening.

James Michener's blockbuster novel of the hippy era, *The Drifters*, uses Mocambique Island as a focus for what is bad about Africa's history of the meeting of cultures. Novelist's license permits him to alter history and exaggerate, but I always felt a strange personal affront. I wished he could have chosen some other place to use to expand his political ideas.

Years after my visits, in 1985, I drank a beer in a hotel in eastern Zaïre with a French geologist who had visited the Island a few times between 1979 and 1983 and he told me that the historic buildings, including the Captain-General's Palace, were being looked after by the FRELIMO regime and its army. But there was no commerce in the town and the inhabitants were starving at times. He had been looking for coal in the northern provinces of the country but his mission was abandoned because the roads had become impossible to travel because of rebel activity.

My sojourns in Inhambane, Sofala and Moçambique Island deeply altered my concepts in the 1970s. During those last years of the Portuguese regime, in the oldest European colony in Africa, there seemed to be a particular harmony between native African culture and the 1,000 years or more of influence from alien Arab and European civilisations. The intrusion of the 20th century was often peripheral, to be seen in discrete pockets and everywhere lying on the land with a light hand. I felt an intuitive kinship, even integration, with history in Mozambique that I have seldom felt elsewhere with such simple emotion. The relative lack of technical and political 'progress' and the strength of long traditions had a profound effect on my view of Africa and the purpose of my life. I was almost forced to travel and learn in the years that have followed and only in one other country, Zaïre, have I felt anything similar.

Since 1974, hastily applied Marxist collectivism damaged agriculture and eliminated Portuguese and local private-enterprise industry. The emerging middle-class was persecuted and most Mozambicans of Portuguese descent emigrated to South Africa, Portugal or Brazil. Barter deals with Eastern Europe extracted food resources exchanged for inappropriate aid.

The awful civil war was perpetuated by superpower support for neo-colonialist dogma alien to Africa. The Roman Catholic missions were harassed and hospitals and schools closed. The infrastructure collapsed; intellectuals, liberal-thinkers and traditionalists alike were re-educated in work-camps. Severe famine became intermittent, only alleviated by the richness of the land. Refugees fled to South Africa, Zimbabwe and Malawi, threatening local economies. Peasants feared all authority. In the 1960s and early 70s the country was improving its infrastructure, awakening to political awareness and nobody starved because of artificially-induced famine.

A whole generation matured knowing only insecurity, fear, hunger, brigandage and the breakdown of traditional values, morals and culture.

*

NOTE in 2007 : This chapter was written in 1989 when there seemed to be no end to the dreadful civil war in Mozambique. Within a few years thereafter, with the ending of the Cold War, there was peace at last. A new government discarded Marxism and the social structure changed. But Mozambique remains one of the world's poorest countries.

INDIA

CHAPTER TWO : CHRISTMAS DAY

'On safari', off the main road, near Mysore, January 1987. (Chapter Four)

My journey to India really began on Christmas Day 1986 in Natal, South Africa. Natal was named by the great Portuguese explorer, Vasco da Gama, because he passed by the coast on Christ's birthday in 1497, leading the first Portuguese fleet into the depths of the Indian Ocean.

The reason for my travelling when most of my world was celebrating with family around tinselled fir trees had been forced on me arbitrarily, which gave the symbolism strength. It was the airlines that dictated my symbolic coincidence with the first major European exploration of the Indian Ocean since the end of the Roman Empire.

I tried to fly from England to Bombay to link up with an expedition around the southern coast of India, but all flights from Manchester, London and the main continental airports were fully booked around the holiday, unless I wished to fly first class of course. The cost of flying first class, however, was greater than going to Bombay via South Africa, so it seemed to me that since I was embarking on a project that required travel on both sides of the Indian Ocean, I should start at the end of the African Continent, the gateway to the East for Europeans since 1497. The problem was that the only connecting flight with vacancies was on Christmas Day itself. Thinking of Vasco da Gama, I recognised an implacable quirk of fate and plunged ahead.

A few days before, I had driven out with Miriam, a friend who was going to accompany me to India, to Phoenix, an Indian residential area close by the urban sprawl of the Black township of KwaMashu to see one of the refuges established in South Africa by Mohandas K. Gandhi, who became the Mahatma and an inspiration to hundreds of millions of people in his own lifetime. I had only superficial knowledge of Gandhi and his works, but since I was going to India to taste a few of its many powerful flavours, I felt I should start by seeing where he had lived for many years in Natal, and where his path to greatness began.

Gandhi arrived in Natal in 1893 at the age of twenty-two, and left for India twenty-one years later, in July 1914, a hefty slice of most men's lives. Maybe most people do not realise how long he lived there. What is quite clear was that the twenty-one years that he spent in South Africa was the maturing and tempering period of his life and without that long experience, he may not have achieved his greatness. He would certainly have travelled a different psychic path through life.

That warm December morning when we visited Phoenix, Natal, produced poignancy. We drove north from Durban on a motorway through industrial estates, wealthy middle-class Indian suburbia, along the fringe of an old-established White working-class suburb and then into the strange African mixture of shantytown and government housing estates which is seen throughout that Continent but which is most visible in South Africa. There was no crisp demarcation between segregated areas, as many might suppose. The politically keen eye sees many images in South Africa that are not, in fact, there. As smallholdings with cottages and shacks merged into

28

the vast council estate that is KwaMashu, I was beginning to get concerned about directions. I was almost ready to give up and return to the city to seek comprehensive instructions when we spotted a battered University of Natal noticeboard advertising the Gandhi Memorial clinic. A rough, dirt road led off the motorway towards a conical hill richly populated by great old mango and avocado trees, jacarandas and monkey-puzzle trees.

On the slopes of the hill there were small houses and shanties and, in universal African style, there were people tending small stalls selling fresh fruits and sundry household goods. It was a weekday, but obviously there were many on vacation from the Christmas factory holidays and we were greeted by cheerful waves and shouts from an impromptu bar where beer was flowing. Further up the hill, neat rows of simple dwellings had been built and there were Black women about and running, calling children. We passed a new concrete-box museum and at the top, a gravel driveway curved round a clump of aged trees. Ahead was a battered, formless colonial style bungalow, much added onto, with the black smudges of recent fire damage, gaping window openings and an air of desolation. But the grounds were tidy, there was a line of washing and several people sitting in the shade of one of the trees. An elderly African came to his feet and walked slowly towards our car.

"This can't be it," I said looking about, dismayed.

"It was looted and fired by Zulu rioters. This must be it," Miriam paused. "Didn't you know?"

I shook my head vaguely as I went forward to the old man and greeted him in Zulu. We shook hands and I waved to the house. "Is this the place of the Mahatma Gandhi?" I asked.

"Yes. This is the Gandhi house," he replied slowly. We stood for a moment, looking. "You can see what was done by some ignorant Black people," he went on quietly, without emphasis. "They came in the night. Many of them, some were drunk. It is very bad."

"Who is here now?"

"Only the caretaker and his family. He is my relative."

"I would like to take photographs, is that alright?"

"Of course. But first you should meet the caretaker and ask him."

We walked about until another elderly Black man emerged and we went through the ritual of polite greetings. Two or three toddlers hung onto his trousers, watching me with big eyes. They were his grandchildren, come to visit. The house and the adjoining printing press founded by Gandhi in 1907 had been ransacked and looted on a wild night of rioting during communal political violence a year or so previous. He could not explain the motives, and the nearby memorial clinic operated by the University had escaped. The material in the museum, financed by the Anglo-American Corporation, had been removed. I asked why there were no Indians about, was it not a place of importance to them? He shrugged.

We stood on the hilltop and wandered here and there. I photographed the damaged buildings and gazed over the surrounding countryside. To the west, the vast mass of KwaMashu spread to blue hills, and on the other side the white bulks of new apartment blocks in the Phoenix township disfigured the gently rolling landscape of coastal Natal. Ten miles away, I could pick out the skyscrapers of Durban and the blue of the Indian Ocean beyond. I tried to imagine how it had been in 1914: there would have been no buildings in sight but for a few Zulu kraals scattered across the wild coastal bush, nothing moving but for some cattle and goats in charge of herdboys. A red dirt track must have wandered up to the hill, and in the valley below a steam train would have passed occasionally, sounding its whistle, heading for the sugar and tea plantations of White settlers further up the coast. It would have been tranquil and simple and I could sense the gentle beauty of a contemplative and serving life there.

We said goodbye to the old Zulu caretaker and his family, watching over the birthplace of an important global philosophy, where I sensed the spirit of a great personality still hovering.

At the bottom of the hill, the beer-drinking had been progressing and the friendly waves and calls were more gay and cheerful. We were offered mangoes and watermelons. I could not imagine those easy, happy Black people marching up the hill brandishing petrol bombs and pangas. But somebody had led a mob there for some complicated reason.

*

Christmas Day was clear and hot with brilliant blue sky and I was sunk in my usual nervous pre-departure turmoil while waiting for the taxi. Had I got all my gear properly packed and marked, did I have tickets, passport, different kinds of money and did I remember where I had put them? Had I called the taxi for the right time, was the taxi going to come at all on Christmas morning? I always remember previous disasters at the time of departure. The inconvenience of lost baggage on a flight from Paris to London can be born with resignation, but a missed connection in Kinshasa or a lost wallet in Lusaka is earthshaking. But, the taxi driven by a very large Zulu cab-driver who lived in KwaMashu, near the Gandhi ashram, was one minute early.

The Durban airport building was almost deserted and echoed to our footsteps. There were a few families travelling with distracted children, missing the conventional celebration that their friends were having. Rather than Christmas, it seemed like a day of disaster when everything was slowing down and nothing was normal. The hot sun and brilliant summer colours of the formal plantings of this southern season helped to disorient me. A young White man was at the check-in counter, obviously standing in for the everyday female staff, fumbling with the computer terminal and apologising for the delay. He tied very long strips of baggage labels on my camp bed and suitcase.

"What's all that?" I asked.

"You're both going to Bombay aren't you?"

"Sure. You don't mean the bags are being checked all the way?"

"Why not?" He grinned at me. "There's nothing wrong with South African Airways."

"But what about changing airlines at Joburg and Nairobi?" I asked weakly. "And it's Christmas......"

"You've got to take a few chances in life, haven't you?" His casual colonial accent and cheerful grin charmed me and I laughed. "You've got time for a couple of shots of Scotch in the bar," he went on. "Don't worry about a thing, man." I took his advice, it was Christmas after all.

Flying north over the summer greenness of South Africa before the dark shadow of night covered the continent, there was some atmosphere of Christmas. The British Airways stewardesses had tinsel tangled in their hair and I was given a double ration of miniature bottles of whisky before dinner.

Miriam was concerned about transiting at Nairobi, there were many travellers' tales of passengers from the south being harassed and refused entry. "Wait and see," I said. "It will be all right."

The Kenyan immigration officer sat at his raised desk in the arrival hall, looking serious. "You have come from Johannesburg," he stated. "How long were you in South Africa?"

"About two weeks," I replied.

He leafed through my passport. "You have not got any of *those* stamps in here?" He watched my face carefully, gauging my understanding.

I laughed. "Not at all. I know what to do."

"That is good!" He grinned at us. "So, you are welcome." He carefully stamped the entry visas and seeing that I was watching, he said: "It is still Christmas Day, I think you would like to have the date clear for a souvenir....."

It was one-thirty in the morning when we reached our hotel. A Kamba waiter was still on duty in the lobby and he carried our bags. I was getting undressed to fall into bed when he was at the door again with a bottle of iced beer, misted with condensation. "This is for the thirst, after Christmas celebrations!" He embraced me, calling me, 'brother'.

Is there any way that I cannot love Africa?

*

The last time that I flew over the Indian Ocean was to the Seychelles, the idyllic archipelago about halfway between Africa and India. It is claimed to be unique in that the larger islands are all great granite domes and towering masses rearing out of the ocean whose shores are either white coral sand or peninsulas and capes of jumbled grey rock. This geological formation suggests that they are closely related to the mountains of Southern India, specifically those along the western rim towards the very end where I was now heading. As India and Africa slid apart over millions of years, somehow the Seychelles seemed to get stranded in mid-ocean.

The Seychelles, although a numerous and widespread archipelago, healthy and fruitful with plenty of monsoon rainfall, were not settled until European pirates roamed those seas. In a negative way, I found this fascinating because it demonstrated, by exception, how important the monsoon wind systems were to the early navigators and traders from Egypt, Arabia, the Persian Gulf, India and the Far East.

For more than 3000 years, civilised man has been sailing the Indian Ocean. In earliest times this maritime trade clung to the land, coasting around the desert and rugged mountain ranges that separated the Mesopotamian and Indus Valley Civilisations, providing an alternative to the tortuous porterage through the few

32

mountain passes and the dangers from hard lands and hard men. As centuries passed and empires rose and fell, ships were improved, sailors' knowledge of the wind systems became confident and mathematics and astronomy contributed to a sophistication of navigation enabling men to venture away from the security of coastal waters. At the beginning of the Christian era, ships were regularly calling on East African shores from Egypt, Arabia and India; firstly because of accident, then from adventurousness and later through bold and deliberate use of the wind systems.

By the 10th century AD, Islamic Arab and Persian colonies existed on many secure island bases and at defendable strategic sites at the mouths of important rivers whose valleys provided access to the great African plateau. Arab navigators charted the coast to Cape Corrientes at the Tropic of Capricorn near the town of Inhambane. But this colonisation by Moslem Arabs was not a cohesive territorial empire, and although the city states controlled by local dynasties often clashed with violence and jealous fury, it was a colonisation by traders. Traders thrive on trade and provided foreigners paid their dues and dealt with resident middle-men, all were welcome. Indian fleets sailed to East Africa and so did the far off Chinese, long before Columbus crossed the Atlantic. Indians as well as Arabs and Persians travelled the interior, looking for new products to try, persuading African kingdoms to deal with them according to their established customs and stimulated the extraction of valuable metals and the collection of ivory and slaves. In turn, they introduced exotic food crops, domestic animals, artifacts, culture and technology.

The Indian Ocean is bounded in the north by the Asian land mass, and it is this principal difference from the Atlantic and Pacific Oceans that produces the special wind systems which made it friendly to the sailors of the great early civilisations. Whereas, the Atlantic and Pacific have regular trade-wind belts in the Northern Hemisphere, the bulk of Asia prevents this in the Indian Ocean. Instead, there is the extraordinary seasonal cycle of the reversing monsoons. Between East Africa and India, the wind blows steadily from the south-west from May to November and from the north-east from November to May. It is a great natural pendulum, not precisely timed, for every year the moment of change must vary, but it never fails. It is a giant atmospheric engine that brings rains across India to the great barrier of the Himalayas where it provides the deluge that feeds the rivers of Northern India and Central Asia which irrigated the evolution of Civilisation. On the ocean surface, this regularly reversing wind system carried ships back and forth from Arabia to India and Africa. A similar system in the Eastern Indian Ocean allowed fleets to move back and forth from Malaysia and Indonesia to the east and south of India. Southern India became the entrepot connecting trade between Europe and the Middle East and Africa, Indonesia and China. But the Seychelles Archipelago did not become settled, because its location placed it outside of the regular routes. Lying in the centre of the western system, traders sailed around it and it slumbered peacefully, neglected by man, apart from occasional lost navigators, until the aggressive Europeans began to swarm in.

Flying to the Seychelles at the end of the north-east monsoon three years previously, the plane travelled through a blue and white forest of great cloud mushrooms rearing up, 25,000 feet, from the calm floor of the Ocean, and I remembered the strange sensation well. Now, coming into Bombay in the dawn we were surrounded by the purple flickers and distant flashes of several small tropical storms, the night-time manifestation of the mushroom forest.

Miriam and I were joining a commercial overland expedition that ran sturdy trucks with custom-designed bus bodies around Africa and Asia and we were to rendezvous with their trans-Asia vehicle for the southern India portion of its route, essential to my project. However, the address the company had given me was totally inadequate. A harassed woman in the taxi booking-office did not recognise the address on the paper I handed her. I called on bystanders and my slip of paper was passed from hand to hand. I was introduced, for the first time, to that typically Indian gesture: the waggle-waggle of the head from side to side, usually accompanied by a grin, that can mean many things but is most often a friendly and sympathetic inability to explain or advise.

I was utterly charmed by the waggle-waggle throughout my journey, more obviously expressive than a European shrug or negative shake of the head. However, lost at dawn outside the airport with a milling crowd and yelling touts, the accumulated stress of my Christmas journey all the way from Natal was not alleviated by a series of smiling waggling heads. I was beginning to feel the numbing desperation at the start of one of those feared travelling disasters.

"Come. Come with me. Come!" A persistent voice at my waist finally had me looking down at a shock of black curly hair and two bright intelligent eyes. Rudyard Kipling's Kim was plucking at my arm.

"Why?" I asked.

"Come. I know everything. Just come with me, sir."

I looked to the booking office for help, but I was forgotten. A scrum of new arrivals besieged the window waving address slips and sheaves of ten rupee notes. I breathed deeply. "OK," I said.

I followed the bobbing shape of the boy through the crowd to a kiosk in the middle of the forecourt, leaving Miriam to guard our baggage. Inside, there was a woman clerk in khaki skirt and shirt sifting through paperwork and a cheerful fellow rocking in a chair looking out at the melee of taxis and buses. My champion engaged him in a long explanation while he looked me over.

"Sit down, sir," he said at the end of the story. "Bombay is very big, you know." I nodded. "We are not going to help you unless you have some more information. After all, I am the duty officer of the traffic police, but there are limits to my imagination."

He smiled encouragingly and the boy's eyes flickered back and forth between us. I told him that I knew our rendezvous was a private house with a garden by the sea, and a lively discussion began between him and the urchin. I watched the two of them, quite amazed. The boy lived on his wits as a pimp or tout, the inspector was obviously a man of power in the cut-and-thrust world of airport transport, but they conversed as equals, concentrating on this annoying problem of a lost foreigner at five o'clock in the morning. The English phrase 'Seven Bungalows' was repeated several times and the two heads nodded and waggled. A conclusion had been reached.

"This boy will explain to the taxi bureau. There is a beach called Versova in the suburb whose name you were given. There is a section with some old houses and many apartments which is locally known as 'Seven Bungalows'. I think that is where Europeans could meet at a private house."

The inspector smilingly accepted my thanks, the boy beckoned me back to the taxi office and we were bundled into the next vehicle in line. The boy accepted his fee from me and disappeared like a whiff of smoke to the next needy passenger. I had learned two lessons in my first hour in Bombay: hopeless problems can be solved in India, and people will go to considerable efforts to be friendly and helpful. The boy's motives had been commercial, what else, but the commerce had been mutually fruitful and pleasantly executed.

As the taxi hooted its way through the early morning traffic, I saw that Bombay never rests, and was charmed by a camel wandering politely along a thundering bus-route. Cows munched on garbage tips and there were the infamous street-people still wrapped in their shrouds in lines on the pavements while hurrying feet stepped over them and auto-rickshaws beeped and roared past their sleeping heads. We rounded a corner and I glimpsed the steel grey of the Indian Ocean between high-rises. The driver stopped for directions and a smiling young woman spoke in educated English: "The 'Daria Mahal'? Oh, yes. It is just over there with the green gates." Coconut trees sheltered a large cream-painted house, a mansion, with a high protecting wall and a *chowkidar* on duty. We were told to wait, and the driver who had been surly and preoccupied with the possible problems we might present became talkative with relief. A middle-aged man in white shirt and dhoti appeared. He weighed us up, his eyes taking in the camp-beds and battered bags.

"You have come to join the Overlanders, I'm sure." His hand was dry and limp, but there was an amused sparkle in his eyes. "Europeans call me 'Max'. Welcome to the 'Daria Mahal'! You must be very tired. My people will soon fix you up, but first you must take some tea."

No ocean-weary trader a thousand years before could have been more grateful for this welcome.

Max was almost exactly my twin in age, and his father had built this family mansion the year that we were both born. An English architect had designed the large house with its airy reception rooms and family suites on two floors with a marble tiled verandah at the back facing into a garden of carefully selected trees and flowering bushes sheltered from the ravages of the monsoon. Tall, oiled teak doors with heavy brass furniture opened onto the sheltered quadrangle. On the ocean side, tranquil while I was there, a manicured lawn spread to a great stone wall which formed a bastion against the south-westerly winds that blow from June to November.

Max employed four gardeners who tended the lawns and flower beds in an unvarying and leisured routine and I earned his friendship early on by commenting on the neatness and the quality of his grass: "It is a very great pleasure to hear someone from England praising my lawn!" It was a particular pleasure for me to roam about with bare legs and feet in the balmy air in the grounds of this oriental mansion, listening to the endless cawing of the flocking pariah crows disturbed by the wheeling kites, and watching the fishing boats putting out from the nearby fishing village of Versova.

"The fishing community is very conservative," Max told me. "The City of Bombay wants to build a road through their village and a bridge across the creek to the Madh peninsular which would save many miles, but they told the authorities: 'If the bridge is built the Commissioner's body will lie in the water first.' " Max laughed. "That was some years ago and there is no bridge, so you see Indian fishermen are very forthright people. And conservative. You must visit the village sometime."

We walked along the beach later that day and it became increasingly smelly as we approached great racks of drying fish with swarms of swallows and swifts flying endlessly round and round in an elongated live wheel, hawking for flies. Human excrement patterned the beach and I began to have difficulty picking my way through it. Men, women and children squatted nonchalantly along the whole of the village frontage with strollers passing at arms length. It was my first contact with this Indian habit, so at odds with usual behaviour in Africa. It became a commonplace sight which I was used to after some days and I could only explain it by assuming that it was evidence of many centuries of close-packed urban life. Were the cities of Sumeria and the Roman Empire surrounded by hundreds of squatting citizens out in the open at all hours of the day? Fortunately, in front of Max's 'Daria Mahal' the beach was clean because the immediate hinterland was wealthy middle-class suburbia, and in the late afternoon I watched youngsters playing cricket, the national game of India.

I slept for a time in the afternoon, the special dead sleep that follows long air journeys that shift you so easily from one culture to another, one geography to another. I woke up with that terrible first thought, "where am I?" The maniac insect beeping of the auto-rickshaws in the road behind Max's high garden walls and the gentle grunt-grunt of the rotating ceiling fan told me I was in Bombay. After returning from the walk along the beach, while we watched lateen sails of ancient Indian Ocean culture returning to Versova, our overland truck arrived.

Mike, the young Australian leader, greeted us and introduced us to his co-driver Craig; Phil, a youngster who had just written his 'A' Levels, two English girls in their twenties and two well-travelled Australians in their early thirties. Miriam, my contemporary, and I completed the group. We seemed a congenial and relaxed party and the truck was spick and span. Designed for Overlanding in Africa, it could cross a trackless sand desert or flooded rain-forest roads with a hard-working team of passengers and skilled drivers. Basically, it was a twelve-ton Mercedes-Benz truck with turbo-charged engine on which a specially-designed aluminium bus body was constructed.

There were large lockers for cooking gear and tents, food and vehicle tools and spares. The fuel capacity was enough for a couple of thousand miles and there was built-in storage for seventy gallons of water. There were coach-type seats for twenty passengers and a strong roof rack for spare tyres, non-perishable food stores and baggage. Since there were only nine of us including the crew, we had plenty of space. Heavily-populated India is not the wilderness of Africa so we would not be camping often, but would be staying in simple guesthouses where we could find parking for the truck in the compound and do our own catering.

After my African safaris, it seemed that the forthcoming 2,000 mile journey would be luxurious, but Mike reassured me: "Some of the hotels we stay at will make you wish for your African bushveld, believe me!"

The next day, setting off through the polluted air and endless suburbia of Bombay, after a breakfast of tropical fruits and real Turkish coffee, I was thrilled to see a painted elephant, hung with bright chains and bells, pausing at a traffic light with its mahout signalling a right turn amidst the massed buses, taxis and trucks. I laughed with pleasure.

CHAPTER THREE : THE DECCAN PLATEAU AND GOA.

Bombay was a collection of islands with simple fishing villages when the Portuguese first established trading posts on them. These islands have merged with causeways, natural silting and land filling over the last 300 years and the great city expires on its northern side into creeks and flat, marshy land. In the dusty atmosphere, as we ploughed through the continuously hooting traffic, the yellow bulk of the Western Ghatts steadily became more distinct; the shadow of the great escarpment that runs all along the eastern shore of the subcontinent behind which the massively dammed Deccan Plateau spreads.

We stopped to refuel on the mainland beside the narrow highway connecting India's most dynamic city complex [16 million people] with the rest of the country. Thundering trucks and buses, belching diesel smoke into the hot yellow sky, carried mottoes exhorting the reduction of polluting emissions. The trucks of India are an artform. Most are built by the giant Tata company, but are usually delivered with only a basic chassis and engine. So, the cabs are all different and the bodies are custom built for the goods that they will carry. They all carry about ten tons, and the road commerce of a subcontinent of 750,000,000 people moves on these creatures of a technology thirty years behind that of Europe. They are an artform because of the design and decoration of the cabs. The interiors are fitted out like miniature boudoirs, temples, seraglios or engine rooms. The exteriors are painted with intricate wreaths of flowers or forest creepers interlinked with mottoes, pictures of saints or jetliners, warriors or houris. If the great temples and palaces of India hold some of the finest classical religious and secular art of the world, then the millions of trucks must represent the greatest concentration of folk-art to be found anywhere. I had often admired the decorated and sloganed trucks of Africa, but they were feeble compared to those of

India. A collection were parked to rest at the filling station at the foot of the Ghatts and I walked amongst them. The station manager joined me and when I said we were heading for Goa, he pointed to a group in a corner.

"Those are from Goa. You can admire them closely." He spoke to the drivers and they clustered around me grinning.

"Come and see," they said. The decorations must have taken days of design and execution and being Christian the artists had liberally incorporated bearded Christs, disciples and saints. Fringes of fine chains hung about like ranks of eyelashes, there were bells on the outside and within the cabs. Plastic flowers burgeoned like tropical gardens, the seats and dashboards were upholstered in scarlet, purple and golden plush; little fans blew air and bouncing animals were strung about. Transistor radios hung on hooks and there were ingenious fittings for torches, tools and thermos flasks. I suddenly thought of pictures of maharaja's elephants in triumphal processions and realised that I was seeing the mechanical ceremonial elephants of the common man. Only the speed of the trucks prevented them from having silk canopies and embroidered umbrellas installed above them. The drivers enjoyed my admiration and one exhorted me to leave my prosaic British truck and join them. Several took up the cry, offering delights, watching to see my reaction, grinning at my expected refusal. I felt relaxed and happy with the spontaneous laughing and teasing.

We climbed the tortuous road up the Ghatts in a convoy of labouring trucks and buses, reaching Poona in the dusk where Mike wanted to visit the famous Shri Rajneesh Ashram. It was one of the communes founded by a charismatic 'guru' to satisfy the hippy-culture of the 1960s and 1970s. The 'guru' was practising, more lucratively no doubt, in the United States and his founding Ashram had no effect on me. A large sign at the well-guarded entrance warned us about all the things we were not allowed to do, especially we were not to leave the conducted tour that was required for all visitors. Heavy, brooding portraits of the 'guru' stared at us like a Central African dictator from the walls of a kiosk where we could buy pamphlets and video-cassette recordings. A suave silk-clad American-accented official arrived after a while and agreed to give us a short tour in the gathering dusk. We saw where older buildings had stood and where hundreds had gathered for open-air meditation in the heyday of the 1970s. There were marked paths where the master had walked. I glimpsed the flickering blue glare of a video display in a meeting room with a small group watching. It was neat and tidy, like a military cantonment or boarding school. I saw few inmates and they seemed to be northern Europeans or Americans, dressed in jeans or flowing cotton dresses; ordinary tourists. Gone apparently were the saffron robes and shaven heads. Phil strayed and was recalled; he told me afterwards that he had seen a meditation group and a girl was 'freaked out', flinging herself around in a circle of people seated cross-legged and holding hands.

That night we had to camp. It was getting late, the next town was hours away, the traffic still thundered on the narrow main highway connecting the populous north and the industrial centre of Bangalore. So we turned down a dirt track and parked in the dark in a field of millet stubble. This was an experience that I was used to a hundred times over in Africa and was interested to see what would happen in India. Immediately, there was similarity. We had hardly got our tents up and started to prepare a simple meal when a delegation arrived from the nearest hamlet. In the black dark outside a circle of light from our lamps, the bobbing yellow glow of a lantern approached, preceded by a barking dog. A circle of indistinct figures gathered to study us and a headman came forward to ask who we were in broken English. I felt I was in Africa. But thereafter it was different.

Without our noticing, someone went away and people returned carrying big brass jars. *"Pani, pani!"* ("Water, water") the spokesman explained. What thoughtfulness: it was so obvious, the most urgent need of all travellers is water. That was the difference between India and Africa. Africans are kind to peaceful travellers, it is a universal human trait. But Africans usually wait to be asked, they are shy and reticent with strangers. Simple peasants at ten o'clock at night on the broad Deccan plateau of India came forward spontaneously with the most natural requirement as soon as they had established that we were genuine travellers.

In the simplest possible way, it reinforced my growing understanding of the base of Indian society whether fabulously wealthy or abjectly poor: many centuries of common civilisation spread over two million square miles. And there was another small symbolic incident: one of our young girls, ignorant of Hindu dogma, made the gesture of offering the leftovers from our cooking pots and was surprised and hurt when there was abrupt refusal from the onlookers. She had not realised that unknown food prepared by casteless foreigners was not acceptable to conservative rural Hindus.

41

This was a complex, deep-rooted civilisation, supported by millennia of cultural continuity little affected by the rise and fall of many ruling dynasties.

The next morning it was clear to me that I had the makings of an attack of 'flu. My throat tickled, my nose was blocked, I had a painful deep cough and the draining effects of the battle within my body was beginning. I cursed the snivelling and coughing family that had surrounded me on the flight from Nairobi to Bombay. It cast a shadow over much of my Indian odyssey, reaching a peak of fever and exhaustion a few days later.

Most of that day we trundled due south along the broad back of the Deccan for two hundred and fifty miles. It was a vast plain with a range of yellow stony hills off to the westward, the Ghatts. Dotted across it were the dark square shapes of houses collected in hamlets surrounded by mango trees and bananas. Cultivated in the damper hollows of the rolling countryside I saw maize and millet, sugar-cane, tobacco and a variety of vegetables. There were some sheep and goats and a few cows and draft bullocks. It was poor countryside and easy to compare to similar tropical scrub plateau in Central Africa, but there was one important difference that I marvelled at. Whereas in Africa wherever there is a similar density of rural population in similar country there are no trees left, long gone from the depredation of goats and ruthless felling for firewood, here in India the plain had a regular scattering of acacias. Despite the vast increase in populations in the last fifty years, trees had been preserved. Maybe it was because of centuries of experience and accumulated wisdom that simple people had learned that there is a definite limit to the damage that they dare inflict on the environment.

In the afternoon we began to descend the Western Ghatts towards Goa on the northern reaches of the famed Malabar Coast. I was excited, for visiting Goa was one of my principal objectives in joining the expedition. Vasco do Gama, leading the first Portuguese ships to sail to India, headed for Calicut because that was known to be the main trading city of the Malabar Coast of India at the time. More importantly, it was ruled by a Hindu dynasty and therefore likely to be sympathetic to the Europeans. Pedro de Covilhão, who explored Arabia, the Malabar Coast and East Africa in 1487, disguised as a Moslem and sailing on Moslem ships, reported this intelligence to King João II and the Portuguese had considerable pre-information on the trade and politics of India. The almost unknown exploits of de

Covilhão, who also penetrated the forbidden cities of Mecca and Medina, must be one of the greatest stories of international espionage.

The powerful Zamorin ruler of Calicut was happy to open trading relations with da Gama. The Malabar cities existed because of oceanic trade and Arab, Persian, Chinese and Jewish trading communities had been welcome. Further back in the past, Greeks, Romans and Christian Syrians had established themselves in these trading cities which had always held themselves independent from the empires and kingdoms that waxed and waned in the Deccan behind the barrier of the Western Ghatts. Tolerance and profitable trading was the rule.

But after the Portuguese appeared, once the Sultans of the dominant Moslem trading states in the Persian Gulf and Egypt were able to assess what was happening, ambassadors and powerful traders exerted their influence on Calicut and other Malabar city-states. Portuguese factories were welcomed at Calicut, Cannanore and Cochin but Moslem-instigated attacks were made on them and it became clear that Portugal would have to obtain an Indian trading base by expensive and undesired conquest.

Two thousand years of peaceful commerce was brought to an end by the rivalry between the Moslem Turks and Arabs dominating the spice and silk trade of the Eastern Mediterranean on the one hand and the Western Christian nations of Europe on the other. Sadly, the wars of the Crusades which had created medieval turmoil in southern Europe and the Levant, were inherited by the hitherto peaceful Western Indian Ocean in the 16th century. The Palestinian cancer of the Middle Ages began to spread.

In 1509, Franscisco de Almeida commanded a Portuguese fleet which decisively defeated the combined forces of the Turks, who ruled Egypt, and their Arabian allies of Oman and Hormuz, and the Portuguese thereafter became the masters of the Indian Ocean for a century. Albuquerque succeeded de Almeida as Viceroy of India and established a powerful fortress at Diu (north-east of Bombay on the Kathiawar Coast), successfully invaded Hormuz at the entrance to the Persian Gulf and occupied the Omani trading cities of Sohar and Muscat. This convulsion of martial activity was almost miraculous because of the small size of the Portuguese nation and its distance away around the end of Africa. Thereafter, the Portuguese made the Malabar Coast secure in their interest. They attempted to take Calicut by storm, were repulsed and therefore the city was smashed by bombardment and Albuquerque decided that the Viceregal seat should be founded elsewhere and Calicut never recovered. Goa was selected because of its excellent harbour of bays and twisting rivers and defensible promontories. It remained the capital of the Portuguese eastern empire in the 16th century, through decline in the 17th during onslaughts by the Dutch, to the moribund years of the 19th century.

We stopped in our truck at the summit of the Western Ghatts to admire the spectacular view, before descending to the Malabar Coast. The slopes of the mountains were a preserved and impenetrable rain-forest. Spread below us were a series of descending ridges, clad in tall trees, each ridge standing out sharply against a background of intensifying silver-blue haze against the lowering sun.

I loved a sign which proclaimed: "NATURE BUILDS THE FOREST - A WONDER = MAN DESTROYS IT - IS HIS BLUNDER". We all got out to take photographs and stand gazing into hundreds of square miles of primaeval jungle. A warm air, rich with the sweet breath of millions of giant trees, flowed up at us. I remembered clearly my awe at my first sight of the great rain-forest of the Congo Basin in Zaïre from a low escarpment near the town of Beni, but this view down the Western Ghatts was grander. It was just as primaeval, but there was a difference in terms of people. Beyond this forest, at the coast, sophisticated civilisation had been at work for more than 2,000 years. It was the barrier of these mountains and forests that had enabled the coastal cities to maintain political independence until the Portuguese-Arab conflict brought four centuries of European imperial control. I felt a powerful historical vortex standing there, feasting my eyes and breathing the oxygen-rich air.

The road tumbled down the escarpment through the forest and we paused at the border post between the inland State of Karnataka and the Union territory of Goa. There were armed policemen at the post who checked the vehicle papers before sending us on and this reminded us that there was civil unrest in Goa. Before Christmas, people had been killed in rioting and the borders had been closed. The problems were complex and the newspapers I read confused me with references to local politicians whose roles were unclear unless one had been following the affair. Apparently the underlying issue was a move to obtain federal statehood for Goa which would give local politicians more authority and prestige. However, this prompted opposition and demands to incorporate Goa either into the State of Maharashtra which abuts to the north, whose capital is Bombay, or the Deccan State of Karnataka to the east. This, in turn raised the emotive issue of language, always a sure way of stirring up violence.

44

Until India seized Goa without warning or negotiation in 1961 by military invasion, the official language had been Portuguese for 450 years, but naturally there was a lingua franca of the people. Whereas, since independence, the powerful federal states of Maharashtra and Karnataka had established official regional languages, Goa had not formalised its local dialect, Konkan. Some politicians proposed that Goa should adopt Maharashtra as the official language and this had sparked rioting. Political interference with culture, or the threat of it, is always a fused bomb and self-seeking politicians seem to have a universal knack of causing turmoil and misery amongst the populace that they profess to be serving. (The problem was resolved by introducing federal statehood shortly afterwards.)

Mike and his co-driver, Craig, had never been to Goa and were relying on route notes provided by their head-office in England from the last expedition a year before. So, they were astonished to find that the bridge across the Mandovi River connecting Panaji, the capital city of Goa State, and the north coast, where we were to stay at the resort of Anjuna, had collapsed in July 1986. It was a reinforced concrete span that had sheered and fallen into the river like crumbled biscuit. We drew up at the side of the busy street and Mike looked back at us with a whimsical expression on his face.

"Nobody bothered to tell me about that," he said. "Any ideas?"

We stared into the busy urban bustle with neon lights coming on in the dusk. "Let's sleep on one of the famous beaches," somebody called out. "The hippies did it, so can we."

Mike laughed. "That's what I was planning ... on the other side of that bridge. I'll try to get some information from somewhere."

We parked by the waterfront and Mike gave us an hour to wander about while he tried to find out what to do. Miriam and I walked in an overgrown formal garden to the ferry station where a small car ferry replacing the bridge was faced with a queue of vehicles that disappeared down the street. I was feeling rotten and depressed for there were many things I wanted to see in Goa. The plan had included days for lolling on the long white beaches made famous by hippy communes in the 1960s and 1970s or exploring the winding streets with cafes and quaint shops, the colonial churches, forts and palaces. Particularly, I wanted to visit the Basilica of Bom Jesus with the tomb of St. Francis Xavier, the Jesuit missionary who opened the Roman Catholic onslaught on India and China in the 1540s. There was the ambience and charm of Old Goa and the cultural mix of Panaji to experience. Here was the oldest city of continuous European colonial influence east of Africa to study and understand. All I had read told me that Goa was a jewel of slow evolution. Goa was unique and the current political disturbance suggested that irrevocable changes could be starting which would erode its character and style. There was also my psychic link with the man at Sofala whose Goanese father had been to school in the old Portuguese fort there before the sands swallowed it.

Walking slowly back to the truck we saw buildings with unmistakable Portuguese facades combined with subtle touches of oriental flamboyance, and there were many shops bearing Portuguese names: Fareira, da Souza, Gomes. Some street signs were unchanged since the Portuguese were thrown out. We all gathered anxiously around Mike.

"As usual, there's the good news and the bad news. There's no way we can get across the river without bribing the ferry captain at about midnight, because he's only allowed to take cars and vans. Anyway, tourists have been moved away from the beaches because of the riots." He paused and rubbed his face; it had already been a long day. "The good news, if you can call it that, is that the roads south are reported to be open and we can get to Colva Beach about thirty kilometres away where we can find restaurants and accommodation. It's the best tourist beach in India, they say, about twenty miles long." He looked at me and shrugged. "If we get sorted out properly, I'll drive back to Goa to-morrow for the sightseeing I know you especially want, Denis." I gave him a smile.

"Sounds all right to me," said Geoff, one of our two Australians. "The guide book has a good write-up on Colva."

"I can't wait to get on the beach. I've been dreaming of it all through the dust in Rajasthan." Rowena's voice was excited in the back.

"Maybe I'll still get to Bom Jesus after all," I said to Miriam.

Driving back along the river through Old Goa town I caught a tantalising glimpse of the flood-lit facade of the great 16th century Dominican Sé Cathedral. I felt happier.

But, an hour later the atmosphere in the truck was tense again. After driving around the town of Margoa getting conflicting directions to Colva Beach and ending up in cul-de-sacs, we were driving on a narrow track through a coconut plantation. About every quarter of a mile we came to a road block of rocks, palm logs and tar barrels filled with sand. We had to get out to manhandle some apart and scraped through others. It was quiet and eerie and the countryside

46

was deserted. Peasants' houses we passed seemed empty and there were no lights anywhere. We were lost but eventually reached the seafront at Benaulim Beach where there were a few darkened resort cottages and a lit-up open-air restaurant. A solitary German Landcruiser and a gaily painted British bus with a 'D' registration numberplate (1966) were parked on a wide tarmac apron beside the sand. Suddenly all seemed normal. The warm air, the scent of the nearby tropical sea and silhouettes of palms were a tonic. The girls ran onto the sand and I heard their enthusiastic voices calling. Craig went off to investigate the 'L'Amour Beach Resort' which advertised camping and bungalows. The moist salt air cleared my nose. "It's going to be alright!" I called to Miriam.

We ate a mediocre seafood platter and drank beer in the open palm-thatched restaurant and were jolly, shrugging off Craig's report that 'L'Amour' was closed because there were sure to be other places along the coast at Colva Beach when we found it. Three hours later it was nearly midnight and nothing was right. Every hotel, resthouse or camping resort at Colva Beach had turned us away and Craig, tired and careless, trying to take a short cut across an intersection, got us stuck deep in soft sand in a stand of coconut palms.

"Bastard! Bastard, bastard!" Mike swore in controlled fury, flinging shovels around and unshipping the trans-Africa expedition sandmats that the truck luckily carried. Then he laughed and punched Craig playfully on the shoulder. "It's all part of the service, courtesy of Craig. This is an Overland expedition, after all. The only trouble is, I've not driven across the Sahara!" It took two hours of shovelling, heaving the heavy steel sandmats about and manoeuvring with howling engine to get out of the sand, as I knew it would. We were all exhausted and covered with dust and fine sand that sweat had turned to paste on our bodies. I had cut my hand on the jagged steel of an old sandmat and I was not comforted by nostalgic comparison with similar experiences in Africa.

Returning to Benaulim Beach, Mike decided, in desperation, to confront the owner of the 'L'Amour Resort' and hammered on doors until a round gentleman in a dhoti emerged. I would have been furious, it was well past midnight, but he was patient and kind. He explained that no matter what the tourist offices said, the situation was dangerous. Gangs of terrorists were intimidating the private hotels and guesthouses and he had been threatened several times that he would be burnt out and killed if he took in tourists. There had been killings locally. The objective was to cause uproar by terrorising the tourist industry which was vital to the local Goanese economy. Already, a big German package tour company had cancelled all block-bookings in the expensive resort hotels for two years. He shrugged and his head furiously waggled.

"Is it safe to sleep in that car-park by the beach?" Mike asked.

"Oh yes. It is quite safe in a public place." Waggle-waggle. "Nobody will harm you; nobody is quarrelling with the British here. But it is so shameful. We have never had such troubles in Goa, not in my lifetime, even when the Portuguese were still in charge."

At half-past three we were all in bed at last: a line of nine sleeping bags lay in the lee of our truck. The metallic ticking of its cooling engine merged with the soft swish of the Indian Ocean as I drifted away.

I awoke when the sun reached my face and the red glare of my eyelids penetrated my dreams. Some of my companions were already up and moving about sleepily. It was a beautiful morning. I was stiff from the activity and contortions of battling with the sandmats but my head seemed clearer from the moist sea air. I climbed into the truck to change into a swimsuit and joined Craig and Denise, our young nurse from Cheshire, on the beach. The sea was a pale blue lake lapping gently along the ruler straight line of white sand and I plunged in. It was glorious in the tropic ocean and I allowed the gentle swells to lift and carry me. The last time I had been immersed in the Indian Ocean was at Kunduchi Beach in Tanzania more than a year before. I was thinking idly about that, ducking my head under and splashing about lazily, when movement at the corner of my eyes caught my attention. Fishing craft were coming in to land.

By the time that I emerged and dried myself off, the fishermen had beached their vessels and a small crowd had materialised to carry in the catch. There were women in saris, a few older men in dhotis and boys running about clad in ragged shorts. The fishermen were small and wiry, very black from years in the sun and practically naked, wearing nothing but pouches holding their genitals held on by strings tied to their waists. Cheerful grins and a waggle or two greeted me when I went over to watch. "You want buy fish?" a boy asked me, looking up at my face closely. I ruffled his curly hair and shook my head, but he took my arm to show me the prize catch of the morning: a ten foot hammerhead shark with gaping killer mouth and blood oozing from its gills. "Very good," he assured me. A circle of disciplined pi-dogs watched the gathering of the catch, waiting to pick up any discard. Further away, gulls stood guard. Turning away from the people, I examined the fishing craft and a surge of excitement filled me.

They were huge dug-out canoes, maybe thirty or forty feet long, hewn from forest monsters with sides built up with rough cut planks. Smaller dugouts were projected parallel on long outrigger booms, and they had stumpy masts carrying long yards with lateen sails bent to them. They were giant outrigger sailing canoes. And the last time I had seen their like was at Bagamoya on the Tanzanian coast opposite to the ancient trading centre of Zanzibar. At that time, I had admired them and had been excited for they were living proof of the cultural links across the Indian Ocean as far as Indonesia. Indonesians had sailed from Sumatra and Java to Madagascar and East Africa over centuries and had colonised Madagascar itself, founding the Malagassy race. I had been so pleased to see the dugout catamarans of Tanzania, and now I was seeing them again, in the same pattern unchanged by technology, in use for the ancient fisherman's craft. I hurried into the truck to get my camera.

"Come and see the dug-out catamarans," I said breathlessly to Miriam who was pulling on her bikini. She looked round at me in astonishment.

On the beach, three men were dragging the shark away on the end of a rope followed by dancing boys and a dog, and some girls from the old English bus were preparing for a day of topless sunbathing, their pale pink-tipped breasts proving that they were recent arrivals. I photographed the magnificent canoes and on close examination found small Christian images nailed to the masts. On one canoe there were flowers tied to the wooden Christ and a crow was perched on its head, squawking.

Later, Mike returned from talking to the owner of the restaurant and gathered us together. "I'm afraid there's no point in trying to stay on here. The news this morning is that nothing has changed. We could camp here on the car-park, but that's not much fun and the police wouldn't put up with it for long. So, I've decided to carry on and get out of Goa. We'll have extra days by the sea down south somewhere. I'm very sorry to disappoint you, Denis."

That was that. The others had no particular special need to see the old churches of Goa, and I had to accept it. I walked away, feeling sick with frustrated anger, and sat on the beach staring sightlessly at the fishing canoes. After a while, I focussed on them and realised, as always, that there seems to be a subtle balance to life's experiences. If we had stopped in Panaji or the popular resorts to the north where most tourists go, I would have seen the colonial buildings and relics, but I would have missed the ancient dug-out canoes on this magnificent empty coast with only a few rough guesthouses and simple fishermen's villages. Benaulim gave me a vision of the Malabar Coast as it was before the Europeans came. How could I know what was more important?

Before leaving Goa State, we found a colonial mission complex. There was a fine old Portuguese church, well-maintained and bright in a fresh coat of white-wash, with an elaborately carved door. School buildings, a nunnery with Roman tiled roof, a walled garden, a large old public well, all with giant trees standing about, surrounded a public square. People waved at us and children screamed with delight and as we progressed further along the Malabar Coast, I was enchanted by the greetings of waysiders, especially the shouts and screams of running, waving children. On the Deccan Plateau, people had been friendly, but not excited by us whereas on the coast there was spontaneous greeting and the openhearted flow of feeling from children. I thought that maybe many centuries of peaceful trade with strangers from ancient Greeks and Chinese onwards had created a culture that was steeped in peaceful familiarity with foreigners and found pleasure in them rather than suspicion or strangeness. Significantly, it was that coast that had the longest and most intimate contact with colonial Europeans.

Goa's people were predominantly Roman Catholic and every village had its church. Before it was abolished in the counter-Reformation, the Inquisition had flourished in Old Goa in the 16th century. But the zealots' main target had not been the Hindus who, being ignorant 'natives', were new souls to be harvested. It was the heretical Syrian Church that needed to be taught the error of its ways. It is fairly certain that the Apostle Thomas brought Christianity to India a decade or two after Christ's death, and later I was to see where his bones are reputed to rest in a suburb of Madras.

By the 3rd century, Christianity was an established faith along the Malabar Coast with bishoprics of the Eastern Church served by priests from Persia and Syria. De Covilhão, travelling in India as a spy in 1487 reported the existence of an established Christianity, and the fact that the great Omani navigator, Ahmed Ibn Majid, willingly advised da Gama about the route to Calicut from Malindi in Kenya may not seem so worthy of surprised comment as many writers suppose. Travelling in Goa, I saw Ibn Majid as a professional sailor, not a politician or religious fanatic. He was thoroughly familiar with

50

Malabar and its religious and racial tolerance, therefore he would not have felt personal antipathy toward the European Christians, brother navigators of the perilous seas. Maybe he had a clearer view than his masters back home: free and expanding trade has always been beneficial to traders and merchants and competition forces new life and virility on stagnant monopolies.

The Moslem princes feared that the Portuguese would take away their lucrative exports of Arabian horses to the Deccan kings and would interfere with their control of the Middle East spice and fine-cloth market, so they reacted to the Portuguese arrival with war. In fact, the Portuguese were not interested in horse-trading with their enemies on the Arabian peninsular and there was an insatiable demand for spices and other Oriental products in Europe.

There was no need for war. The Portuguese had no intention of establishing a formal colonial empire in the late 15th century; it was in reaction to Arabic and Turkish belligerence that they became belligerent in their turn. This long-running military confrontation in the Indian Ocean bled Portugal white and caused economic depression and civil turmoil in Arabia. Empire building through military force became tradition in the Indian Ocean and when the Dutch, French and British followed in the 17th century, they came already prepared for war and confrontation..

A Portuguese Catholic church in Margoa.

The seagoing fishing catamarans at Colva.

Christian fisher-boys of Colva

CHAPTER FOUR : MYSORE AND 'OOTY'

The coast south of Goa was really spectacular.

Green clad rocky promontories pushed out into the ocean and white sandy coves lay in their lee. Bluffs spread from the foothills over which the road climbed and there were views from the crests over steep cliffs into valleys. In several places, lines of scrub-covered sand dunes paralleled the shore with lagoons, papyrus swamps and emerald rice paddies sheltering behind. Coconut plantations grew along the shore and casuarinas stabilised dunes exposed to the monsoon. Palm-thatched villages nestled amongst the coconuts, surrounded by mangoes and bananas. Women were planting some of the paddies, flooded by irrigation canals and men were ploughing with water buffaloes.

I saw a number of distinctive Portuguese-style shrines or chapels and there were several substantial villas. Hemispherical Roman tiles or Mediterranean pantiles became standard roofing where the family could afford something better than palm thatch. We had left Goa, but a gentle Portuguese influence continued. It was an ecstatically fine coast, infinitely varying, with a peaceful rural population and the backdrop of rainforest and the high escarpment of the Western Ghatts. If I were ever on that coast again, with the freedom of my own vehicle, I would be happy to beachcomb there until I sighed with boredom. We passed two fishing villages on the beach verges with fish drying-racks as at Versova and they had large sailing catamarans drawn up on the sand which I loved. In extraordinary contrast, I was astonished to see two rusty supertankers stranded in a deep cove, half demolished, with a Lilliputan army at work around them and mountains of scrap awaiting despatch. It was as if with the end of whaling, man has taken to flensing his own marine gargantua in the most primitive way.

We spent New Year's Eve at a Youth Hostel in the Jog Falls nature reserve, where a river falls into a deep rock canyon with smooth walls. Thin white veils of spray were falling then, but at the height of the monsoon it would be an engorged spectacle. The Youth Hostel and several guesthouses nearby were filled with tourists who had come in gaily decorated buses from all over India and had stopped there overnight. With the kindness and goodwill that I had already come to expect without question in India, one of the rooms was emptied by a party who were ready to cram in with others to give us space. It was like the Black Hole of Calcutta with nine of us sleeping together like sausages and I would have preferred to be under the stars, but we could not refuse the hospitality. We had a quiet evening in the cool dry air. The interesting part of it for me was the company of the other tourists. At one point, about a hundred jolly Indians were watching us cooking and eating our meal by the side of our truck and a battery of flashguns were fired at us. At midnight gongs were struck, there were cheers and Mike fired off some crackers that he had brought along.

I chatted to a bunch of middle-aged gentlemen later, who offered me swigs from their bottles of poisonous Indian brandy as they crowded close to me. We talked about how the Raj had changed India, both for the better and the worse. We discussed Mountbatten's alternatives before Partition, and India's close relationship with South Africa's Apartheid theory. We talked, in an increasingly fumblingly way, about the ineptitude of politicians. We agreed that ordinary people, like us, should be left alone and do not need dogma. They were from Hyderabad and were going to follow the same route as us in the next few days. They were all small businessmen and had escaped their wives and children for a bachelor frolic. As the brandy bottles emptied they asked me how we had arranged to share the three women and one lad amongst the five men in our party. They did not snigger, it was a serious question.

In the morning, woozy from the brandy, the night in the Black Hole and my growing fever I declined the opportunity to climb down to the bottom of the great gorge. I had several delicious cups of coffee at a stall on a terrace looking into the depths of the gorge while Mike ate a hearty breakfast of several fried eggs on unleavened bread. Sitting in the sunshine, dreaming, I was startled when a small hand took mine and I looked down into the smiling eyes of pretty twelve year old girl. Without a word being said, she began to paint my fingernails a bright magenta and engulfed by a strange mood I let her

54

continue. When my companions returned they took little notice, although Miriam thought I had been somewhat extravagant. I left the nail varnish on for several days to remind me of the strangeness of my Indian New Year.

Later that day we stopped at Halebid to admire the carved glory of the 12th century Jain temple built by the local Hoysala dynasty. A fluent guide took us round. Thousands of figures of gods, their familiars and heroes were carved from blocks of soapstone, and there was a huge monolithic statue of Shiva's sacred bull. Amongst the deities there were many figures of farmers, domestic workers, various labourers, soldiers, dancers and musicians, and a frieze of erotic postures and positions. Knowing that, apart from one major cult that preached spiritual liberation through total satiation of all fleshly desires, Hinduism and its Buddhist and Jain offshoots are intensely spiritual religions, I had often puzzled about the famous erotic statues on Indian temples. Our guide explained that they, together with the other illustrations of daily activity, were educational in times when only the upper three castes were permitted literacy. Worshippers not only studied personifications of religious and historical legends but also learned the recommended manners of everyday. Erotic temple carvings were the sex-lessons which were part of the general curriculum prepared by the priests.

How simple and sensible it seemed, in contrast to the Western tradition of elevating the church above the mundane and preaching against pleasure. My understanding of the great vogue that Hinduism and its offshoots had amongst the hippy-culture was extended. It also showed how prescribed life had been for the lower castes and how disciplined these ancient religions had been, even into the most private of human physical activity. Perhaps this aspect was missed by many hippies, seeking spiritual and behavioural 'freedom'.

Halebid was the capital of the cultured Hoysala Dynasty that ruled the province in the 12th century, but further on we drove slowly through the ruins of the fortress of Shrirangapatnam where Tippu Sultan, the last of the independent Moghul southern dynasties, was defeated by the British in 1799. Ten miles away was the modern capital of the Maharajas of Mysore where we stayed two days, so we had a brief taste of 700 years of history of the southern Deccan.

The wealth of the Indus-Ganges valleys of northern India attracted many overland invaders from Central Asia over two thousand years. Aryans were the first and they brought the basic Vedic culture that was so well established and dominant that it has underpinned Indian society since then. They were followed, in succession, by Persians, Alexander's Macedonians, Bactrian Greeks, Parthians, Scythians and White Huns in the centuries up to 500 AD. The Mauryan and Gupta empires extended classical Indian Hindu-based culture and entrenched the enduring feudal system of government that prevailed into the mid-20th century. After the rise of Islam, Moslem Arabs and Turks invaded and the Moghul dynasty reigned until the 17th century when, in decline, it was gradually succeeded by the British Raj. Southern India was relatively untouched militarily by all this and the coastal trading cities hardly at all. Armies came south and temporary Imperial rule was established, but the problems of logistics always proved too great. Imperial overlords eventually broke away when they became sure of their security or were deposed by revolting local kings and regional dynasties were founded. Nevertheless, the ancient Aryan Vedic civilisation and culture infused the whole of the subcontinent and absorbed whatever racial mixes were added from the northwest and no matter what dynasties ruled, until the Moslems and modern Christians came.

In this context, V.S. Naipaul wrote in *India: a Wounded Civilisation* (1977):

> Yet it is fundamental to an understanding of India's intellectual second-rateness, which is generally taken for granted but may be the most startling and depressing fact about the world's second most populous country, which now has little to offer the world except its Gandhian concept of holy poverty and the recurring crooked comedy of its holy men, and which, while asserting the antiquity of its civilisation (and usually simply asserting without knowledge or scholarship), is now dependant in every practical way on other, imperfectly understood civilisations.

I understand what Naipaul is saying and I cannot disagree with this very brief conclusion, but I wonder if it matters. Humanity needs a massive civilised inertia to counteract the flashes and thunders of more volatile and therefore dangerous nations and ideologies. With great continuity of calmly and gently evolving culture, India has been a valuable core-civilisation, just as the massive continuity and inertia of illiterate and non-technical Africa has been a valuable core-society on the other side of the Western Indian Ocean. Both these great pools of human wisdom are now dependant, as Naipaul stated, in every practical way on other civilisations. We are now observing, in our own time, the often disastrous effect of the consequences.

Mysore was a good city but the influenza fever was catching up with me. It is famed for its woodcarvings, especially in sandalwood, and we haunted the souvenir shops at different times. The Cauvery Craft Emporium had the most exquisite inlaid work in a great jumble of furniture, trays and ornaments at prices which were extraordinarily tempting. People were friendly and kind: Rowena, one of our English girls, went into a shoe shop to replace a pair of sandals and they insisted on mending her broken strap without charge.

The main tourist attraction of Mysore was the Palace. After Tippu Sultan was deposed by the British, the British installed the present Maharaja's ancestor as Ruler and Mysore was administered as a Princely State. It is perhaps not often realised by many to-day, or forgotten, that there were 565 autonomous Princely States, governed and administered by various Maharajas and Rajahs, covering an area of over 600,000 square miles in British India. In the decade or so after independence, privileges and duties guaranteed by solemn treaties that Mountbatten had persuaded the rulers to accept, were gradually removed by legislation.

Indians are great tourists and we visited the Palace in the company of thousands of trippers, pouring through the rooms open to the public in a constant stream like magical flood-waters. The opulence, oriental splendour and rich colours of the decorations awed me. The circular wedding chamber with marble columns and the golden council chamber were especially lavish while the endless wall-painting in the vast Durbar Hall, illustrating a Dassera procession at the peak of Mysore wealth and power, held my attention. I suppose what I found most significant was the great size and extravagance of the palace. A socialist would have predictable comment to make, but I do not see it their way. People do not resent the signs of power and wealth in their head of state: it is a source of communal pride which all men need. In any case does it matter whether the State is one man, a politburo, or a parliament? It is how the state is governed that matters in the end. In the West we are far too smugly sure of our own system which has spawned some extraordinarily wicked governments.

That evening my fever increased its grip. I had no energy and I had to write my diary and think about the things I was experiencing with a great effort of will. So I did not appreciate the visit to 'Ooty' in the next two days as much as I could have done. Ootacamund was the British hill-station for the government of Madras Province and resort for South India, high in the Nilgri Hills, at the end of the Western Ghatts. Climbing up to 7500 feet from the dry Deccan plateau our labouring truck passed through the glistening neatness of tea gardens and coffee plantations surrounding workers' villages. The people looked different: hairy with rough black skins and ugly lined faces, mountain people descended from the Dravidian race who occupied the subcontinent before the Central Asiatic invasions and who were of the same ancient neolithic race as the aboriginals of Malaysia, Indonesia and Australia.

In 'Ooty' I looked in vain for the publicised fading glory of lanes of well-preserved Kentish and Surrey bungalows languishing in neat cottage gardens of rambling roses and honeysuckle. The quite substantial town of tenements and rows of small shops rested in a bowl around the flat area of the decayed race-course. The lanes in the 'English' part of town were potholed and dusty, the gardens overgrown or dead.

We all put up at the YWCA (which nowadays accommodates both men and women) lying on the hillside above the race-course, and it had some of the charm I was seeking. It was a double-storied rectangular block with simple rooms furnished with squeaking iron bedsteads, wardrobes with groaning doors and armchairs with faded chintz-covered cushions. A long-disused fireplace with dark mantelpiece gave the room an immediate feel for the 'good old days', and I sniffed the stale air smelling of slightly damp, clean linen and dusty curtains almost with pleasure before opening the ill-fitting windows to let in the thin dry air of the mountains and to watch the sunshine sharpen and the shadows turn very black as evening approached. The tall eucalyptus and fir trees spreading their scents from the hillsides above reminded me of the South African highveld and sound had that well-remembered flatness of altitude. The YWCA was a success for me as I climbed into bed early, lit by a dim 40 watt bulb.

There was a book with stained and faded linen covers on the window sill; it was T.E.Lawrence's *Seven Pillars of Wisdom*, and the flyleaf was inscribed: 'Eliza Bingham, 1943'. I lay, feeling weak and fevered, clasping that book in a clammy hand, listening to the murmuring talk of my companions eating dinner around our truck outside the window, and was transported back forty years. As I slipped into sleep, I wondered about Eliza, who had maybe slept in

58

that room in the same squeaky bed, and her choice of stirring literature. Had she chosen it romantically when going off to wartime India, or had a parent, aunt or fiance given it to her as a parting gift for a young, adventurous girl? Why had she left it behind? Where was Eliza now?

Early in the morning there was hoar frost on the race-course and the icy thin air cleared my blocked sinuses. The fever had finally left me in the night and I joined the rest of our party on the narrow-gauge train from 'Ooty' down the mountain to Coonoor. The journey was a submergence in nostalgic Raj and superb natural beauty. We had awful milky coffee in the bare waiting room before boarding the train whose steam engine hissed oilily and belched sulphurous smoke. The line ran through upland meadows and pine trees at first. There were even some of those English bungalows except that the brick and stone originals with tiled roofs had ugly cement block and corrugated iron additions extending them. But I did see some roses.

Coming to the edge of the mountain, we looked down several thousand feet over mist-wreathed tea gardens into the haze of the lowlands towards the Indian Ocean. There were several villages below us, looking very like their counterparts in the south of France and Italy from the heights, with their crooked streets, tiled roofs and churches with stone bell towers or Hindu temples with their southern style gopurams which looked similar at a distance. I noticed that none of the villages had both church and temple and it was obvious that the people segregated themselves into one religion or the other. We stopped for long waits at the few stations which were brightly painted and other passengers got out to stroll and puff cigarettes in the sunshine. Cows and horses munched the grass in the station yards and encroached on the line. One of the stations was named Wellington. Further down, we entered a deep gorge, whose sides were too precipitous for agriculture and as far as the foot of the mountain there was dense tropical rain-forest with smooth slabs of grey granite dome showing in patches.

The narrow, twisting road and the incredible little railway had been superbly engineered and built to follow this gorge up to the 7500 feet heights of the Nilgris in the 19th century, solely to provide relief from summer heat for the British officers of Madras Province and their families. They were monuments to arrogant power with more imaginative boldness than any Maharaja's palace. Anyone can build palaces. But the road and railway were still being used, almost unchanged, a century and more later. Maybe, they were symbols of what Naipaul had been hinting at when he wrote about the stagnation of Indian Civilisation compared to the virility of others.

Mysore - the Maharajah's Palace

CHAPTER FIVE : IN IBN BATUTA'S FOOTSTEPS

On the way to Cochin on the coast from the foot of the Nilgri Hills, we passed through two cities on a road that was once again a thundering highway traversing the endless village of urban ribbon development. Coimbatore was a forgettable dense mass of traffic and people but Trichur intrigued me considerably with its massive red-walled fort in the centre with a great Chinese-style main gateway. We had no time to stop, but the gateway tuned my eyes to notice an increasing number of Chinese influenced architectural features on the southern Malabar Coast and reminded me of the many centuries during which this part of India engaged in trade with China.

Regarding ancient trade in the Indian Ocean, *The Periplus of the Erythraean Sea* is an important work. It was written as a guide-book by an anonymous Alexandrian Greek about 100 A.D. Of this coast it says:

> Mouziris [the modern Cranganore, where Thomas the Apostle probably landed], belonging to the same kingdom is a flourishing place with ships from Ariake [inland of the Gulf of Cambay] coming to it, and also Greeks. ...

Twelve hundred years later, Ibn Batuta, the famous Moroccan traveller in Asia and Africa, was writing:

> It is at this town [Panderani, a few miles north of Calicut] that the Chinese vessels pass the winter. ... We stopped at the port of Calicut, in which there were at the time thirteen Chinese vessels, and disembarked.

To-day, there appeared to be a considerable residue of Chinese architectural style as we travelled towards the end of India: especially in roofs with their upward-curving gables and carved decorations of a general delicacy of design. I saw a number of modern, middle-class villas in that style which was not especially exceptional, they could also be seen in Los Angeles, Sydney or Cape Town, but I noted older commercial buildings and houses and a mix with Portuguese style in some old churches. The occurrence of Buddhist temples by the roadside south of Cochin reinforced a Far-Eastern pervasion which I guessed at and was confirmed by the conclusions of historians. Buddhism branched away from the Hindu mainstream in the 4th century BC and was an important cultural event in north-west India. Its spreading path was over the Himalayas to Tibet and China where it gained most adherents, because Buddhists were persecuted in India by Hindu purists.

Its reinforcement on the south-west coast by prolonged contact with China is an interesting example of a cultural full circle. South Indian cuisine was also similar to Chinese, it is delicate and relies on simple lightly-spiced vegetable and soupy dishes eaten with many variations of fried rice. Of course, the natural ingredients of any region provide the base of its cuisine, but I found many interesting ways of cooking rice and vegetables and I kept thinking of China. Southern cuisine is vegetarian and this has religious roots in the purer forms of Hinduism, less affected by Persian and Arab influences from the north, and by the strictness of Jainism and Buddhism both of which are opposed to violence against all forms of animal life.

As we travelled more deeply along the southern Malabar Coast, I was finding a necessarily superficial look at its history and culture increasingly fascinating. Apart from anything else, the people dressed differently: plain colours or simple checks and plaids rather than more elaborately woven or printed designs. White predominated. Many men wore lungis, either to the ankle or folded to a length just above the knee, replacing the universal western slacks or jeans and the occasional dhoti of Bombay and the Deccan states.

EXTRACT FROM MY DIARY : 5 JANUARY 1987 :

Approaching the coast at Cochin, we crossed several wide inland waterways that have provided communications from Calicut as far as Trivandrum for many centuries. Built-up areas spreading. A number of Christian schools: St.Anthony seems a favourite along with St. Joseph, and naturally the Portuguese, St.Francis Xavier. Amazing designs of some Roman Catholic churches become common with elaborate filigree and decorated facades (a definitive

Indo-Portuguese style?) Other modern ones have extraordinary steeples with several life-size effigies of Christ, Apostles and Saints on platforms. I presume these churches are a modern development of Dravidian styled Orthodox Syrian churches: a sort of Hindu-Christian cultural mix evolved over nineteen hundred years? Fascinating. Beginning to see Buddhist temples. Mosques and conventional Hindu temples about but churches of both orthodoxies dominate.

Through 'old Cochin', an area of higgledy-piggledy houses and warehouses in vaguely Portuguese and later European colonial styles, then into modern suburb of Ernakulum. Drove around looking for our hotel. Got stuck in a narrow street of small shops and litter of vehicles. Everybody cheerful and grinning at us: lots of shouted advice and laughter with heads waggling and hands waving. Malabar Coast people really are very friendly! The height of our truck nearly brought down telephone wires, Phil got on the roof with a shovel guiding and lifting the wires, (imagine the crackling phones and cut-off conversations...) We knocked down a Communist election poster and collected a line of Party flags strung across the alley with our roof-rack: nobody seemed concerned. Auto-rikshas were pushed almost into shops to clear a way for us. ... Eventually Mike found our small, modern concrete-box hotel, Biju's Guest House, simple and clean, and we are allocated shared rooms. Water comes out of the taps - excellent!

We all walked some distance to a modern, air-conditioned restaurant where I had a large plate of highly-spiced Szechuan stewed beef (for Christian and Moslem visitors) and prawn fried rice for Rs25.00 [about £1.40]. I'm still feeling exhausted from the fever so fell into bed and slept well until awoken by mosquitoes. Put on ceiling fan and slept again until a cannon fired at 04.15 am and loud temple chanting began nearby. A muezzin joined in from a nearby Mosque at 05.15 am. I still slept off and on until half-past seven when four cannon shots were fired. Cochin is a funny city. I'm sure I will love it. ...

We did our formal sightseeing in Cochin by courtesy of the local government tourist organisation. The double-decked motor launch left from the Sea Lord Jetty, a marvellous Indian name, and cruised the extensive harbour, stopping four times for us to get out and be rushed along by our authoritative tour-guide, a large lady with gold pins in her nose wearing a plain maroon sari. The harbour was an excellent one, and it is obvious why it had been an ocean port and trading centre for so long. It was at the centre of the series of lagoons, lakes and connecting rivers and canals that stretch along nearly two hundred miles of flat coast lands from near Calicut to Trivandrum, where rocky hills come down to the sea. At several places these internal waterways burst through to the ocean to spill the massive monsoon rainfall and it was where these breaks were wide and deep enough for ships to use them easily that the ancient and modern ports were situated. Cochin harbour had a wide entrance, suitable for to-day's large container ships and tankers, and the extended and complicated estuary had plenty of room.

Sailing the harbour were long canoe-shaped, roughly-built cargo vessels propelled mainly by the poles of two of the crew and therefore they had to navigate with care, keeping to shallow water in contrast to most ships which prefer the deeps. A few did carry stumpy masts on which they hoisted simple square sails made from palm matting and I watched them, dredging my memory, until I suddenly recalled where I had seen similar craft before. It was on the Niger River in West Africa, and I have a photograph of one near Onitsha taken in 1961, identical in every detail even to a boy crouching over a charcoal fire on the deck, preparing a meal. Scattered across the estuary's milky blue mirror, small dugout fishing canoes crawled like water beetles while one of the two occupants periodically stood to toss his throw net, another image that is repeated across the world.

Beyond the modern quays of Willingdon Island lay the promontory that divided the harbour from the ocean and on it were the places I had come so far to see. The waterside there was clad with old wharfs and lines of godowns, low lime-washed buildings with red tiled roofs discoloured by the mould of many monsoons. I could imagine Chinese junks, Indian thonis and Arab dhows parked there with armies of coolies loading and discharging them in the 15th century, before being supplanted by tall-pooped Portuguese galleons, then Dutch and finally fat English Indiamen as the three European nations took over each other's eastern trading systems. There were a few ugly motor-barges there that day: the style of Western technology can never compete with the aesthetics of bygone days when man relied more on nature. Our launch pulled in at the passenger jetty at Mattancherry where we debarked to be hurried through the old Portuguese Palace and the famed Jewish quarter. The Mattancherry Palace was given by the Portuguese to the Rajah of Cochin as part of a deal they made to extend their trading base in the middle of the 16th century. But there is little to show of that time, because the Dutch renovated it after throwing the Portuguese out of Ceylon and India south of Goa during their wars with the Hapsburg Empire in the early 17th century. It is a dull palace, not much more than a large house, with a dour northern European look to it. But its history is real enough and I caught a whiff of it in the brief time we were allowed. There were particularly fine murals and some intricately carved woodwork, but it was hopeless trying to study them in the rush of bare-footed tourists racing through in ten minutes.

I found Jewtown had a more powerful ambience. The narrow street with tile-roofed shops and godowns crowding it was blocked by a large handcart loaded with sacks of sugar and rice that a gang of sweating turbanned men wearing lungis were busy with. I stopped to photograph the timeless scene. Further on, though, there was a metal sign with the legend, *J.E.COHEN : TAX ACCOUNTANT*, on it. Back to the 20th century, I thought, then on reflection realised that it was not so. Probably J.E.Cohen's ancestor had been practising there a thousand years before, because the Jews have been in Cochin that long and taxes are endemic to civilisation. A white-haired Jewish elder showed us over the synagogue [1568] with blue handpainted Cantonese floor tiles, finely carved sandalwood furniture and the calfskin Torah on wooden spindles. Our Indian guide told me that there were only seven Jewish families with thirty members left in the community, but the evidence of resilience and extraordinary racial integrity of the Jews amazed me once again in Cochin. Standing in the little synagogue, surrounded by the ancient trading town, I was conscious of the simplicity and endurance of that racial strength.

Fort Cochin was at the end of the promontory. The rusty steel slab of another Russian container ship from Black Sea ports slipped through the harbour entrance as we bustled in to the jetty. Coconut palms rustled and casuarinas sighed in the sea breeze. There were no taxis or buses parked around the few soft drink stands and curio stalls and I was suddenly grateful for the space and relative quiet at the end of the land. The only activity was around the line of Chinese fishing machines built along the edge of the channel. These incredible structures are correctly a much-publicised tourist attraction and often quoted as the definitive evidence of powerful Chinese influence on south India. They were massive arrangements of cantilevered rough-hewn spars fastened by a web of coconut fibre ropes from which a large net was suspended. The finely balanced machine was tilted by the three or four operators to lower the net into the tidal currents and after an interval decided by long experience, the machine was tilted back again, raising the net out of the water before being hauled to shore. I watched two or three operations of this ancient activity, delighted as always with the ease and lack of physical effort with which all old, well-tried equipment is used. Near the rank of fishing machines, the remains of the original Portuguese fort could be seen, built on and extended by successive regimes, and I was sad to find a granite plinth, with a typically Portuguese inscription with words running together, lying in an open area half buried in the sandy ground. I picked out a name, which looked like Gofre de Suamo, and a date, 1581.

The principal monument at Fort Cochin was the church of St.Francis, built by Portuguese Franciscans about 1505, which makes it probably the earliest Roman Catholic church in the East. It stood some distance along a quiet road shaded by great old trees and lined by double-storied bungalows with wide eaves and verandahs to combat the monsoon, belonging to the British Raj. The church was mould streaked and not as attractive or architecturally authentic as the many Portuguese churches I had seen elsewhere on the coast. The Dutch had rebuilt the facade during restoration in 1779 and it had subsequently been maintained by the Anglican Church after 1795 when the British took over the Dutch colonies in India. It had a forlorn air and I found it sad. The typical colonial whitewashed 'Cape Dutch' gable, at home at the Cape of Good Hope in South Africa, seemed out of place there. Within, it was gloomy and shabby; the Anglican Church of South India was obviously not particularly active and I wondered if it should not be given back to the Catholics for the sake of historical posterity.

Vasco da Gama died of illness in Cochin in 1524 whilst he was visiting in his capacity of Viceroy of India and we were shown a marked rectangle in the floor of St.Francis' church where he had been buried. Da Gama has always fascinated me and I tried to get excited about that plain polished slab in the floor, but the emotion I sought eluded me. It was the seediness of the church that may have caused it, no doubt, but the psychic reason had to be the fact that Da Gama's brother had exhumed the hero's corpse and shipped it back to Portugal to have it entombed in greater style at his home. A coach load of hot and bored American and German tourists arrived as I walked away, and I preferred studying the fine official homes of the British Raj secluded within gardens of brilliant bougainvillaea, frangipani, giant old mangoes and banyan trees. I seemed to pick up more live vibrations from them.

On the way back to the Sea Lord Jetty, we stopped at tiny Gundu Island where a government-supported community made matting products from coconut fibre with traditional wooden handlooms in a complex of simple sheds scattered amongst palms and casuarinas. From there I studied two Indian thonis at anchor nearby. The thoni is the traditional commercial sailing vessel of South India and they still operated up and down the Coromandel and Malabar Coasts to Sri Lanka and the Nicobar and Andaman Islands. They used to sail to East Africa and Vasco da Gama's fleet anchored alongside four of them when he arrived at Malindi seeking a pilot to Calicut. Thonis are long, slim vessels, considerably larger than a Thames barge, and usually carry two or three short masts on which are hoisted massive, long jointed yards for lateen sails similar to Arab dhows. But thonis also carry an additional suit of sails spread on subsidiary yards, set on stays or sprouting from the bows to catch tropical zephyrs when the monsoon is not blowing. The ones I saw in Cochin did not have the rakishness of Arab dhows, they were bluntly designed for maximum cargo and I guessed that as they have retreated from trans-oceanic voyaging, they have been coarsened by the need to be more economic in a coastal trade. However, like all traditional sailing ships the purity of their lines could not be disguised. Sitting in the shade of an irregular tiled roof on the verandah of a coir mat store, watching those ancient craft, I felt the emotion and excitement I had been seeking.

I knew that Hindus lose their caste by travelling on the sea and so I had wondered how the nation had built up a great medieval maritime trade. After understanding the culture a little better by travelling there, it became clearer. There are four main castes: very roughly, the Brahmins or intellectuals and priests, the warriors who were usually the rulers and administrators, the commercial castes who traded, lent money and often organised craft guilds, and the peasants who were divided into other workers' and artisans' sub castes as the civilisation became more technical and complex. These castes had depreciating rights and privileges down the scale. Then there were the outcastes with no rights or privileges. The name is precisely appropriate, and it was one of Gandhi's crusades to attempt to upgrade their status in society. From time to time, over centuries, 'upwardly mobile' social and working groups were able to gain some recognition for sub castes with finely graduated improved status by exerting their economic or political power and by forming craft guilds in the cities.

Sailors and fishermen, because of the taboo on sailing the seas are, by clear definition, outcastes and this explained to my satisfaction the almost belligerent conservatism and cohesiveness of the modern fishing villages we visited, starting with the one at Versova on the fringes of modern metropolitan Bombay. Because fishermen handle produce that all castes eat, they have to be allied to the peasant caste, however, and the subtlety of the socio-theological convolutions are typical of the complication posed by this ancient religion to Westerners who try to see everything in black-and-white. I learned that Tamils have a name for the sailors' sub-caste: Paravan. However, the low status and lack of recognition of the great worth of seamen by the Hindu religion, a culture and faith that was created by Central Asian Aryans and evolved amongst inland people, had two obvious and major results. Firstly, because of the lack of status and prohibition on literacy, sailors and fishermen were easily recruited by foreign religions; it is no accident that Christianity gained such a powerful hold on the Malabar Coast from the 1st century. Secondly as soon as the Moslem Arabs became more aggressively active in the Indian Ocean from the 9th century, they captured most of the Indian trade from Indian ships because Hindu Princes did not have navies. The military caste could not sail the oceans without losing caste. This was reinforced by a general purifying Hindu movement at about the same time, in reaction to the onslaught of Islam. India increasingly became the mid-ocean entrepot rather than participating in all aspects of trade and the tolerance of the Malabar Hindu rulers of foreign communities sustained this role until the Moslem-Portuguese conflicts.

Interesting simple evidence of this sensitivity to international trade is given by Ibn Batuta:

> I saw the infidel (Hindu), the sultan of Calicut, wearing a large white cloth round his waist [a lungi] and a small turban, bare-footed, with the parasol carried by a slave over his head and a fire lit in front of him on the beach; his police officers were beating the people to prevent them from plundering what the sea had cast up. In all the lands of Mulaybar, except in this one land alone, it is the custom that whenever a ship is wrecked all that is taken from it belongs to the treasury. At Calicut however it is retained by its owners and for that reason Calicut has become a flourishing city and attracts large numbers of merchants.

I particularly enjoy this image of the Ruler, simply dressed, personally supervising the salvage of a valued foreigner's flotsam. It is so 'Indian'.

Regarding the abandonment of the Hindu religion, I later discovered that the communities at Versova and on the nearby Madh peninsular near Bombay were strongly Christian and I remembered the Christian effigies fixed to the masts of the great catamarans at Benaulim Beach. The strength of Christianity and Islam on the southern Malabar Coast is evidenced by the number of churches and mosques without reference to supporting statistics, (about 25 per cent of the population of Kerala State is Christian), and the ancient Syrian Church has had its adherents there since the Apostle Thomas was the first missionary, reputed to have landed at Cranganore in 52 AD.

Vasco da Gama met Indian ships at Malindi on the Kenya coast in 1498 and it is recorded that his men thought that they had found Christian sailors on the East African coast when they abased themselves before an image of the Virgin Mary, but were disappointed when they discovered that they were Indian. The modern assumption has usually been drawn that they were Hindu rather than Moslem which led to the misunderstanding. I cannot accept this lazy assumption: I am sure that the Indian sailors whom the Portuguese met were indeed Christian and the disappointment was not that they were Hindu, but that they were of the Syrian orthodoxy within an Indian cultural envelope, which was probably as alien to Western Catholics in those days of the Inquisition as Hinduism would have been.

In *A History of India* (1966), Romila Thapar makes interesting comments:

> Indian ships were by now [300-700 AD] regularly traversing the Arabian Sea, the Indian Ocean and the China Seas and were seen at every port in these areas. .... The 'Island of the Black Yavanas' is mentioned and it may have been a reference to the negroid population of either Madagascar or Zanzibar. ..... Indian contacts with the east African coast date to a period in prehistory and by now this contact had developed through trade. Chinese traders were also competing at east African ports. ...
> ... Trade with China reached an unprecedented volume during these centuries. [900-1300 AD] ... It is believed that there was an Indian settlement on the [Chinese] mainland opposite Formosa.

69

She also wrote with reference to the 8th century:

> Yet the law-makers were declaring it a great in for a Hindu to cross the sea, to cross the 'black waters', ... Ritual purity was becoming an obsession with both Brahmins and the upper castes. ...

From Cochin we continued southwards, following ancient travellers. *The Periplus of the Erythraean Sea* (ca 100 AD) states :

> Nelkunda [Kottayam] is nearly 500 stades from Mouziris [Cranganore], and likewise the same distance by river or sea....

Ibn Batuta wrote in the 14th century:

> I decided to travel thither [from Calicut to Quilon, it being a ten days' journey either by land or by the river, if anyone prefers that route. I set out therefore by the river, and hired one of the Muslims to carry the carpet [his only possession] for me. Their custom is to disembark in the evening and pass the night in the village on its banks, returning to the boat in the morning. We did this too. There was no Muslim on the boat except the man I had hired, and he used to drink wine with the infidels when we went ashore and annoy me with his brawling, which made things all the worse for me. On the fifth day we came to Kunja-Kari which is on the top of a hill there; it is inhabited by Jews, who have one of their number as their governor, and pay a polltax to the Sultan of Kawlam [Quilon] . ...
> ... On the tenth day we reached the city of Kawlam, one of the finest towns in the Mulaybar lands. ... There is a colony of Muslim merchants; the cathedral mosque is a magnificent building . ... This city is the nearest of the Mulaybar towns to China and it is to it that most of the merchants come [from China].

Our party was going to take the inland waterway ferry from Allepey to Quilon, a journey of about eight or ten hours, and although I was free of all fever by then, I still felt enervated so decided that I would travel in the truck with Mike. I told Miriam that it was because Ibn Batuta had given the journey a bad write-up, but I think she thought I was not being a conscientious researcher. When we saw the

70

desperately overcrowded boat with late passengers already sprawled on the metal roof in the blazing sun, I think she may have wanted to join me, but pride would not allow that. I watched them depart along the canal in a cloud of blue exhaust smoke trailing in the stagnant air, and was sure I had made the right decision. But I did have a pang of regret: I had been carrying a sharp image of Alan Whicker recording one of his TV programmes from a canoe in this same canal, sheltering under an umbrella in the drenching monsoon rain, and had wanted to be there ever since, whether I was following some particular historical trail or not.

However, Mike and I had a quiet and restful day together. We visited a fishing village, which conformed to the expected tight-knit communal style with a large Portuguese-style church and Christian school nearby, and watched purse-seine nets being hauled while engaging in badinage with a group of young lads. Mike asked me to look after his expensive watch while he surfed with the boys on their rough catamarans. We drove slowly along the coast road, crossing canals and open waterways on bridges and stopping at wide estuaries with empty sandy beaches, and we both swam in the milk-warm sea. I saw more Chinese fishing machines on an island. I noticed simple river craft being poled along with neatly constructed, curved bamboo roofs.

Everywhere were coconut palms. In the villages there were more strange churches with multiple images on odd shaped spires, conventional Portuguese style Catholic churches, mosques and more Buddhist temples. Chinese roofs were quite often visible and considering that Kerala is nominally Communist I was interested to see estates of pleasant middle-class, architect-designed, two-garage villas amongst the palm groves, mangoes and ornamental trees along the sea shore. On the road we actually passed a late-model Mercedes Benz, an extraordinary sight for there were few private cars in India and most were Indian copies of the 1950's British Morris Oxford.

We reached the pleasant city and ancient port of Quilon in early afternoon and after locating the ferry station, Mike suggested that we have lunch in the nearby eating place where we ate a vegetarian meal served on banana leaves and eaten with our hands. The aloofly friendly proprietor who sat on a stool at his cash desk did not look like a local, he was too tall and had a pale coffee-coloured face with an aquiline nose. Maybe it was Ibn Batuta, down on his luck, I thought: perhaps he bartered his carpet for the little restaurant. I wandered the streets taking some photographs and had coffee in a

71

dark little bar while Mike went to a movie and had a beer with some lively students.

When the ferry came in well after dark and our companions disembarked, sunburned and subdued, Mike shepherded them to Ibn Batuta's eating house where he had asked me to organise a selection of all the dishes available including fresh-caught sea fish, served on the banana leaf plates. Rowena was a bit disconcerted at eating with her hands but it was one of our happiest dinners together and Mike was in good form after a relaxed day away from his passengers.

*

NOTE : I will always treasure that day especially, because Mike was tragically killed in an unnecessary accident later that year. He was climbing on the top of the same Dragoman safari-truck en route from Katmandu to Pakistan to free wires which had snagged the roof-rack, when he slipped, or misjudged the movement of the wooden pole he was using, and was electrocuted.

The ferry from Aleppey to Quillon - our party scrambling aboard.

CHAPTER SIX : HOLIDAY AT KOVALUM

For the next few days we had a holiday at Kovalum Beach, a tourist resort just south of the city of Trivandrum which is at the end of the waterway system and capital of Kerala state. We had been travelling and sightseeing strenuously and apart from my 'flu, some of the others had been suffering from severe bouts of diarrhoea. We were missing the planned relaxing days of beachcombing in Goa.

We made camp on the large flat roof of a guest house which had a tap and kitchen sink used for weddings and other functions and there was a rough thatch shelter from the sun, so it was quite extraordinarily pleasant. We brought up all our kitchen gear and laid out our camp beds and sleeping bags.

Early the first morning I was woken by chanting down on the beach and went to investigate, to find that in amongst the tourists, there was a functioning fishing community and the chanting accompanied the hauling of the nets. Most of the haulers were middle-aged, wiry fellows wearing lungis and turbans, the skin of their torsos and arms burned black and ribbed and strained by worn and stringy muscles. They ignored the topless European girls bouncing about and young men poking lenses into their faces. As the bulging purse at the end of the net reached the low surf they waited for the best wave and, with a crescendo in their song, heaved it ashore. Women and boys then rushed forward to empty and assess the catch. These long heavy purse nets were laid by large planked surf boats with upturned ends, precisely the same as those used in the Oman on the Arabian Gulf and that used to be operated by Indian fishermen off Addington Beach at Durban, Natal. It was good to see the origin of another cultural transfer around the rim of the Ocean. Hauled up on the beach nearby were true catamarans, boats made by lashing several logs together, selected to make a rough canoe shape, with a balancing

73

outrigger. Young men used these to fish with lines or by diving for lobsters off the rocky points that enclosed the Kovalum beaches.

Before Kovalum became a tourist resort, it must have been an idyllic place. Two wide, shallow beaches of fine sand were enclosed by rocky points coming down from the steep coconut palm clad hillside. The fisherfolk had made an extended village within the palms and tilled small vegetable plots. For half the year, when the weather was fine, they would fish and, when the monsoon blew, there were the coconuts to harvest and patches of rice and vegetables to tend. Now, tourist guesthouses, shacky boarding houses and some quite smart villas were spreading amongst the palmgroves. A package-tour hotel stood on a bluff. Along the beach there was a rash of rough little restaurants, boutiques, snack-bars and curio stalls. One of the restaurants advertised a video movie programme accompanying dinner each night. It was beginning to approximate a Mediterranean resort and the advertisements were in English, French and German. Local teenage boys hovered with their eyes on the shapely bare breasts of good looking blonde girls and peddlers swarmed with piles of lungis and turban cloth being sold as scarfs (at two or three times the price in town), trashy plastic souvenirs and warm soft drinks. I supposed that most of the foreign tourists had come seeking the simple beachcombing life with an Indian flavour, but they were finding that the style of the Costa del Sol that they had run away from was catching up with them. The main difference that I could see was that Kovalum was 'dry', but there was plenty of *ganga* to smoke to make up for the lack of liquor. However, the sun was very hot, we were now about eight degrees from the Equator, the sea was warm and still clean.

Miriam and I walked to the end of the further beach, where I was excited to see another bunch of traditional catamarans, lying like giant bananas on the sand. A smiling young man joined me.

"You like this boat?"

"Oh yes," I replied. "It is a very old design."

He waggled his head. "We always build like that. They go easy on the sea. You want one; only thirty rupees for half-day?" I declined, and he studied me. "You camping?" I nodded. "All right, I know what you want. I get crayfish for you."

My face lit up. "Yes!" I cried. We discussed sizes and quantity. He would have what I needed the next morning. He pointed to an old thatched cottage and a couple of shacks at the head of the beach, set apart from other buildings. "Go there at ten o'clock. Ask for Coconut

Salesman Raj."   We agreed and wandered back, discussing the 'special' dinner I would prepare for our group. A leper stopped me and asked for the Celtic cross that I wore on a chain and I had to refuse, but allowed him to touch it and was rewarded with a lipless smile. Other fisher boys offered to hire me catamarans, they were cheeky but cheerful, laughing when I refused and teased them. Life-guards with canary-yellow swimsuits and baseball caps were setting up warning flags and I looked at Miriam with a helpless smile. She said: "Come on, relax. Suffer and enjoy it!"

After swimming next morning, we went to look for Coconut Salesman Raj. At the stall he had pointed out, a boy said he was still fishing but showed me half a dozen crayfish that were already waiting, still alive with waving feelers. I pretended to be angry at the delay to tease the boy and he promptly gave me a cool mango juice which I then had difficulty paying for. I sat for a while exchanging insulting remarks with him before he suggested that I visit the cottage opposite where there were fine things to see.

Curious, I followed his advice and entered an Aladdin's cave of delights. Miriam could not suppress an exclamation of astonishment. Two Kashmiri gentlemen from Srinagar had set up shop in this simple fisherman's house by the tropical ocean and had filled every space with carpets, woven cloth, jewellery of every kind, carved ivory, leatherware, ebony and sandalwood pieces, batiks and exquisitely embroidered napkins and tablecloths. We sat for a couple of hours or more talking idly with the Kashmiris and looking at their goods. They were soft-spoken and gentle; superb salesmen. I bought antique necklaces from Tibet made of chunks of rough turquoise, red coral and beaten silver. I queried the coral and was told that it was imported to Tibet from coastal lands and much sought after as a living stone from the incomprehensible ocean. What irony to be buying it made up in old necklaces and bracelets there on the beach at Kovalum! The silk carpets of a myriad designs were breathtaking and incredibly cheap. One of the partners explained that they had a small weaving factory in Srinagar where they had a staff of designers who travelled in Iran and Pakistan to look for unique old patterns which they converted for weaving on their modern computerised looms. I complimented him freely because the product was excellent. I asked what they were doing in a hut at Kovalum.

He waggled his head slowly. "Usually we are in Goa, but there is communal violence there this year." I nodded. "So we came to have a look down here, travelling in our van. It is very cold at home at this

75

time, so we always come to the Indian Ocean in January. It is our holiday."

I gestured at the carefully laid out stocks of fine crafts. "But, you are working."

"Not very hard." He smiled. "You and the lady are the only customers this morning so far. Anyway, it is always a pleasure to sell such things. ..."

Coconut Salesman Raj had returned and I bought a dozen assorted crayfish from him. A group of young Germans were buying rubbishy souvenirs from a stall further on and I thought that a fine piece from the Kashmiri gentlemen would probably cost them less than the overpriced slogan-printed T-shirts, plastic baseball caps, glass-bead and shell necklaces and coarsely woven lungis they were buying. But the style of the beach-stall was raucous and the atmosphere cheerfully commercial and that is what they preferred.

We walked inland along a rough dirt track and came to a village. There was a row of simple wooden shops and tea houses and gaily decorated pick-up trucks were there to act as taxis. Again, the culture impact of tourism was obvious; most of the shops were converted to selling T-shirts, rugs and cheap jewellery. German slogans advertised the wares. The tea houses sold Coca Cola and commercially bottle mango juice. If we were in a city it would not have surprised, apart from the European language signs, but this place had the structure of a simple village by the sea. We needed to buy rice and sugar and the tourist shops did not sell these needs of the real world so we walked further until we found a grocery off to one side with rickety counter and dirt floor. Inside there was the timeless perfume of spices, lentils, roughly polished rice and herbs. I waited my turn amongst a half dozen housewives who looked me over curiously and gave me shy smiles. The purchases after being weighed on an ancient spring scale were poured into squares of paper which were then neatly screwed into cones. The housewives brought their baskets, but we had none, so the proprietor went into the back of his shop and came out with a well-used but serviceable plastic bag. I wanted to pay for it, thinking back to the value that such things have in villages in Africa and undoubtedly also have in a poor little store in India, but he refused money, waggling his head and grinning at me. I thought of the mountains of plastic discarded daily in the West. To try to compensate I bought some sticky sweets that Phil and the girls would probably like and a big paper cone of peanuts.

I had the roof-top camp to myself to prepare the dinner and enjoyed myself on my own. I made fried rice with pineapple and brinjal and a huge bowl of stir-fried onions, garlic, ginger, cabbage, tomatoes, leeks, susu, okra, cumin seeds and shredded carrots with plenty of coconut oil. I boiled the crayfish lightly, peeled them and soused them with salted coconut milk, lime-juice and oil. There was pawpaw to follow. It was good and everyone was pleased.

One evening, the younger members of our party decided to indulge themselves at the 'video restaurant' and Miriam and I went to one of the simpler eating places, the Rockview Restaurant, because we liked the look of it. The roof was rough thatch, the floor beach sand and it was enclosed by low bamboo matting so the night breeze drifted gently through. We sat on hand-sawn plank benches. There were a few other diners and they were an interesting mix: a lone Japanese girl with long black hair wearing a minute bikini, a middle-aged Indian couple properly dressed for an evening out (he wore slacks and shirt with a tie, she a fine sari), two Italians with curly beards talking animatedly, and a very relaxed, dreamy-eyed Scandinavian boy, drawing on marijuana cigarettes. A serious, almost sullen, youngish man passed round menus and asked us to write our choice on a scrap of paper; evidently he was illiterate in Western script. We waited a long time, chatting idly and watching pink crabs emerge from holes in the sand-floor to grab scraps of fallen food before scuttling back again.

The sunlight slowly faded and western rock music started up from along the beach. A huge moth came to the light and had the Japanese girl screaming in alarm until one of the Italians gallantly removed it. A young Indian woman, with an old lady hovering, produced our dishes from the back and the man served them without a word. We had egg curry and fried rice and it was delicious. Later, an old man with rheumy eyes came in and sat near us. He studied me for a long time with a toothless smile and made remarks to the waiter who eventually came over to me and spoke in fluent English.

"This is the father of my wife, who cooks for me with her mother, and he lent us some money for this restaurant. He likes you and asks me to explain all this." I listened with surprise. They exchanged glances and the old man nodded encouragingly. "He was a coconut climber but retired when the tourists came." The young man smiled for the first time. "He is still very strong, even though he is seventy years now."

The elder cackled, he could obviously follow the conversation. He reached out a thin hand and clasped my wrist with a powerful grip, grinning and wagging his head. He brought his face close to mine to peer at me with his fading eyes. I smiled and nodded. He released my wrist but then held onto my hand for a long time.

Seine-net fishermen at Kovalum

CHAPTER SEVEN : LAND'S-END

We woke at 07.00 and breakfasted on the beach, watching fishermen hauling their nets, for the last time. Kites were soaring and crows croaking. The road all the way to Cape Cormorin was lined with prosperous villages and we drove first through coconut plantations and then many rice paddies. There were some old 'Chinese' houses and more modern middle-class villas.

The guide-book said that the old princely state of Travancore, now merged into Kerala, carried out extensive land reform before independence which has resulted in increased agricultural prosperity, which will hopefully not be damaged by any socialist ideas of communal farming. The land became very flat later, with the granite Cardamom Hills marching like a dragon's back in the east. These hills were just like the central mountains on the Seychelles and I could imagine the sea covering the flat lands once, creating lovely rugged islands with headlands and bays.

Entering Tamil Nadu state there was a subtle change, more untidiness in the villages, road signs faded and battered, less use of Western script, clearly not as prosperous as Communist Kerala. Is it governments' ideology or the common people's collective will which are more important, I asked myself? It is the people's will, of course. Governments' task is to harness it no matter what ideology is employed; if an ideology fails, another must be devised; the old one must not continue to be forced on the people like a stubborn donkey being beaten to the ground. I could think of South Africa and Tanzania, at opposite ends of a political spectrum in my continent of Africa, where stubborn donkeys were staggering bloodily along.

Quite suddenly we were in Kanyakumari, tourist-pilgrim town at the end of India. There were many souvenir shops loaded with sea-shell necklaces, coral and conches, wooden bangles, carved gods, flower garlands, T-shirts, sweetmeats, lungis and saris. People seethed, buses parked everywhere. We were the only Europeans I saw all day. We parked by what I thought was a very crude concrete memorial, the Mahatma Gandhi mandapam with a geometric spinning wheel decorating it, and had an excellent vegetarian lunch, as much as we could eat, on banana leaf plates in a crowded 'canteen' with young boys rushing to serve. The lunch cost Rs 8.00 each (about 45 pence) for three vegetarian courses and a mountain of unleavened breads.

Miriam and I walked down to the end of land to an ancient, weather-worn temple with a ghat leading into the sea at the very southernmost point of the sub-continent. Men were standing in the sea washing or staring out in meditation or thoughtful wonder at being there at that holy and geographically unique place. I also stood staring southwards towards the Equator and then to the west, towards Africa. I meditated in my own way. Sofala was over there. And Durban with Ghandi's ashram at Phoenix, burned by a mob of Zulus. Behind me milled the energetic Indian crowd and the crude drawing of Gandhi's spinning wheel emblazoned on its concrete block of a building. The sun struck down on the glittering blue sea and there were many black spots of fishing catamarans as far as the horizon.

There were large pilgrim groups spilt out of the buses, some in plain black or green lungis and some big, bald older men with pale eyes, white beards and saffron robes. Where were they from? This place was sacred to Parvati who failed to win the hand of Lord Shiva and so remained a virgin in her incarnation as Kanya. Offshore to the east was a great smooth granite dome of an island with a finely architected temple complex built in 1970 to commemorate the Swami Vivekananda who meditated there for forty days in the 19th century before going on a pilgrimage over all India teaching his philosophy. I found the aspect and proportions of the temple very pleasing. It complimented well with the ancient pillared temple at the bathing ghat, both of which conflicted with the awful Gandhi memorial. Fine aesthetics and crudeness, cheek by jowl, is too often visible in India.

We drove out on the Madurai road looking for a place to stay or camp on a beach. By chance, Mike saw a signpost and we took a track down to the sea which was now the eastern, Coromandel Coast to a preserved historical monument, the Vattakotal Fort, standing amongst a plantation of coconut palms, brooding over a black sand beach.

It was a Dutch colonial fort, built after they took over the trading system of this area from the Portuguese in the mid-17th century and began to impose a formal colony. It was beautifully built of giant granite blocks with smoothly cut faces, but the joints were a series of gentle curves, like a stretched jigsaw, fitting precisely together without any mortar. Was this for strength and adhesion or just the whim of the masons? They could certainly cut clean straight lines if they wished, and since this was a fort I assumed then it was for strength, but later on I saw exactly the same style of dry-course walling at the great temple outside Trichy so I suppose it was for aesthetic pleasure. I marvelled at the vast walls. The upper parts were finished later with firing embrasures built of roughly laid clay brick and lime mortar, (by the British?) I was amazed at the exact quality of this dry-stone walling: it would have been famous in Europe with hundreds of visitors and TV documentaries, but the place was deserted and there was no mention of it at all in the guide-book. The local craftsmen were truly fine and the stone must have been quarried in the far Cardamom Hills.

A rather dim but smiling, head-waggling caretaker appeared and let us in, indicating that we could camp. The interior had wide ramps up to the platforms around the walls and a great bastion projected out into the sea where a battery of cannon would have stood. Despite the bastion standing actually in the sea, there were no major cracks in the walling after three hundred years! A white Portuguese-style church was visible amongst the coconuts about two miles along the seashore to the north-east.

I watched fishing boats returning to the coast from the far distance, from the direction of Sri Lanka. There was civil war there then and the Tamils were seeking an Apartheid-type separate state whereas the two people had lived together for hundreds of years with easy communications. To-day's ideologically inspired politicians who start the weary round of terrorism, indiscriminate bombings and guerilla war in the later 20th century sicken me. Do any of them ever care for the ravaged ordinary people whom they are stridently 'representing'? Oh, for the days of simple unashamed dynastic supremacy and ideologues confined to universities and religious faculty!

A fishing boat with lateen sail slipped past the old ramparts below me and I watched it with slow excitement. When the sun began lowering I went down to sit on the strange pitch-black fine sand under the silent walls of the lonely fortress, surrounded by coconut palms.

I imagined the rough Netherlands soldiers and the earnest administrators of the *Vereenigde Oost-Indiesche Compagnie* supervising the army of masons and labourers who built the walls. Were the Dutchmen also amazed at the sophistication and prowess of the craftsmen engaged to build a remote colonial fort? Had they any respect for the ancient civilisation that they had come to conquer with cannon and gunpowder?

As the sun set in the west, the full moon rose out of the sea in the east, a serene and beautiful sight. I moved to a felled palm bole and sat on for quite a while and thought about personal time: I was married on a wintery day in Staffordshire exactly thirty years ago that day, in another era. There is no possibility that my wife and I could have foreseen how we would separately have celebrated that thirtieth anniversary. She was with family in frozen England, I was alone on a black-sand beach on the Coromandel Coast beneath a Dutch rampart looking towards a rising tropic moon and the old spice island of Ceylon. I was late for dinner.

Dinner was inedible to me: badly cooked spaghetti and dehydrated 'bolognaise' mix from our emergency stores, purchased in Johannesburg maybe two years ago when our truck was on a trans-African safari. I could not eat it, but the strange symbolism was not lost on me. It was followed by bananas spoiled by lumpy, tasteless custard. Our English girls apologised, explaining that they had been lusting for 'European' food for a change. They blamed the South African dehydrated mix, obviously long past its proper 'shelf-life', but I knew that Parvati was punishing them for failing to press their thoughts towards her culture in that place.

Afterwards I went down to the beach again and sat in the moonlight which was a silver flood. I thought, inevitably, about Sofala and the hippo. From there my thoughts strayed here and there to all of the history and speculation of the Indian Ocean peoples and their commingling over millennia across the waters. I thought about what I was doing and the wonder of being there that night. I was nostalgic and thoughtful. It was extraordinarily peaceful, waves gently swishing, air balm, my thoughts roaming far away. I wondered why the Dutch had built this fort there and could not fathom it.

Months later I was re-reading Gavin Young's *Slow Boats to China* and came across his statement that he had been told that the modern regional port of Tuticorin, further north, replaced an older port close to Cape Cormorin used by the Dutch which had subsequently silted. By whim of fate we had camped there, beside its guardian fortress.

In a shift of mood, influenced by unsatisfied appetite and the doleful moonlight, I recognised that this journey around the coasts of India was not a 'fun-safari': I was enjoying it, because it was something that was important to me and I was pursuing understanding that can only come with physical and psychic contact with India and its people. I wished we could stop for a while in this lovely loneliness to let our souls catch up. But, life is an endless balance, as always. The organised expedition with the others had enabled me to see the places and acquire an understanding I would never have gained in the pages of books, nor on a Cooks' packaged-tour. Baying at the moon is a profitless activity.

It rained twice in the night and it was windy so I had to get up and climb out naked to crawl around in the wet darkness hammering at loose tent pegs.

Bathing ghatt at Cape Cormorin - the very end of India.

The famous Chinese fishing machines at Fort Cochin, now a tourist attraction but still used commercially when we were there.

Considering the purpose of my Indian safari, the east coast of the
Indian sub-Continent may not appear to have many direct links with
Africa. However, trade is not concerned merely with direct contact.
Trade is a spider-web of interconnecting routes of fleets and caravans
linked by market places, stimulated by dreams of profit, bazaar-gossip
and espionage.

The east coast, which I traversed as far as Madras, did have
importance to Africa, because it was the Empires and Kings based
there who first controlled and encouraged India's Far Eastern
activities. China was a vast and powerful trading empire under its
succeeding dynasties. It was the Pandya kings of Madurai and the
Pahlava dynasty of Kanchipuram with its seaport at Mahabalipuram
who launched and sustained the eastern trade. Colonies were
established in Malaysia, Indonesia and Sri Lanka and the Hindu
religion established there. When Hindu fundamentalism stimulated
by Islam contributed to the decline of indigenous Indian seafaring,
Arabs dominated the Western Indian Ocean and the Chinese the
Eastern. But as I had discovered at Cochin southwards, and as
described by Ibn Batuta, Chinese merchants and sailors also made
bases on the Western shores of India. Chinese ships sailed to East
Africa and there are written records of at least one large fleet that
cruised there. Chinese wares from the 13th and 14th centuries have
been unearthed in Great Zimbabwe and are common in archaeological
digs along the whole African east coast. Madurai and Mahabalipuram
were part of the system that had immense influence on the socio-
political development of medieval eastern Africa.

We stayed in a rough concrete box of a hotel in Madurai, but
the taps and fans worked. I went into town with Miriam in an
autoricksha and had a silly argument over the fare for the first time in
India. There was instant hassle at the great temple gates from peddlers

and beggars: the most persistent I came across in India. We walked around taking pictures and admiring the extraordinary wealth of stone carving on the giant gopurams. This is the famous Dravidian art of south India. We were followed by a whining beggarwoman who kept scratching my bare arm in the most infuriating way. I could have struck her. There was a spasm of amusement when we saw a decorated elephant lean up against a crowded tour-bus and put his trunk in a window and was given several coins for its mahout from the passengers. We bought some beautiful gold-threaded braids in a silk shop we entered to get relief from the crowds. We were supposed to be cooking, so looked for the produce market in vain for some time, getting confusing directions.

Twice I was approached by drug peddlers: "I've got very good ganga; also stronger. Very good quality. Come with me, please!" and was asked, with the universal knowing leer: "I can show you and your lady something special with beautiful young girls and boys? You will enjoy it. Come! Come!" Madurai was different. Eventually we found the market, but were disturbed by the strangely unfriendly people. We could not find sugar or spices stalls, and nobody would explain. Why? We travelled back to hotel with another angry autoricksha driver, charging high fares. Was it Madurai or some personal doom that made the city so unwelcoming that day?

I showered and washed my hair before tackling the sugar problem. Outside the hotel, I asked several food stalls without luck; eventually a well-spoken and polite middle-aged lady directed me around a corner. I could find no shop, but there was a bar open to the street with several drunken young men who called out to me insistently and I reluctantly joined them. They laughed and joked, then, to my surprise, decided to escort me to a shop further along which sold me sugar at a very cheap price. I asked why they were drinking and celebrating and they told me it was the Pombal rice-harvest festival all this coming week and they could drink as much as they wanted because they were Christian. They belonged to the parish of St. Joseph.

After dinner, Miriam and I walked in the street and had a couple of iced mango juices at a street stall where a cheerful old man lovingly demonstrated his patent chai-boiler, heated with charcoal shavings, with smiles and lots of head waggling. So the day ended well.

As I drifted to sleep, listening to the noise of traffic, I reflected that Madurai was known to the Greeks and Romans. It was an ancient

86

dynastic capital, two millennia old. The great temple complex was fine, but some people were ugly in spirit that day.

Our route took us on to Madras via Tiruchirappali, Pondicherry and Mahabalipuram. I enjoyed all three places and we had some good times, but it was Tiruchirappali, commonly called Trichy, on the wide Cauvery River that impressed me most. Trichy had a quite different atmosphere to Madurai which enveloped me as soon as we entered the city, and I felt lighthearted and easy. There was a distinct feeling of serenity and quiet gaiety. In retrospect, I'm not surprised: Madurai was the capital of militant kings for a couple of millennia, Trichy was a religious centre. These distinctions actually do work, I have invariably found, and I often wish that we took greater practical cognisance of them in the West.

Mike did not have any fixed objective for a place to stay and almost on a whim turned off at the first hotel he came to. The Aristo Hotel was a gem, a colonial relic standing in about three acres of private land in what had been the European cantonment. Gentle, elderly servants dressed in lungis, tunics and turbans spoke in old-fashioned Indian pidgin, learned by ear during the Raj rather than by rote at school. I sat on the wide verandah with hanging vines filtering the sunlight and watched birds other than crows and mynahs hopping about amongst canna lilies and geraniums. The endless roar, punctuated by the battlefield shocks of vehicle hooters of an Indian city, was visually repelled by the quiet lawns and flowerbeds and the impenetrable thicket of a mass of mature bougainvillaea that formed the garden wall. The insistent insect buzzing of autorickshas with their nasal bleats like loud computerised sheep was partially at bay.

Faded portrait photographs of stiffly posing aristocracy from Europe and British India hung haphazardly about the open lobby and the entrance verandah. Stained and faded letters from distinguished visitors praising the hotel were framed and fastened to the wall. I asked the receptionist about them.

"Oh yes, indeed. In the 1930's and 40's this was a famous hotel, all over India. The owner was a personal friend of many of the most senior Princely Rulers, and as you can see he was known to the Royals and others in Europe. Those were great days, you know? Trichy was a resort of the rich and famous."

I nodded, smiling at his pride. But looking at the photographs and stilted typewritten letters on crested paper with flourished signatures there was the inevitable feeling of sadness at the decline of the hotel and the society that produced it. How can the degrading of any part of a society serve the common good? Society and civilisations progress by the improvement of the wealth and achievements of the masses towards its higher classes, not by pulling down the mighty to the level of pettifoggers and clerks. Perhaps that is the greatest disservice that the architects of socialism have done to us all; the creation of smug satisfactions at the destruction of excellence.

"Sir?" A servant had silently arrived at my elbow. I smiled up at him and wise old eyes instantly crinkled in reply. An impulse to ask for a large whisky-soda *stengah* and a cheroot was reluctantly put down; the whisky would have been vaguely-flavoured raw rum there nowadays and cigars unobtainable. While I contemplated, and he waited, tray and napkin held ready before him like shield and banner, Phil and Miriam arrived and sat down with cheerful chattering. We had fresh lime sodas and talked about the sightseeing possibilities.

But first, I had to contend with the lay ladies of the local Christian Convent. Laid out on a bench were a collection of handkerchiefs and napkins: pieces of fine lawn and muslin embroidered with classical English designs by the girls of the school. I looked around at the tropical environment and the sepia aristocrats in their crooked frames. I looked at the earnest ladies in saris with tiny jewels in their noses selling these goods and I saw in my mind the shiny heads of black pigtailed hair bending over the needlework. How did they feel about the stylised English motifs they struggled to reproduce in immaculate stitching? I was assaulted by another kind of nostalgia. Here were these English Victorian wares being offered, incredibly cheaply and so genteelly, to a bunch of roughly-dressed overland travellers like us, with such bland belief. Inevitably, I bought several pieces for my family at home. It was a lesson in faith.

We took a bus to the centre. City buses in the south are practical vehicles: simple rectangular shells with sturdy metal seats crowded together and the windows have no glass. In mid-morning our bus was not full and we bucketed down the long straight to the great rock-temple that stands like a vast sphinx in the centre of the old town. We got down and found that we were still a long walk from the foot of the slab-sided pink sandstone mass covered with temple buildings, but we were determined to go up. The experience of Madurai had put Miriam off autorickshas in Tamil Nadu, but I was hot and enervated enough to take a chance on annoyance and wandered over to where a dozen of the little black beetles squatted in the shade of the Christian cathedral with its tall spire punily trying to assert itself against the giant Hindu sphinx a mile away.

I spoke to the first driver but he waggled his head and I was going towards the next when a roly-poly man in Western dress rushed forward.

"You are wanting temples and sightseeing?"

"Oh, yes. That's what I'm wanting, and it's very hot to-day." I smiled at him, suddenly desperate that I should not be hassled in Trichy.

"Don't worry, sir. Many many people from all over come here. From Delhi, Bombay, Hyderabad, Madras. Even Calcutta and America. Where are you from, sir?"

"England."

Waggle-waggle. "That's good. You are welcome, Sir. This driver here is very reliable, he is specially recommended for foreign tourists. He will take you and the lady to the rock-temple then across the river to Srirangam Ranganathaswami temple then back to hotel." He grinned. "At hotel is waiting baths and cold drinks." He had summoned a bean-pole elderly driver as he talked and pushed him forward like a prize goat or fine length of cloth for my approval. I laughed. Correctly interpreting my laugh, the tout proceeded to haggle with me over the price, which we did with good humour. No doubt it was a special price for rich foreigners, but at Rs40.00 (about £2.20) what could I complain about? A single journey in Madurai had been more than that and our tour in Trichy would last all afternoon.

We rattled through winding back alleys where women and children were drawing pictures on the pavements with coloured chalks and powders set into pastes with water. Some were religious, some classically geometric, some vaguely western. It was a feature of the Pombal rice-harvest festival and we saw them all the way to Madras. Children waved and called to us and the women smiled. Trichy was all right.

At the entrance to the rock temple we left our sandals in a hall with hundreds of others casually waiting for their owners under the eye of the old temple elephant, rocking gently on her chained hind legs. Her golden eye looked at me with all the wisdom of the universe. Her trunk was moving continuously towards the people round about, soliciting alms, but never actually touching: a very polite trunk. An indulgent father gave a handful of coins to his excited little boy who rushed in repeatedly to place them one after another in the natural cup at the end of the trunk. Each coin was hefted to the mahout who stood beside with a clinking bag.

A wide stairway tunnel had been cut through the living rock up to the summit and the whole mountain was honeycombed with side corridors leading to dim, incense-wafting artificial-cave temples. We were awed. On the summit, a collection of pillared temples had grown towards heaven from the sandstone over centuries and we joined several hundred tourists and pilgrims wandering about or sitting and talking, some picnicking. The city was spread below and its roar came up in waves as the gentle breeze shifted. In the mid-distance the broad Cauvery River snaked past with ruler straight irrigation canals radiating away across the endlessly flat emerald landscape to the misty horizon. "Whew!" exclaimed Miriam, waving her arm at it all. We watched for a long while, picking out women preparing the evening meal in backyard kitchens, boys playing Indian cricket in small open spaces, a beggar sitting outside a little neighbourhood temple, a group of men bending together in earnest discussion, butterfly-like women in saris gathered about street stalls, autorickshas buzzing along trailing faint wafts of blue smoke, a growling bus trumpeting its musical horns and its driver leaning out of the cab to wave gaily to a friend. Trichy is so flat and crowded and we were silently suspended above it like aliens in a flying saucer. Its heart was bare to us.

Our faithful autoricksha driver was waiting at the entrance and he whisked us, without a word, across the Cauvery River to the Ranganathaswami Temple complex. I had read the guide-book but it did not prepare me for the reality. The complex sprawled over a large area, rectangular in shape with a series of walls each with its gate crowned by a tower with the now-familiar but endlessly fascinating intricate mass of carved gods, heroes, spiritual familiars, legendary animals and illustrations from contemporary life. The gopurams of southern India are a marvel. Between the outer walls there were apartment buildings, hotels and shops. As we progressed inwards, the religious functions increasingly dominated until at about the fourth gateway we entered holy ground where we had to deposit our dusty sandals.

Now, the particular experience began. I felt transported 2,000, even 5,000 years, to the atmosphere of any great ancient city of the Middle East. I could have been in Babylon or Damascus, Mohenjo Daro or Persopolis. The pillared buildings, secular or spiritual, the open forums, the many gopurams with massed carvings, the

90

containing walls, the shrines and images were executed in Dravidian style and dedicated to the complexities of Hindu religion. But the form seemed to me to be universal to this period of the great classical civilisations which traded together and exchanged knowledge and culture for those millennia while we Europeans still adhered to primitive living in nomadic settlements within the great forests of our northern continent. I suddenly had an intimacy, a psychic rapport, with the Assyrians, Egyptians, Persians and Indians, that no amount of book-reading or looking at diagrams and pictures could ever give me.

Within the inner complex, I was not in a museum, nor was I in the sombre majesty of a Norman cathedral. There were hundreds if not thousands of people milling about. There was a regular market selling produce of the land. There were moneychangers and curio sellers, temple officials and guides, priests and ascetics, excited children, solitary soft-eyed wandering cows with gilded horns, pariah dogs, crows and kites wheeling above, groups of robed pilgrims walking together or meditating and squatting around a swami, listening to his stories or philosophy. There were many tourists in smart western dress, and a very few other bemused Westerners like us. Painted elephants hung with tinkling bells and jangling chains stood rocking at the entrances to shrines collecting alms, and in one great hall chairs and banners were being set up for a gathering to celebrate Pombal.

I thought of Jesus Christ in the Temple of Jerusalem and understood with absolute clarity the *humanness* of his puritanical Jewish revolt against the colourful Asiatic culture that infused Palestine, but I also suddenly wondered at the lack of Christianity of his splenetic outburst in the particular Gospel story. His behaviour seemed that of an angry ascetic of the Essene cult rather than that of a tolerant preacher of love. Wandering in the Ranganathaswami Temple that afternoon transported backwards through two millennia of time, immersed for an hour or two in the everyday of an ancient Civilisation, I received insights I could not have found in any other way.

Incense tinctured the air and beyond the murmur of the many voices and the swish of hundreds of bare feet on old stone and packed earth, there were chants and the clash of cymbals or gongs from the holy sanctuaries. An attendant took us through a chained gateway up stairways onto the roof of one of the buildings where we could look over the temple-city and photograph the series of gopurams. I was intrigued to be told that the largest of them all at the main entrance was just being completed.

"You mean it is being repaired?" I asked, looking at the spider-web of bamboo scaffolding enclosing it.

Our guide smiled. "No, Sir. It is just now being completed. They have been building for some years and the artists have come from all over to make the carvings. It is the biggest gopuram in India."

"My word," I said to Miriam. "All those tens of thousands of carved statues! I was sure it was several hundred years old. How wonderful that the technique and craftsmanship is still virile. In Europe we would probably add on some easy and simple modern tower, like Coventry cathedral."

"That is the difference in our civilisations," she observed, thinking about it. "We seem to be always innovating whether it's good or bad. So often bad. They are perpetuating tried classical traditions. Who knows what is best?"

Neither is better, I thought. Both are essential. If only humankind had the wisdom to integrate both and exploit the best of each stream of human endeavour without stress and turmoil. Maybe in modern India it could be successful.

We drove northwards on flat country, intensely cultivated where irrigation canals cut across the land in miles-long straight lines and dusty and dry with scrub bush in between. It was hot and the air was hazy, the sky brazen. In many villages the rice had been harvested and was being threshed. Some villages had simple machines driven by coughing petrol or diesel motors, in others we saw water-buffaloes or oxen with painted horns being driven round and round as they had been for centuries. Others had discovered a new way: bundles of harvested and dried rice were laid out on the tarred road to be threshed by the traffic. In between the passage of trucks, buses and the occasional car or jeep, women and children ran out to rearrange the battered bundles or replace them with fresh stock. I presumed that at the end of the day when the traffic eased they would carry the chaff away and sweep up the piles of rice grains.

One evening we arrived at Mahabalipuram, seaport of the Pahlava kings at the height of their power in the 7th century AD. These kings replaced nomadic herding and sporadic cultivation by an organised system of agriculture introduced by the Mauryan Empire, which despite inevitable exploitation by bad landlords when feudalism flourished was the backbone of Indian prosperity and cultural stability until the 20th century. What Africa was trying to do in the 1980s with pressure for instant success, Indian kings and emperors achieved over long time periods more than a millennium ago. This was a theme I kept repeating to myself over and over.

No doubt there were many faults in India's rural communities and agriculture that a sociologist or technical person could point out to me, but this continuity and inertia appeared to me to be praiseworthy. Despite the enormous increase in India's population in recent years the long-established and stable peasant society had been able to employ new crops and improved technique to stave off famine. In Africa where there is similar geography to India, socio-political turmoils and ethnic civil wars have resulted in chronic disaster involving hundreds of thousands every year in the post-independence period. India escapes this despite much higher densities of population. Severe poverty and degradation in many overcrowded cities in post-independence India are the result of other social upheavals: massive urbanisation fuelled by a drive for inefficient centrally-planned industrialisation, and triggered by the horrendous national trauma of politically-convenient instant racial partition in 1947, Mountbatten's misguided and short-sighted *apartheid* programme, when millions of people in the sub-continent left the land and fled to the cities.

Mahabalipuram is famous for its Jain shore-temples, built in the 7th century AD., and to-day it is a place of pilgrimage and a holiday resort. Being Pombal and a week-end, tens of thousands came for an outing from nearby Madras and in the evenings orderly snakes curved around and around in the main square, queuing for buses. Many were young men. There was hardly any litter. I watched these happy and disciplined masses with awe comparing them in my mind with Blackpool or Scarborough at the end of a bank-holiday week-end in high summer. Mahabalipuram, an easy few hours from Madras, is also known to the backpackers from Europe and North America and we suddenly met numbers of our kinsfolk again, lolling in the cafes and teahouses drinking coffee or sodas and smoking ganga, or lying on the beach encouraging the blazing sun to scale their fair northern skins. We had hardly met any European or North American travellers for the hundreds of miles since Kovalum Beach and I saw them as a sudden intrusion into our odyssey. There was an expensive Youth Hostel complex with rooms for Rs170.00 per night (£9.45) in a main building and several chalets. This was beyond Mike's budget, so he found a 'camping' with plenty of room for tents in grounds with mango trees and coconut palms for shade. After pitching tents, still damp and mouldy from the rain at Vattakotal Fort, we had a few jolly drinks from stocks on the truck and went along the road for a dinner of prawns which was advertised at a tourist restaurant. We had a happy evening, with lots of laughing and joking, but the food was not a great success. It was even less of a success at 3.00 a.m. when I had to stagger hurriedly to the toilet in the light of the moon and there were several wan faces at breakfast.

The Jain shore-temples, eroded by the weather, stood solid and grey on the sands of the beach. The east coast was an endless featureless beach, hundreds of miles of golden sand, and when standing by the sea the haze of humidity fuzzed the edge of that ruler straight line that divided flat land from silvered ocean. I did not see where the ancient harbour could have been and I guessed that there may not have been one. In the calm season, the ships lay off the beach at anchor. During the monsoon, they must have been either away trading across the oceans or hauled up on the beach for repair or safekeeping. With thousands of local trippers and a sizable number of White backpackers about I was unable to feel any emotional rapport with the place. Nevertheless, I was glad to have been there and to have an intellectual sensation of an important source of ancient Eastern trade.

Our little group was breaking up and although we had not acquired great cohesion, we had been friendly to each other. After Mahabalipuram we drove slowly along the coast road to Madras where we were to scatter and the truck would be serviced to await the next group for the return journey. The crew were cheerful at the prospect of a break for they had been hard at it all the way from Katmandu, a prodigious journey. The road passed along an artificial coastline where the dunes were stabilised and buttressed by millions of casuarina pines planted to prevent flooding during the monsoon.

Periodically, we passed government flood disaster depots where emergency equipment was stored. The monsoons are particularly fierce in the Bay of Bengal. Two nuclear generating stations lurked in the haze of humidity with power lines marching with shiny skeins off into the interior.

There were no villages that I can remember.

CHAPTER NINE: GATEWAY TO INDIA

I had not been looking forward to Madras, expecting suffocating crowds like Bombay, so I was pleased to find it airy with wide straight boulevards radiating out from the downtown nucleus on the ocean front. Unlike Bombay which is squeezed into its island like a stretched stocking, Madras was founded by the British on a piece of land within a protecting loop of the Cooum River and grew into its present shape over the flat plain with measured planning. This does not make it an exciting city, but it is an easy one to tolerate.

Mike took us to the Guru Hotel in an area with many reminders of the Raj: Victoria Crescent, C.-in-C. Road, Mount Road, Montieth Road. We trooped along, in our best safari clothes, wrinkled but clean, to the Connemara Hotel for a farewell dinner party. The Connemara is one of the grand hotels of southern India, large and urbane, finely-furnished and well-kept, with the polish and suavity of success. Unlike the poor old Aristo in Trichy, the Connemara had grown with the years. The floors were marble, the ceilings high with turning fans studding them and on the main staircase there were examples of temple carvings. We invaded the red plush and polished mahogany of the upstairs bar in our cheery, motley group and were served excellently with quiet courtesy. The atmosphere of international luxury was strange after weeks of rough travelling.

Miriam and I walked back to our simple Guru Hotel, followed by an autoricksha driver for most of the way who tried hard to sell us a wide array of hallucinatory and sexual delights, suggesting greater and greater variety of the latter as we refused the more mundane. Vice peddlers in India intrigued me by offering their wares determinedly to mixed Western couples. Was this because they thought that we would both be equally interested in their pleasures, European women being assumed to be emancipated, which might well be so, or was it because they did so out of learned experience with other foreign tourists? I would like to have found out.

I enjoyed sightseeing in Madras. We went on a bus-tour that visited the Fort St.George complex of the Raj. Some of the buildings were well-preserved, including St. Mary's church with many memorials and marble statues like any old Anglican church in a historical town in South Africa. I was interested in the Dravidian Kapaleeshwara temple complex devoted to Shiva. This temple and place of pilgrimage was founded before Christ and lay within the present city but well outside the British central Fort St.George area. The awareness of these southern Indian temple-complexes being a living picture of ancient cities that I had discovered at Trichy recurred there, but the Pombal festival was over and the number of visitors were fewer.

Nearby, almost as an afterthought, our tour-guide pointed out the Portuguese Catholic cathedral of Saõ Thomé (commenced in 1504 and completed ca.1520) as we drove past, built on the reputed site of the tomb of the Apostle Thomas. I felt a strong psychic shock and shiver of emotion, goose-pimples stood up on my arms. Rattling along in our bus I thought about St. Thomas who had settled finally at Kapaleeshwarah, perhaps because it was a famous already-established religious centre. I wondered if he been happy ending his days at an old Hindu temple, so many weary miles and years away from Palestine and the excitement of following a great young preacher? By then, tempered by decades of close intimacy with Hinduism, Buddhism and Jainism with ideals not very different to those of his own Jewish Master, he must have been a very wise and holy man. I hope he was much honoured and respected. How well had he retained the simple puritanical faith of Jesus after many years of living within the complex caste systems, sophistication and power of Indian civilisation and culture? Was it possible for any man to do so, I wondered, when the basic principles of belief were little different? It is a pity we know so little of the later life of St. Thomas whose experiences and psychic development must have been so different to that of his colleagues struggling with Western Civilisation and the Roman Empire. What amazing dialogues would have resulted had they met?

Miriam and I had travel reservations to make and the manager of the Guru Hotel told us that the airline offices were quite close by. We had not travelled in a trisha, a ricksha pulled by a man peddling on a bicycle extension, so engaged a bent old man who seemed to need the business since he was always waiting at the hotel door. He quoted Rs20.00 and I said to Miriam with some surprise that it must be quite a long distance. Hardly had I settled to enjoy the experience when he pulled into the car park of the offices; we had travelled about a hundred yards along a broad level avenue. Miriam's angry consternation and our rider's guarded caution sent me into a paroxysm of laughter which astonished them both.

"You should see the two of you," I wailed.

"I don't see what's funny," Miriam retorted. "He's an old devil."

"Of course he is! But in his eyes we were foolish rich devils to agree to the price."

I caught his eye and seeing that I was not angry, he allowed a shy smile to creep over his worn face as he waggled his head. When we had to return the next day with our load of baggage and camping gear, he cheerfully manhandled it all and conducted us to the airport bus for practically nothing, waiting until the bus pulled away with a grinning face and a twinkle in his eyes. That old trisha rider will remain sharply in my memory of Madras and southern India. I hope that our excessive fee for a brief ride eased his life a little.

After interminable dreary delays we arrived in Bombay in the late evening and this time I knew the way to Max's home at Versova and could direct the taxi. It was remarkable to be back there with the same traffic sounds, the bleating of the autorickshas overlaid by the swish of wind in Max's coconuts. It was like returning home and the *chowkidar* greeted me with a genuine smile of welcome. We spent nearly a week in Bombay, relaxing in the garden, and doing gentle sightseeing. At last my soul was catching up.

Max created a pleasant routine: every evening as the sun began to set across the Indian Ocean a servant brought out white painted cane chairs and set a tea tray on a low table. Max would appear and politely invite us to join him. We would sit on the lawn watching the red ball fall into the sea and converse. The tea was a blend and strengthened by cinnamon and a few cardamom seeds and was accompanied by exactly six 'Marie' biscuits. We talked of many things, gently probing each other's lives and opinions over the several evenings: an exploration of the lost art of the slow creation of friendship that was a grand experience in itself. We discussed the Indian economy, Margaret Thatcher and Rajiv Gandhi, the gold-smuggling trade between the Arabian Gulf and Bombay, the threat of China, the arrival of hundreds of thousands of peasants in Bombay and the shanty towns they were building, the universal 'black' labour market and the grey economy, the desperate need for India to modernise its economy and eliminate widespread corruption, poetry in the East and the West, our grown children and the changing ways of modern youth, the influence of Heaven on mundane Earth, the habits of crows and kites. Always when the red ball had sunk behind the Indian Ocean, we bade each other good evening and parted with politenesses.

We spent a day on the Madh Peninsular, visiting the fishing villages, mingling with the fishermen, watching catamarans returning with crab and shrimp and exchanging smiles with the bold-eyed village girls spreading them to dry in the sun. I watched a young man proudly washing his small fishing boat adorned by brightly painted motifs with black soupy water from the stinking pollution of the Madh channel. We watched a practised street side cook frying samousas in Versova next to an open sewer where joking men battled in the filth to mend a pipe. We crossed with a happy jostling crowd on a snorting pedestrian ferry where the City of Bombay had been prevented from building a motorway bridge by the intransigence of the fishing community. I inspected a crumbling 16th century Portuguese fort and thought of those days when history took drastic turns. Beside a small Hindu temple under a peepul tree there was a memorial to de Almeida Rodrigues de Alcaiende surmounted by a Christian cross. There were cattle-egrets in golden mating plumage and a herd of water-buffaloes steadily moving across an empty grassland. Indian cricket was played by schoolboys, very seriously, on a field and a school-master used a political party's loud-hailer to simulate a commentary.

Walking in the streets around 'Seven Bungalows' amongst the high-rises where simple apartments were selling for 2,000,000 rupees [Max's *chowkidar* was paid Rs300 a month] a young man with a painted face strung a python round my neck. I ate a mountain of prawns Goanese style in the Channel Nine restaurant and did not suffer afterwards.

On another day Max arranged for his regular taxi driver, Mr Kamal, to take us to the city to visit the cave temples on Elephanta Island. Young women selling themselves as photographic models abused me because I did not want their services and monkeys groomed each other on the rocks beside the temples carved from the living heart of the island. An expert guide gave us an excellent encapsuled description of the dogma of the Hindu religion there and showed where the Portuguese had labouriously hauled up cannons to blast the carved images. How aggressively intolerant and unchristian Western Christianity proves to be over and over again.

We had *tiffin* in the grand Taj Hotel. We walked the downtown streets and spent an hour in the shade of the huge ceremonial arch of the Gateway to India, completed in 1924, overlooking the great sheltered harbour, watching the ferries and tourist boats. In that place, high officials, administrators, soldiers and traders of the British Raj had come and gone. For three thousand years a series of conquerors had entered through one or another gateway to India and their dynasties had ruled and declined, until Western technology also surged through those gates, an insidious anonymous invasion, and nothing was the same again.

I was so thankful that I had come to India to try to gain an understanding of this great nation of ancient civilisation on the other shore of the Western Indian Ocean. There were many geographic similarities to eastern Africa which it had crucially influenced, but there were extraordinary differences, all human.

The Old Fort Museum and a magnificent bronze cannon in Madras.

99

The Gateway to India in Bombay and the statue of King Shivaji, founder of the seventeenth century Maratha state.

EAST AFRICA

The 'aquatic men' at Tiwi Beach - my most important experience during
the East African safari   (Chapter 18)

CHAPTER TEN : A LETTER FROM OMAN

A letter from my son, James.

Ruwi,
Muscat,
SULTANATE OF OMAN
1st December 1987.

Dear Dad,

I have visited the Ministry of National Heritage and Culture in Muscat a couple of times. The first time, they said that your letter to H.H. Sayyid Faisal Al Said had not been received. When I took the copy of your letter I was given various excuses. The truth is that I think it is almost impossible for you to get a private visa at present. Tourist visas will not be issued for some time until 'international' hotels are completed where 'packages' will be accepted booked through tour companies. If you could be sponsored by a university or some contracting firm then it would be easy. Oman is not open to tourists, and that's the end of it. So I have visited the dhow-building centre and taken a number of colour-slides as you requested. It was very interesting and I'll describe it all for you as best I can. I've also bought some historical reference books which have been published here that you probably can't get in England to add to your library and I'll bring them home on my next leave.

I went to Sur twice to see how they still build dhows. Sur is about three and a half to four hours drive from Muscat and is connected to the capital by a good metalled highway that takes the long, inland route. The coastal plain is rough terrain and there is no through road beside the sea. Sur is a small town that is entered down a wadi. There are lots of ancient agricultural terraces of alluvium and limestone rising up on both sides of the main road. It is a typical Omani town with many old, somewhat scruffy one or two storied buildings. TV aerials sprout on the roofs now, but the streets are relics of times when few cars were about: not that long ago in Oman. A new road is being built around the town along the bayfront. The bay is large but has a very narrow mouth, no more than 150 metres wide. On the south side there are limestone cliffs, and on the north is the sandy beach and a flat area where most of Sur town is situated. The majority of the dhow-building takes place on the north shore of the narrow mouth.

The first occasion that I visited Sur it was raining (or threatening to). It was dark and dismal and a strange sort of quiet wariness was felt as we waited for the storm to come. Most of the dhows are now built by Indian or Pakistani craftsmen - migrant workers are found at every level of society and in every commercial and government organisation in the Gulf. There are still Omani dhow-builders, but they rely a lot on Indians to do the labour. Logs of timber are imported from the Indian sub-continent to Sur where they are cut into planks by hand. The planks are cut to whatever length the logs dictate. The 'dhow-yards' are a maze of offcuts and mountains of sawdust.

Most dhows are built as fishing craft without masts for sails. The "thud-thud-thud" of diesel engines tells you how they are propelled these days. The average dhow is built about a frame of wooden ribs and each plank is hammered to ribs and beams with large iron nails which looked as if they had been locally cast. The planking is covered by an oil mixture of some sort which gives new dhows a deep orange glow. Many have decorative carvings on the stern and bows. On my first visit, a very large dhow was being built with beautiful carvings on the stern and a fine bird for a figurehead. It had been commissioned by one of the aristocratic Omani families and after her sea trials was to be sent to England to have radar, latest electronic gear and luxury fittings installed. Her hull was an excellent example of ancient design and craftsmanship.

The second time that I visited Sur was during a week-end camping party at nearby Qualhat which was an Indian Ocean trading centre from the beginning of the Islamic period (approximately 700 AD). It was sacked by the Portuguese in the 16th century and finally ruined by an earthquake. Marco Polo is locally reported to have travelled there, but I have also read that he never left Persia. On this visit it was a very hot and sunny day and Sur was quite different. The town was quiet and seemed deserted. We

103

crossed the mouth of the harbour on a little ferry, like a barge, and walked around the village on the southern side to see the ancient fort there. The village is inhabited by fishermen and had a lazy atmosphere although some young children came up and were curious about us.

The large, ornate dhow that I had seen building last time had been launched but was resting on her keel because the tide was out. Children were playing on her deck and on other beached dhows. Some of these dhows were being caulked by their crews with a foul mixture of boiled fish, tallow and who-knows-what! It smelt so disgusting to our noses that one of my friends had to leave otherwise she would have been sick.

You asked about dhows stitched together in the ancient fashion. I did actually see some lying, rotting, on the beach at Taqa on the southern coast north of Salala, near the ancient port of Abysoppulus, fabled to be part of Saba's spice trade route before the Christian era. They were surrounded by modern aluminium hulls. There are lots of dhows of various types lying on the beaches of Oman and the net-fishermen still use the smaller ones to pull out from the land with oars to hand their nets. These are mostly being replaced by fibreglass boats and outboard-motors these days, except in Sur where the old traditions are still being kept.

I hope the colour-slides help you; every one says more than I can put into words.

Lots of love,
James.

*   *

Ahmed Hamoud al-Maamiry writes in *Oman and East Africa* (revised in 1985):

> The Omani Arabs were not the first visitors to the east coast of Africa. The Sumerians who lived in Iraq about 7000 years ago were the first people to make voyages on the open sea. .... The Assyrians also made sea voyages and it is quite possible that they reached the east coast of Africa where they left the witchcraft which is still being practised amongst the

coastal people. ... Another interesting connection between Assyrians and East Africa is the use of the sign of a horn called in Swahili, 'Siwa', in writings and sculptures to indicate strength and chieftainship.

The Periplus of the Erythraean Sea, the Alexandrian Greek trading manual on the Indian Ocean written about 100 AD, is definite about Arabian influence, and indeed control, of trading stations in East Africa,

> Chapter 16: From here after two courses off the mainland lies the last mart of Azania (East Africa), called Rhapta, which has its name from the aforementioned sewn boats, where there is a great deal of ivory and tortoiseshell. The natives of this country have very large bodies and piratical habits; and each place likewise has its own chief. The Mopharitic chief rules it according to an ancient agreement by which it falls under the kingdom which has become first in Arabia. Under the king the people of Mouza (a city just north of the entrance to the Red Sea) hold it by payments of tribute, and send ships with captains and agents who are mostly Arabs, and are familiar through residence and intermarriage with the nature of the places and their language. ...
> Chapter 18: And these are almost the last marts of Azania on the right hand. ....

There has been considerable scholarly effort devoted to identifying Rhapta. It was certainly on the coast of Tanzania, and many have suggested that it was situated at the mouth of the Pangani River, close by the modern port of Tanga. The Pangani is one of the major rivers of East Africa and has its source at the Kilimanjaro massif. There is a report of a Greek trader, Diogenes, who, before Christ, travelled up an East African river and sighted mountains with snow and lakes, and thus supported the concept of the Nile rising in many fountains at the 'Mountains of the Moon'. Since there was regular trade along the coast, there would have been many anchorages and safe havens known to pilots. G.W.B.Huntingford, an expert on *The Periplus* believed it is likely that Rhapta was either at Kisiji (about 60 miles south of Dar-es-Salaam) where there is a small river, or in the vast Rufiji Delta opposite Mafia Island. Rhapta was obviously a place of importance, it was held in tribute to Kholaibos of Saue, the King of Mouza, a powerful trading manufacturing and seafaring state on the south-west corner of Arabia, traditional home of the Sabaeans. (Queen of Sheba in Solomon's day).

An early Arab geographer, Ibn Hawqal wrote in the 10th century that there was a race of 'white' people living on the East African coast which has led some historians to conclude that they were descendants of Alexandrian Greek traders. They may have been, for Greeks certainly traded in East Africa and Southern India, but it is much more likely that they were Omani Arabs or Persians.

The modern *Africa Pilot* (1980) states:

> Between Kikunya Mouth and Ras Pembanyasi 32 miles ENE (the piece of coast north of the Rufiji where Kisiju lies), the coast is mainly sandy with no marked projections and is fronted by a drying sandbank which extends as much as one mile offshore in places; several rivers with wide mouths flow into the sea along this coast and, although all the mouths dry, the rivers are accessible to small craft at high water.

Although sands shift over the centuries, this may not seem a suitable area to establish the most important market port of that early era on this coastline, so perhaps Mafia Island or Kilwa was the location for Rhapta. Kilwa Kisiwani particularly assumed great importance in medieval times. In 975 AD, Shirazis from Persia took control of Kilwa where they found Arabs already in occupation. The Shirazis bought the island from the Lord of Kilwa 'for as much cloth as would go around it'. In the 14th century, Kilwa was the powerful city-state controlling the gold trade with Great Zimbabwe and I always believe that tradition and old knowledge rather than chance applies to the choice of the site for a city. I have to admit, however, that this could be rather sentimental and from a negative point of view it is likely that Rhapta was established on a sandy island or seashore, because otherwise its remains might have been found by now, and Kilwa has been well explored by Chittick. Similar difficulty surrounds the precise location of ancient Sofala on the Mozambique coast, as I described in Chapter One.

[Note, September 2008 : Thanks to Prof. Felix Chami of the University of Dar-es-Salaam it has now been established that 'Rhapta' lies closely north of the Rufiji Delta, some 50 kms from the sea. It was the chiefly capital of neolithic farmers and fisherman who were trading with seatraders well within the first millennium BC. There was obviously a settlement at the seaside, since buried by floods and cyclones, where seagoing dugout canoes were employed as well as fishtraps in river estuaries.]

At the end of the 15th century, the Portuguese explored the East African coast and I can quote the Vasco do Gama *Roteiro,* or *diario,* of his voyage:

> After we had been here [Quelimane, near the northernmost modern Zambezi River mouth] two or three days [about 25 January 1498] there came two chiefs of this land to see us; they were so haughty that they valued nothing that was given to them. One of them was wearing a cap on his head with the hems worked in silk, and the other was wearing a cap of green satin; and there had come in their company a young man who, as we gathered from gestures, had come from a far-off country and said that he had seen great vessels like those that carried us.

Quelimane was not a major trading port, but it was strategically placed at the mouth of a river in the Zambezi delta system that Vasco da Gama's fleet had approached to obtain fresh water and to careen their fouled ships, but the people were in close contact with Middle-East and oriental trade.

Further north, da Gama reached the Arabs and Swahilis themselves at Moçambique Island:

> The men of this land are ruddy in colour and of good physique. They are of the Muhammadan faith and they speak like Moors [Arabs]. Their clothes are of very thin linen and cotton and of many-coloured stripes. All wear caps on their heads hemmed with silk and embroidered with gold thread. They are merchants, and they trade with the white Moors [Arabian Arabs] four of whose vessels were here at this place, carrying gold, silver and cloth, and pearls and seed-pearls and rubies and the like: men of this land use all these things. It seemed to us from what they said that all these things had been carried here from India, and that the Moors had brought them, except the gold; ... In this place and island which they call Moncabique was a chief whom they called Sultan.

A Turkish admiral, Kâtibi Rûmî, compiled a sailing compendium with charts in 1554, during the reign of Sultan Suleiman Khan (1519-15660. It was known as the MOHÎT, *The Mirror of the Indian Ocean.* Down the East African Coast there are a number of recognisable ports of call on his maps: Bandar Maqdaso (Mogadiscio),

107

Malandi (Malindi), Mombasa, Wasini, Zangibar, Kilûa (Kilwa), Mosambig (Moçambique Island) and others. The interpretation of his latitudes show good accuracy and it is also possible to clearly identify the following along the southern Mozambique shore: Khôr Kuwama (Zambezi or Cuama River), Sofâla, Kiluane (Ilha de Chiloane), Sar-Nôh (Cape Corrientes). I have been fascinated that the modern place names on the eastern African coast have had such integrity over at least five hundred years in the literature of diverse people.

It is especially important and noteworthy that the MOHÎT locates two places south of Cape Corrientes: Waân at about 25 deg S (possibly the Aguada da Boa Paz) and the significant Sagara at about 26 deg S. Undoubtedly Sagara is Delagoa Bay, which shows that Arabs were in contact with the Tsonga-speaking traders of that area, at least in the 15th century, and there was exchange of intelligence even if there was no great trade in goods.

Finally, in order to complete the trail between the Indian Ocean traders and Africa, especially the southern interior, Peter S.Garlake writes in *Great Zimbabwe* (1973):

> In the mid-tenth century, the Arab geographer Masudi visited the coast and made the first mention of Sofala and the gold that reached it from the interior. So the products of the first mines, opened in the late first millennium towards the end of the Early Iron Age, seem to have very quickly entered overseas consciousness. ...

As the Zimbabwean gold trade waxed, so Kilwa and other East African Arab and Swahili cities burgeoned. Garlake summarised:

> ... the circumstantial evidence linking the fortunes of the two people [coastal Arab and Swahili and inland Zimbabwean] is strong enough to demonstrate conclusively that trade between the two groups was so considerable and closely linked that their economies were interdependent and waxed and waned together.

CHAPTER ELEVEN : AEROFLOT AND ELEPHANTS

I stood in the echoing cavern of the international arrivals concourse at Nairobi Airport, watching the perspiring Russian diplomats being greeted by broad untidy people from their embassy, followed by groups of neatly dressed Black men returning from conferences and indoctrination in Moscow. The Aeroflot flight had arrived. After some delay, young people in jeans and sweatshirts carrying their loaded backpacks started coming through: Aeroflot from Western capitals to Moscow and then to Nairobi, a two or three day journey, was one of the cheapest ways of getting to East Africa. At last I spied the anxious face of my nephew poking up above the crush, carried on his six feet four inches bean-pole body.

"I made it!" he said with a wide grin. "Am I glad to see you."

"How was the journey?"

"Not too bad, but an eye-opener. Have you ever been to Russia? No? It's an experience, I can tell you. I don't know where to start."

"Let's get a cool drink," I said guiding him away from the crowd. "Have you eaten recently?"

"Only Russian food, and that's weird."

We had hamburgers and Cokes while Jonathon wound down. "Moscow was amazing. Like a 1950s 'B' movie. The cars and trucks were the sort that I have never seen except in photographs or old films on TV. The transit hotel was just basic. And we were ordered about by these serious faced people. We weren't even allowed out of the door; there were guards on it. They wouldn't change a dollar traveller's cheque and I had no money for two days, it was bloody desperate. They would take Western plastic, but I don't have any. I shared a room with a very nice Danish guy and that saved me from going mad. We made friends with two Danish girls and they had two bottles of schnapps so we drank and talked for about twenty hours non-stop. They were the friendliest people I've ever met. We talked and talked about everything. ... And I met a couple of smashing English girls, fourth year veterinary students, they must have been ahead of me and they've gone. I must tell you about Aden ..."

The Aeroflot plane had stopped at Aden and they had been let out into the airport building. Aden had made a big impression. The temperature was over 100 deg F and the airport had not been repaired after the last bout of civil war. The plate glass windows were starred from heavy machine gun fire and the side of the runway was littered with damaged vehicles and burnt out fighter planes.

"Nobody would explain what had happened." he said.

"There was a rebellion against the Communist government and the Soviets went in and put it down very fast."

He shrugged, "If South Africa or America do something like that everybody is screaming at them, but the Russians do what they like."

"The Soviet Russians are masters of media control and disinformation," I said. "Anyway, we've got to visit an old man and then we'd better begin to get sorted out. After you've had a sleep, I think."

"When I get over being here with you, I'll need one. Is this really Africa? I can't believe it! Fucking marvellous!"

"It's interesting that you stopped in Aden," I mused as we walked to the car. "It's at the centre of the old Sabaean Empire which sent ships to East Africa two thousand years ago."

"History is what this expedition is all about for you isn't?"

"More or less," I said.

He laughed. "More-or-less. You say that a lot don't you?"

"More-or-less." I smiled. "It's true of most of life isn't it?"

During the next weeks I was determined to visit as many of the historically important places on the East African coast that time and money allowed. I had seen some before, but not with particular purpose and not soon after my journey around the Malabar coast of India. I also wanted to consider older puzzles which I believed were linked to the Indian Ocean: the evolution of mankind and the rapid expansion of Bantu-speaking Negro people over the southern half of Africa. The roots of those activities were here. I was glad to have Jonathon as a companion and we were going to have a great time. Apart from being my nephew, he was my god-son and I had promised him for years that we would have an expedition together before he

110

grew out of travelling with a middle-aged uncle. He was twenty-one that year. Having Jonathon as a companion was going to make this particular safari different to any other.

I turned off the freeway to Nairobi down Enterprise Road, heading into the industrial suburb of Nairobi. Smart factories and depots belonging to multi-nationals with familiar names were neighbours of dirty anonymous buildings along a potholed road. Trucks and cars swerved from one side to the other to avoid craters in the tarmac and ragged people lounged in groups on the sparse dusty grass of the verges. "Who are they?" Jonathon asked. I glanced at them. "Looking for work, I suppose. A million people live in the shanty towns around Nairobi, scratching a living. There's no dole here and crime is widespread."

We pulled up in the yard of a half-demolished colonial farmstead with new construction going on all around. A concrete mixer was running and dust hung in the air. "We're calling on an old man, the father of some friends back home, and I've got to hand over some presents. I've met him before and he lives a miserable life."

We went to the dilapidated bungalow which had been the farm residence twenty years before. The farm had been owned by one of the great White-hunters and colonial 'characters' but was now an industrial suburb that had created a fortune for land speculators after independence. In what had been the living room there was the smell of old dirt and stale cooking. Broken furniture and mechanical tools lay about. A refrigerator with a twisted door stood next to a disembowelled electric cooker and wires hung nakedly from a fuse-box. Cracked, dust-caked glass in the windows was framed by rusty iron burglar guards. A sullen Black woman with a snot-nosed child was ironing on a table and gave me an indifferent glance.

"He lives in one room here with a large African family," I explained quietly. The modulated tones of a BBC Overseas Service newscaster came from behind a door in the corner. I nodded in that direction, went over and knocked.

The old man got up to greet me with a warm smile. "Hullo there! So you came to see the old crock again. Sorry it's such a mess, but these bloody people don't care and it's not really my business any more. If I talk too much they'll turf me out, you see. Take a seat, if you can find one.... And who is this, then? Not your son is it?"

"No, this is my nephew Jonathon. How've you been?"

"Can't complain really. I'm seventy-four after all. But I've got this fever that comes and goes. Yesterday I couldn't get up at all and

I can't eat. I feel so weak. I went to the doctor's a month ago, I think I told you last time, but he's a bloody shyster anyway, like them all nowadays ......"

I listened to the old man's rambling, desolated in my heart for him. He was dressed in crumpled clothes and had not shaved for several days. In England he would have the appearance of an alcoholic vagrant, an old-fashioned 'tramp', but he was nothing like that. He was a sick old White man living in squalor in an African shanty; with thousands of pounds in the bank that he had no use for in Kenya and could not take away to live with his family. He was alone; his pals were either dead or long gone to live in Clacton or Bognor. As I automatically responded to his talk I wept inside.

"Have you eaten to-day?" I broke in.

"Well not really. You see I haven't been up to the supermarket this last week. My eyes are getting worse and I didn't feel up to driving. The insurance won't cover me anymore and I couldn't face some policeman on the take stopping me. It costs money every time somebody with a uniform looks at me and they know me round here of course." He laughed. "You've got to take the rough with the smooth, I suppose....."

What smooth? I thought, bitterly. "Come on, we'll take you shopping. Jonathon will carry your things and I'll be your chauffeur. Have you got money?"

"Ho, yes. I've got money." He shuffled to an old cabinet, painstakingly unlocked it and extracted a thick wad of two hundred shilling notes. "I find it difficult to get to the bank, they keep me waiting so long these days."

A thin hand gripped Jonathon's arm. "Look over there, boy," he said pointing to a massive eight-wheeled Mack truck with rusting machinery on the back. "That's my old American Army tank recovery vehicle. I've pulled more breakdowns out of the mud than anyone else in East Africa. They don't build them like that any longer: beautifully engineered, two separate gearboxes, six-wheel drive and a twenty-ton winch. That ten-ton mobile crane is mine too."

"Is that what you did?" Jonathon asked.

"Yes..." He paused. "I used to be the biggest private contractor in Kenya. I could tell some stories of those days."

"Come on," I said, gently. "Let's get you stocked up."

That evening we ate in Buffalo Bill's, a bar-restaurant near the concrete box hotel where I had booked us into a cramped double room. Buffalo Bill's was a well-known pick-up joint and as dark

112

approached with tropical rapidity the girls arrived like a storm of butterflies. The music was almost drowned by dozens of loud male voices and feminine shrieks and laughter. We took a table at the back and ordered steaks and beer and while we waited, we were bombarded by the penetrating stares of unaccompanied women seeking acknowledgement and invitation. I had seen it before a hundred times all over Africa, but it impacted on Jonathon like an electric force-field.

"Wow, I never knew anything could be like this," he said, awed. "Look at that girl there, smiling at me. She's fantastic." A Masai girl with extraordinarily fine classical Nilotic features; smooth brow, slim nose, chiselled lips and large almond eyes was transmitting strongly to him. When she saw my eyes on her, she grinned and stuck out her pink tongue.

"Remember...." I said.

"Yes, I know." He sighed. "Eighty percent of Nairobi prostitutes have the AIDS virus. Isn't it awful?" I laughed, he was not thinking primarily about their dubious future. It was awful for a young man, full of piss and vinegar, to be loose in central Africa in the late 1980s. It was like letting a starving person free in a delicatessen filled with poisoned food.

Later, a guileless teenage girl came and sat down and an older woman followed. I bought them beers and listened to them talk. They were from the port of Kisumu on Lake Victoria, a town which had become economically depressed after the break-down of commercial shipping on the lake following disputes between Tanzania and Kenya and the wars in Uganda. Flourishing colonial development frequently died from the disease of nationalist politics in Africa. She told Jonathon how she had come to Nairobi to be a dancer; she had not achieved success yet, but she was sure that she would be a great dancer one day.

"What are you doing, meantime?" he asked. "I mean, how do you live?"

"I pass the time in the night-clubs. I'm learning how it is in these places, you see. In Kisumu we don't have such sophistication."

I looked at her fresh young face, lit up with energy as she explained her dream to the young White man, and turned to the older woman next to me. "If you are her friend, how can you let her do this?" I asked. She shrugged and said disinterestedly: "It is her life, she has to learn. As I did." I looked at the heavy smudges under her eyes and the sagging breasts pushed out by an undersized bra. I smelled the sharp perfume overlaid by stale beer. She smiled mechanically at me. "Why don't we all go now to your hotel room. Come! Those young ones like each other, you can see that. We can all enjoy together." She took my hand possessively and I summoned the mental effort to get us disengaged.

Jonathon lay on his bed, hands behind his head, staring at the ceiling as I pulled my clothes off. "Aeroflot to Moscow. A Russian hotel like a prison with no money. Africa and ol' Den. That poor old man. And then Buffalo Bill's. All in three days. It's too much........"

Over the next two days we bought the basic necessities for looking after ourselves for the next eight weeks: Primus stove, frying pan, saucepan, plastic plates, enamel mugs, cutlery, panga, hand-axe, some tools, jerrycans and a stock of basic foods like rice, salt, oil and sugar. We had brought sleeping bags and a boy-scout tent with us and I had my trusty camp-bed, veteran of twenty years of safaris. I had been afraid that there would not be space in the small Mazda estate car that I had rented, but it all fitted in with room to spare. You can get away with surprisingly little.

Julius, my old friend from a previous safari, turned up and through him I was able to get information about useful people to see on the coast. In the few days waiting for Jonathon, arranging car-hire and getting acclimatised, Julius and I had renewed our friendship. He was a Kamba from Machakos District and I had visited his *shamba* and knew his family. His father was a fine old man, a retired engine-driver of the defunct colonial East African Railways system. Jonathon was impressed by Julius, "what a lovely man", and we were to spend much time together at the end of our safari.

I do not like Nairobi and I was glad to leave. It was a shabby facade of mouldy European tinsel planted on a bare African plain. The miniature skyscrapers were out of place amongst square miles of shanty towns. The cracked paving and rusting fountains of the ostentatious City Square, dominated by the solitary brooding statue of life-president Jomo Kenyatta before the depressing conference centre and KANU party headquarters with menacing security guards, seemed to epitomise all that is wrong with modern post-colonial Africa. Nairobi has lost the charm of a lighthearted colonial British settler town of the 1930s and 1940s and has gained nothing in exchange. Downtown was a miniature Johannesburg but its second-rate architecture, cut-price construction and unfinished streets had not the solidity and style of power and wealth that the South African city had. The African contribution was not of their tradition or

114

culture; it was the sordid mutation of new urbanised Africa of dirt and poverty that has followed the shattered dreams of hundreds of thousands of hopeful people drawn from the beautiful land that they know to the false grail of the clogged city. Those European and American tourists who view Nairobi with romantic eyes see vibrant colour and excitement of an exotic culture; what they do not see is that it is also exotic to the African and it has served him so badly.

I was in high spirits when we left the diesel exhaust haze of Nairobi streets and headed east for the Indian Ocean, on my quest once again.

The smooth highway to the sea followed the railway line built at the end of the Victorian era, not to develop Kenya but to open up the Eldorado of lush Uganda. It was a monotonous road, the boredom of the miles and the gradually changing landscape broken periodically by the danger of negotiating giant articulated trucks whose drivers were also bored and tired. The trucks carried the burden of commerce for a huge slice of the continent, deep into the rain forests of Zaïre along appalling roads. From the bare Athi Plain eastward of Nairobi, at long intervals, we descended a series of shallow escarpments and on each wide terrace the lower altitude provided increasingly tropical vegetation.

The air warmed correspondingly, until about halfway, at Mtito Andei, there were baobab and fever trees and I was sublimely at ease in shorts and bare feet. The pale hazy sky of the highlands changed to a clearer blue with tufty clouds. We talked a lot, me pointing out features of the landscape and freely distributing African lore and legend, Jonathon telling me about his recent escapades at home and his long-running battle to find good employment and a satisfactory career path in the difficult area of North Staffordshire where he lived. So, time passed quite easily and we did not stop until the car needed to be fuelled.

The petrol station was in a line of small *dukas* and eating houses. Returning to the car we were accosted by a small crowd of ragged and emaciated beggars. I handed out my small change automatically and disengaged myself as politely as possible. Meeting personal poverty in Africa and Asia becomes distressingly normal. In the car, Jonathon was subdued and his face was red.

"What's the matter?" I asked, wondering if my handling of the incident had worried him.

"I couldn't look those people in the eye," he said, his voice troubled. "If I had, I would have signed away my travellers cheques.

I'm glad you were kind, I'm afraid I couldn't face them." It was commonplace to me, but to a young man from England it had been a shocking surprise and I suddenly saw the incident through his fresh eyes. Famine victims are special horrors, specially reported on, and the endemic everyday poverty of Black Africa is not realised in Europe. The packaged tourists hardly feel it either, sheltered by their tour guides. I realised that having Jonathon with me would provide me any number of renewed insights.

On the way to Mombasa, I intended that we should have a couple of days in Tsavo National Park to see some game, enjoy the wilderness and to get used to camping together. Jonathon had been to South Africa when he was a boy, but had no experience of camping in a wilderness. I decided to enter Tsavo East at Manyami gate. The gateman was a wiry little man, friendly and cheerful, glad to see someone. When I signed the registration book, I saw that the last vehicle entered his gate three days previously. Few private cars tour the Kenya parks and the package tour kombis used another route.

"Where can we camp?" I asked him.

"You must go to Voi gate, or Aruba," he told me and I asked him for directions and if I could buy an up-to-date map.

He grinned at me, with embarrassment I suddenly realised. "No maps, not for a long time." He tore a page out of a note book in his desk and drew me rough directions. "Aruba is very good. That is the one where you should camp. But from here the road is not so good, it is better to go first to Voi, then to Aruba. At Voi you can camp and there you will see Eleanor."

"Eleanor?"

He laughed with enjoyment. "The elephant. She can eat bananas from your hand. That is Eleanor."

"They charge enough to let us in, you'd think they could have some maps for sale. Surely they don't want people to get lost," Jonathon grumbled, getting in the car. "Anyway, what's Eleanor about?"

"I'm not sure," I said, puzzled at my mental blank. "But, the name rings a bell."

Jonathon drove along the dirt road in the late afternoon, parallelling the highway a few miles away. It was a liberated ecstasy to be in African wilderness again. The sun was lowering and the light was softer across the plain. I stopped him at a battered signpost that triggered a memory, and we turned down a sandy stretch to the huge whale back shape of a monolith emerging from the flat thorn bush. I vividly remember visiting Mudanda Rock twenty years before and seeing many elephants, so we climbed its rough red surface with anticipation. It is shaped exactly like a giant whale, about 500 yards long and 50 feet high. Cautiously I peeked over the top, and there were no elephants, in fact there were no animals of any kind in sight. We sat down together and gazed at the African plain, silenced by its majesty. There were lion footprints in the sand where the car was parked.

Near the Voi gate we found a deserted campsite with rough open sided *bandas* [a kiSwahili word used to describe simple tourist shelters or huts]. They were scattered about a large cleared area with a few thorn trees. An ablution block with broken unusable toilets stood to one side. We were alone and chose the banda in best state of repair and unloaded our gear into the open shelter with its tattered *macuti* palm-thatch roof before gathering firewood. I made up the fire while Jonathon explored as the sun went down.

"Hey, Den!" I heard his excited call. "There are elephants here, by a little artificial waterhole."

There were two red-brown shapes not fifty yards away, taking their evening drink. They were two cows, and we watched them as they leisurely took their fill before slowly moving off. They did not seem to even glance our way. Jonathon was ecstatic and I was filled with pleasurable feeling. Then I suddenly remembered the story of Eleanor, an orphan raised by Daphne Sheldrick, wife of Tsavo East's famous Game Warden, David Sheldrick; one of the departed old school of East African conservators. She had looked after many abandoned baby animals and I had met youthful Eleanor twenty-two years before. I had forgotten about it, and now here was Eleanor again, although I did not know which of the two she was. What a coincidence.

From my Diary, THURSDAY 19 AUGUST 1965:

.... Drove to Voi and into Tsavo East park. A warm day and rather cloudy. Saw lots of animals down by the river - giraffes, different antelopes, elephants, buffaloes. African game guards were herding a teenage elephant and a baby black rhino, who liked lemon cream biscuits which it took from our hands. We camped there near a loo and showers. After dinner little bright eyes were watching, reflected in the light of the fire.....

The dry wood fire roared smokelessly and made a fine bed of coals for cooking beefsteaks we had bought in Nairobi. I was about to grill them when Jonathon grabbed my arm. "Over there...." he whispered.

In the dusk, I could see a large bull elephant standing by another banda. There was a squeaking sound and the splash of water. "He's just turned on the water tap." Jonathon breathed. We watched for several minutes as he drank from the trough under the tap until I suddenly realised, in the deceptive light of gathering night, that he was walking fast straight towards us.

"Into the car, quickly!" There was strained urgency in my voice.

"He won't come near the fire, will he?" Jonathon asked anxiously as he wound up his window.

"He will," I replied, peering through the dusty windscreen. There followed a frightening quarter hour. The giant old bull stood by the fire and went through all our gear. He solemnly ate our tomatoes, oranges and onions after spilling them out of a plastic bag. He picked up the box of cutlery and utensils and tossed it aside. He examined a jerrycan of water, lifting it to his mouth to taste it before dropping it and deliberately standing on it; it burst with a bang spraying water about, which seemed to annoy him for he then flung our bedding around.

"Jesus!" Jonathon groaned. "He's coming here." The dark purple of the sky disappeared as the giant animal towered over the car. We shook as he leaned against it and I prayed to him not to buckle the panels or try to heave us over with his tusks. Time stopped. The nostrils at the end of his trunk, as big as my hand, flattened on the windscreen as he felt it and smelled us. The radio aerial snapped with a crack. The bellows noise of his breathing came from all around as his trunk explored the doors and side windows. Then suddenly he was gone with a final shudder of the car.

Jonathon lit a cigarette with trembling hands. "Give me one," I said with an unsteady voice. "What an incredible experience! We'd better see what is left of our equipment. And you'd better turn off that tap that he was using..."

He had broken all our eggs, mixed up sugar and salt, eaten our vegetables and bread and thrown everything around, but apart from a piece of the car's aerial and the burst jerrycan nothing was damaged. I had kept a bottle of duty-free whisky from Heathrow, and we had a few stiff drinks, talking our heads off, before cooking a depleted meal.

118

As we prepared for bed Jonathon asked if he would come back, but I reassured him: "Elephants aren't stupid, he has checked us over and that's done now." I slept exhaustedly, without dreaming, but Jonathon told me next morning that he was awake most of the night. As dawn began to break, elephants had come again and stopped to sniff the air with probing trunks by the open banda before moving on.

Driving away from the campsite we met a uniformed game guard and I got out to question him. "A bull elephant came to our camp last night and ate our food and broke our water container," I said after greetings were exchanged.

"You were not hurt?" he asked, seriously.

"No," I said. "But frightened, because I did not know him."

"That one does not care about people," he said gravely. "He comes to our compound very often. Did you see Eleanor? She does not harm anyone."

"Yes we also saw two females, one must have been Eleanor."

He smiled. "It was a good experience for you."

From the luxury Voi lodge, close by, nestling on the upper slopes of a high stony hill there was an extraordinary view across the plain. Jonathon had never seen anything like it. I reckoned that we could probably see across forty or fifty miles of country, as flat as the sea. There was no sign of humanity. Great swirls of dark thorn scrub mingled with the pale gold of grass like the movements of ocean currents. We had cool drinks on the deserted terrace and watched a small herd of elephants and some zebra.

Later, I was conscious of a black swarm moving around the edge of the hill, like a mass of safari ants. "Buffalo," I said, pointing. There may have been up to a thousand of them. We stayed there for a couple of hours, unable to leave.

Across the flat plain, away from the Voi hills on a good gravel road, we reached the Aruba safari camp in the afternoon. There we took a better kind of banda, two rooms with louvre windows, comfortable safari chairs and beds with linen. There was a small provision store but it only stocked cigarettes, warm beer and biscuits. "Well, I wanted to be here for a few days," I said. "But since that ellie ate our fresh food we've only got a few tins of meat and rice. We must move on the day after to-morrow."

We were both disappointed, for Aruba was enjoyable. The bandas were situated amongst old acacia and wild fig trees within a moat dug to keep out the elephants and hippos, for its main attraction was a small lake formed by an unobtrusive dam across a minor tributary of the Galana River. At dusk, drinking a beer, we luxuriated in the dry warmth for we had dropped 3000 feet from Nairobi, and we could hear hippo grunting in the quiet. Later, elephants were drinking with loud hissing noises and snorting and squealing as they bathed, and when we were in bed I heard lions and a hyena. There were no lights in sight but for a twinkle locating the Voi Lodge twenty five miles away and the stars were ablaze.

I was woken in the morning by the scream of a fish-eagle and an elephant family was strolling along the far shore of the lake. Zebras were skipping about and I could see impala antelope and Thomson's gazelle on the skyline. I wandered out and walked on the dew damp grass clad only in a lungi from Cochin, the already warm breeze gently caressing my skin. Drongos, bulbuls and doves were calling and chattering in the acacias. Superb starlings danced at my feet, cocking cheeky eyes at me, waiting for crumbs to be tossed at them. Because of the rogue elephant, we breakfasted very simply on digestive biscuits and coffee before setting off for the Galana River further north across the plain.

I was particularly keen to see the Galana which runs from the Highlands near Nairobi to the sea at Malindi, because the few rivers that cross the dry plains of East Africa were the pathways for migration from fertile plateaux to lush littoral of the Indian Ocean since the beginnings of mankind on earth. The rivers on the east coast of Africa are rare and special because the tilt of the continent draws most of the water from heavy central African rainfall away down the Nile and Congo, leaving only the left over dribbles to flow eastward. From the deserts of Somalia to the great Zambezi delta, a distance of 2,500 kilometres, there are only half a dozen perennial rivers that make the magic connection across lands which are dry and baking for more than half the year. The Galana was one of them.

The road was quite good, hard red earth laterite and sand patches in the beds of streams flowing towards the river. Doum palms appeared, the typical palm of the Nile and the Sahel, with branching candelabra-like trunks. We parked at a vantage point and Jonathon searched for signs of game while I gazed over the scene and thought about it. On the north shore of the river there was a steep escarpment with a level top as far as one could see; the river had been gradually shaving away the great plain for many centuries creating a sharp divide between the flat land on either side, one side a couple of hundred feet higher than the other. From the south, this escarpment served as an unmistakable landmark, and if you were lost you could head towards it sure that the river lay at its foot. The river itself was running, snaking between clean white sand banks and dropping over shallow rapids with lush reed beds in clumps at the bends and on islands in the stream. It was a classical picture of an African river of adventure stories and films. One could imagine intrepid explorers dressed in jodhpurs and pith helmets fording it with long lines of porters, watching for crocodiles in the reeds, waiting to shoot a plump waterbuck, guarding the delightful heroine taking a discrete naked bathe in a cool, clear pool.

I also saw a mind's eye picture that was closer to reality. I saw occasional small gangs of African traders, middlemen carrying elephant tusks, rhino horn, beeswax and tortoise shell plodding steadily ocean wards, singing to help the monotony pass, aiming for Malindi at the river mouth where the Indian and Arab ships waited. Probably they herded some cattle too. A couple of months later, the parties returned, loaded with bales of cloth, glass beads and iron implements, singing more joyfully for they were heading home to wives and children.

Maybe eight million years earlier, baboon-like creatures headed towards the sea, following the vegetation and the water in small bands, escaping a land increasingly beset by awful droughts. At the seaside, they had to stop and adapt and over hundreds of thousands of years evolved into naked, semi-aquatic apes, swimming and walking upright and learning to talk as they gathered the fruits of the ocean and the coastal forests. Later, as climates changed, maybe bands of newly hominid creatures moved back up the river valleys and settled on the banks of Great Rift Valley rivers and the shores of the lakes.

I had a siesta in the warm breeze rustling through our banda when we got back and about three o'clock we went for a stroll around the moat surrounding the camp. We heard the hippos grunting and we watched some of the staff painting a shed by the waterfront where somebody had thought of fish-farming at some time. We were walking slowly back when some instinct made me turn and the scene that I saw made my breath catch and had the hairs rise on my arms and neck.

Over the crest of the gentle rise on the other side of the lake a red-brown tide was flowing, streaming a haze of dust above it. A rustling noise punctuated by faint grunts and rumbles reached across the water. I stood utterly transfixed, looking at the vanguard of a huge mass of elephants surging purposefully towards the water. They were moving quite fast and in unison. Hundreds of legs were swinging, hundreds of trunks curled and swayed, heads were bobbing and ears flapping.

"Ye Gods," I breathed. "Cameras!" yelled Jonathon. We ran for the banda and returned with our equipment. The mass was still coming over the crest. We both made estimates two or three times. There were undoubtedly over five hundred elephants there.

For an hour or more we watched them. They were scattered over an area nearly a mile wide and several hundred yards deep, milling about, moving into the water to drink and bathe, moving out again. There was squealing and deep trumpeting, splashing and hissing of water. Young ones scampered about and old bulls stood stationery for periods guarding the skyline. We went in and made coffee, watching from the open windows, then returned to the moat as they began to move off. This operation was interesting, for it was not like the purposeful surge towards the water, it was a hesitant and almost confused activity. Groups would move off in one direction, stand about, then cross to meet other groups and merge again with the mass. I saw a big group go off then stop still for perhaps five minutes before changing its collective mind and reversing direction. Eventually, there was a determined departure in the direction from which they came, although there were a hundred or more still drinking and playing in the water. In another half hour the last of them cleared the crest, leaving dust glowing in the golden light of the setting sun.

We jumped in the car and drove around the lake to where I thought they might be. But they had melted into the bush by the time we got to the wide swathe of flattened earth where they had crossed the road. They had gone out of sight. When an animal has four legs which are about five feet long, a walk is as fast as a hard jog to us.

A tourist kombi overtook us on the way back, smart safari-suited viewers with binoculars and cameras peering out of the observation hatch.

"Those poor people don't know that there are five hundred ellies just a couple of miles away," Jonathon said.

I agreed. "They won't have seen elephants at all since they are all congregated in that giant herd to-day."

We talked about the event over dinner. It was obvious that the great herd did not move about the plain in one mass and the camp caretaker told us that they saw them like that only intermittently and irregularly. Something caused them to coalesce from time to time: all

122

the families and clans gathering from tens of miles, maybe hundreds of miles, around to go down to the water together. The confused behaviour at the end of the watering suggested that having drunk and bathed there was a sense of release and the giant herding impulse was weakened. No doubt, having left again in one mass, they would gradually peel off as first one dominant cow then another lost the crowd magnetism and led its clan away. What was that great psychic force? What triggered it? I did not know enough of the circumstances and was filled with wonder.

I woke at about two in the morning and went out, naked, into the night lit by the newly risen half moon. I felt close to the reality of my animal ancestry, far from the artificiality of cities and machines. The cool night air tickled the hair on my naked skin and I stayed out there for an hour or more. Away towards the Galana River I heard two different lions roaring and a hyena whooped.

Jonathon at the Voi campsite.

CHAPTER TWELVE : VASCO DA GAMA'S PADRÃO

Twenty miles from the sea, we drove on the last of the interior plateau at an altitude of about seven hundred feet, but signs of the tropical coast were showing. There were coconut palms and dark green mango trees around the small shambas of maize and manioc. I felt kinship with traders two hundred years before, arriving with their lines of porters and slaves carrying elephants tusks and recognising the end of another months-long safari from the arid interior, from the far distant green highlands and the spiritual mysteries of the frozen whiteness of the great mountain, Kerinyaga, later called Kenya by the White men. We descended the escarpment through the intruding suburbs of Mombasa, passed the belching pollution of the inefficient oil refinery with its stink of chemicals and into a tropical downpour, the rain from a low purple cloud so heavy that it was difficult to see the vehicle ahead of our car. Red mud flowed along the verges. Then we were clear and into burning sun and steam on Mombasa Island.

If I dislike Nairobi with its brash mess of bad attributes and distortions of both European and African cultures tangled with struggling 1980s technology, I have warm and relaxed feelings for Mombasa. It is an old city, founded about a thousand years ago, rich in established traditions from simpler eras of slow moving civilisations, sufficiently well founded to still resist the modern cultural onslaught with some strength. In eastern Africa, Mombasa is quite exceptional. There is no other large inhabited city in the whole of the sub-continent north of the great European colonial cities of the Republic of South Africa, which is more than a hundred years of age. Lamu, Malindi, Zanzibar, Mocambique Island and Inhambane are old towns, but they have so far retained the intimate scale of centuries ago. Apart from these, and Mombasa their queen, no town that fruited in medieval time, whether in the interior or on the East African coast has survived.

Such is the strange social history of eastern Africa. These few relics of old Africa are vital to an understanding of the peoples of the continent, because once their history is submerged by technical civilisation and the reconstruction in steel and concrete that seems to follow inevitably, there will be nothing left to which the interaction of Indian Ocean trade and African society can be vitally related. Preserved ruins, monumental relics, manuscripts, cave paintings and sculpture are real historical and archaeological evidence, but living towns and cities that span centuries are the only true means by which ordinary people can feel and believe in the soul of past culture and civilisation. Ruins are sterile intellectual places where the faint strains of psychic contact have to be sought with difficulty and patience; in places like Mombasa or Zanzibar it actually happened there, where people are living now.

I drove around to give Jonathon an idea, and to remind myself. The streets were filled with people, as I remembered, untidy and busy, with a style and atmosphere that is lacking in Nairobi. Nairobi appears more prosperous and though equally busy its people do not laugh as much. Mombasa has a smile on its face. We stopped on Mama Ngina Drive, overlooking the blue ocean, where plump men in T-shirts and baseball caps played golf, their round black faces shining with perspiration and concentration. A cabaret-bar which I remembered from twenty-two years before still overlooked the water, but they were busy and could not sell us needed cool drinks. Government House was now surrounded by a high solid wall, evidence of the lawlessness of the 1980s. But Fort Jesus still brooded on its coral rock cliff with ancient trees shading its walls.

I stopped by some curio sellers where I could see stools made by fixing concentric rings of cane around three stout sticks. They were identical to some I had once sat on at Nia-Nia, a remote junction in the heart of the Ituri Forest in Zaïre, so I had to get out to bargain with the jolly stall-keeper. But the stools were for her own use and passing guests and she would not sell them. "If you come back, maybe you will see the one who sells them. But, why do you want this kind?"

"I saw that kind very far away in Zaïre once. They were exactly the same and I always remember that place."

"What happened there?" she asked.

"We had been travelling for a long time and sleeping in the bush and we came to this bar. It had cold beer and stools like that. And we all danced in the street to 'boogie' music."

She laughed with pleasure at the little story. "We must try to find these stools for you. And what about the girls there?"

"Not as fine as those of Mombasa," I said and her shriek followed us to the car.

"I think these people are just incredible," Jonathon said. "They're so natural and so 'earthy'. You'd never have a conversation like that at home."

"It's Africa," I replied, grinning at him. "But I wish I could find out how the exact same stools were being sold here in Mombasa."

We stopped at the Manor Hotel, the only colonial hotel of quality on Mombasa Island. It was rambling with several verandahs and a court with palms and plants onto which the large dining-room opened. Behind, there was a walled car park with the *askari* watchman on duty. The servants were cheerfully polite and well-trained, and some were old and had been there many years. We had a large room, simply furnished and the doors and windows were rich solid mahogany. I telephoned my contacts at the museum and arranged to call. The shower gushed luke-warm water like a waterfall, the right temperature to wash away the dust and sweat of Tsavo, and I lay naked on the bed while Jonathon pottered about and laundered clothes.

Jonathon was determined to sample the infamous night-life of Mombasa and one afternoon we looked for the Sunshine Bar about which he had been told many stories by a friend who had served in a Royal Fleet Auxiliary vessel based on Mombasa. We found it on the long Kilindini Road which leads to the harbour. Faded photographs of strippers, topless dancers and fire-eaters flanked the doorway and within there was the tawdriness of any night-club seen in daylight. There were stained mirrors on the walls and low red stools and tables were scattered around the dance floor. In a corner the gear for a disco or a small band waited to be activated. In my head I could hear the shattering boom of the huge loudspeakers in that small room and the forced enthusiasm of the bored DJ's distorted voice announcing the next record. I heard the tired rattle of drums and clash of cymbals as an over made-up sweating girl in stale wig and spangled G-string came in to bump and grind. I felt the insistent hand of a bar-girl on my thigh and the warmth of her breath in my ear as she invited another drink. The universal ordinariness of this night-club in

Mombasa struck me as being a fine example of how modern Western Civilisation has downgraded entertainment and reduced the simple pleasures of music, wine and sex to such a lacklustre level of tasteless trumpery.

There were voices coming from a passage-way and we went through to find a long bar decorated with an amazing collection of shells and corals cemented into the walls. Three or four White men were there, salesmen or visiting technicians by the look of them, sweating in slacks and shirts with ties, drinking their cane spirit and Coke. A rattling air-conditioner blew stale warm air around. At the end of the bar there was an astonishing corrugated iron door with a huge padlock on it and as we sat on stools banging came from it. The barman went over and unlocked it to admit a freshly groomed girl. I caught a glimpse of a dusty compound and a shed with a row of doors before the iron door was elaborately padlocked again.

"What the hell?" asked Jonathon.

"That's where the resident ladies have their short-time rooms, I think," I said.

"Ah, the fast-AIDS station."

I laughed. Jonathon was good at puns and irony. He turned to me with his eyebrows raised. "It's not African, is it? There're much better places in Stoke-on-Trent."

Further down towards the dockyard gate there was an old double-storied building with wooden slatted shutters and wide verandahs with trellis work topped by a rusting corrugated iron roof, set back from the street in a sandy yard with an old mango tree in the centre. It must have been a colonial shipping-agent's office, now it was a disco-bar and 'lodging house'. On the trunk of the tree, posters advertising dancing and meals had been nailed up. "I'd like to have a look in here," I said. "A bit rough, isn't it?" Jonathon said, hanging back. I smiled: "This is African."

If I was choosing my own dive, I would have gone for that place. In the large, airy downstairs rooms the original teak office counter was the bar with battered tables and chairs around. Another room was obviously used for dancing since there were a couple of old domestic hi-fi loudspeakers hanging on the wall. The shutters were open and the fresh evening air drifted through. The rough-plastered walls had not been painted in decades and there was an interesting collection of old beer and drinks posters stuck on them. I walked through to the toilet and found the simple urinal trough well-scrubbed with a handful of naphtha balls in it. Jonathon was talking to a plump girl with shy eyes and a dirty dress behind the bar.

"The beer's not cold yet," he said. "They don't really open till after eight o'clock."

"What did you think of that?" I asked as we walked back to the street. He nodded: "Yes, that was African. But it's a bit far from the hotel isn't it?"

We had a happy dinner in the Manor Hotel dining room overlooking the palm court served by a friendly old waiter who remembered the colonial days. "Where is a good place to go now?" I asked him as I sipped an Armagnac with my coffee.

He looked me over and thought seriously before replying. "Well, there is one place, not far. It is called the Salambo and is a disco."

"Is it safe?" I asked.

"It is safe."

"O.K.," I said to Jonathon.

It was a simple basement disco with an entrance fee of fifteen shillings and a big quiet man with watchful eyes at the door. The beer was at standard prices. The music was a mixture of western rock and African 'boogie', and the sound was clear and not too deafening. The place was crowded with mostly Black people but we managed to find a small table and the cruising girls were cheerful and did not hassle us. Jonathon loved it and I enjoyed jumping on the floor to the 'boogie' music.

We got into conversation with a middle-aged fellow in smart clothes at an adjoining table. He was there with two girls, one slim and well-dressed with serious eyes and the other plump and jolly. We discussed the merits of Zaïre music compared to East African boogie. Mbilia Bel, an international Zaïrois singer, was being played. The man said he was a trader from south of Mombasa and he had a couple of trucks which he used to go into the bush in the interior of the Kwale District.

"We are from Kisumu," the jolly girl said.

"Oh, yes," I said. "I want to go to Kisumu."

Her eyes lit and she spoke rapidly to her friend before turning back to me. "You must take us with you. The two of us are related and we need to return home."

"They are nice girls, you should take them," the man agreed. "You will enjoy them."

"I like your son," the jolly girl said, grinning at Jonathon and touching his hand. "And my 'sister' likes you." The serious, slim girl's eyes were resting on me. "But we can change around. We can show you many interesting things on the way, and we know the safe places to put up without spending much money."

The man laughed. "You see. It was good luck to meet to-night. And I must return to the bush to-morrow."

It took some time to convince them that we were headed for Malindi and Lamu first. We had some beers and they told us about conditions in Kisumu, on the shores of Lake Victoria, where there was much unemployment and depression because of the failure of the Lake trade with Uganda and Tanzania. I was reminded of the young would-be dancer at Buffalo-Bill's, who also hailed from there.

"Kisumu used to be a very bright town," the serious girl said. "Now it is quiet, but you should see it. It is very interesting and there is history."

Before leaving Mombasa we spent time in Fort Jesus. When I first visited it in 1965 it had recently been taken over from the Prisons Department and was being converted to a museum. The shell was there but the interior was all red earth, excavations and remains of demolished British colonial buildings. To-day it is a fine museum with green lawns, flower beds and coconut palms within one of the major historic relics of East Africa.

Ibn Batuta also visited Mombasa and wrote:

> We came to Mambasa, a large island two days journey by sea from the Sawahil country [presumed to be the coast southwards towards Zanzibar and Kilwa]. It possesses no territory on the mainland. They have fruit trees on the island, but no cereals, which have to be brought to them from the Sawahil. Their food consists chiefly of bananas and fish. The inhabitants are pious, honourable, and upright, and they have well-built wooden mosques. We stayed one night in this island, and then pursued our journey to Kulwa, which is a large town on the coast.

Because of their early friendship and long alliance with the Sultans of Malindi, the Portuguese did not bother much with fortifying their base in East Africa in the early years. They were always at odds with the Sultan of Mombasa, but neither side were powerful or earnest enough for drawn out warfare. D'Almeida, the conqueror of Oman, sacked Mombasa in 1506 because the sultan refused to accept Portuguese suzerainty and thereafter there was relative peace for a generation. In 1528 Nuño da Cunha, en route to Goa to take up the vice-royaltyship of India, sacked and burnt Mombasa again because the Sultan would not accept Portuguese suzerainty and was continually harassing the Sultans of Malindi and Zanzibar who were allies of Portugal.

In the early 16th century, Duarte Barbosa, a chronicler of the Portuguese Empire, wrote of Mombasa:

> It is a town of great trade in goods, and has a good port, where there are always many ships. It is a country well supplied with plenty of provisions, very fine sheep, which have round tails, and many cows, chickens, and very large goats, much rice and millet and plenty of oranges, sweet and bitter, and lemons, cedrats, pomegranates, Indian figs, and all kinds of vegetables, and good water. The inhabitants at times are at war with the people of the Continent, and at other times at peace, and trade with them and obtain much honey and wax and ivory. This King, for his pride and unwillingness to obey the King of Portugal, lost his city and the Portuguese took it from him by force, ...

In the 1580s a powerful Turkish privateer, Ali Bey, appeared from the Red Sea with the authority of Moslem rulers to obtain local support and the notorious Simba warriors from south of the far Zambezi stirred up the whole coast. Portuguese interests were endangered, a major effort had to be made and Fort Jesus was built. It was not such a fine architectural construction as the Fortress of São Sebastião on Mocambique Island, which was designed by one of the best medieval military engineers in Portugal, because it had to built in a hurry. Local engineers from Goa rapidly completed Fort Jesus under the direction of João Batista Cairato on 11th April 1593, but it was practical and withstood many sieges.

There was peace until a Portuguese-appointed Arab Sultan of Mombasa, Yusif bin Hassan, revolted and captured the fort by subterfuge, massacring the garrison, in 1631. But he wearied of ruling the Swahili people without the military backing of Portugal and may have become a pirate based on Madagascar before ending his days in Arabia. The Portuguese reoccupied the fort when he left and ruled unopposed until 1696 when the Omanis came.

James Kirkman, doyen of East African history and archaeology, describes the siege:

The original garrison had consisted of the Captain, João Rodrigues Leão, some fifty men with their women and children, and about 1,500 loyal Swahili from Kilifi, Malindi and Faza. The Captain died in October and was succeeded by Antonio Mogo de Mello. On Christmas Day 1696 when the Fort was about to fall, it was reinforced from Goa, but the reinforcements brought plague with them. On 20th July 1697, the Arabs attempted to take it by storm but were beaten off by the four surviving Portuguese, seventeen Bajun [Swahili people from the Lamu archipelago], four African men and fifty African women. By the end of August all the Portuguese, except a teen-age boy, were dead and the Fort was held by Bwana Daud, a cousin of the Sheik of Faza. In September the frigate which had brought reinforcements called in on its way back from Mozambique to Goa. It was wrecked on the shoal opposite the Fort and the crew became the garrison. The general, Luis de Mello de Sampião, soon died but his successor, Joseph Pereira de Brito, drove the Arabs from the surroundings of the Fort. In December a new garrison of a hundred men under Leandro Barbosa Soutomaior was landed, and the crew of the frigate with Bwana Daud and his followers were taken to Goa.

But plague stayed and by the middle of December 1698 only the Captain, eight Portuguese soldiers, three Indians, two African women and an African boy remained alive. The Fort was scaled during the night of the 12th December, near the gate in St. Mateus, but the Portuguese held out in the cavalier bastion until seven in the morning of the following day. Then the Captain was killed and the survivors surrendered, but later one of them blew himself up with many Arabs in the powder magazine over the gate, where he said gold had been hidden. A few days later, the relief ship arrived from Goa, saw the red flag of Oman flying over the Fort and sailed on to Mozambique. .... And so Portuguese rule and influence north of Mozambique effectively ended.

We read this bald account in Kirkman's guide-book while we drank iced fresh lime-juice in a sun-shelter high on the walls overlooking the old harbour. It was so tranquil there, so peaceful and the old horrors were long buried. It was hard to try and imagine the agonies of men and women over long months there nearly three hundred years before.

We walked through the old Swahili town that nestles against the Fort. I had enjoyed the old warren two years before, but it had become seedier somehow in the interim. Several houses were abandoned that I was sure had been noisily occupied before. I walked on thoughtfully, wondering what could be done to get life into this important live relic of history. Tourism would do it, but where was the capital and sensitivity to restore the old buildings and open restaurants, little hotels and tasteful curio shops without destroying the style and ambience? It could be an exciting living museum thronged with European and North American visitors by day and also by night if there was good policing. Many thousands of tourists came to the concrete-box package hotels on the coasts north and south of Mombasa Island. After a walkabout in the town and a visit to Fort Jesus they retired to become oiled seals on the lounging chairs beside the swimming pools or drank beer in the cramped macuti sheltered bars in the hotel gardens. They did not spend much time or money in Mombasa because it did not have sustained charm for them, and had a bad reputation for mugging and petty theft. I feared for the old town and was moody.

Overlooked by the Fort and the remnants of the Swahili town lies Mombasa Old Harbour which had been used by the dhow fleets from Oman and the Yemen for centuries before they stopped sailing the monsoons in the 1950s. Old photographs show a mass of ships moored there awaiting the change of the wind. They would take off from Arabia on the northwest monsoon and arrive in East Africa in January to trade, leaving again in April and May when the reciprocal winds began to blow. In ancient time, according to the *Periplus* they carried spears, axes, small swords, awls and several kinds of glassware, and wine with which to make friends. These manufactured goods were exchanged for ivory, rhinoceros horn, tortoise and turtle shell and coconuts. In recent centuries, the dhows brought dried fish, dates, cloth and carpets, ceramics from Persia and China (via the entrepots of southern India), glass beads, metal and wooden artifacts, which were traded for ivory and rhinoceros horn, animal skins, slaves (until the later 19th century) mangrove poles for house construction, charcoal, spices and gum. As time passed and fashions changed, the produce varied, but the trade lasted two thousand years. It was sad to stand there and look around the empty harbour. Only petroleum exchanged for paper dollars comes from Arabia to East Africa these days. How could that be progress?

Before leaving the next morning for Malindi, I called on the curio seller by the Fort and she greeted me with a warm smile: "So you remembered? But I have not seen the one who has the stools...." So we headed north along the fine coastal highway without the means to sit down in whatever campsites we found.

Malindi was one of the more important Arab trading settlements and may have been established as early as the 7th century by Omanis fleeing from the armies of the Caliph, Abd-al-Malik of Baghdad, during the first Moslem conquests. Other fleeing Arabs settled the Somali coast in the 8th century and Persians from Shiraz in the late 10th century set up local dynastic rule all the way down to Kilwa, where they found Arabs already in residence. Ruins that have been explored prove dates of occupation from the 9th and 10th centuries.

James Kirkman wrote, in *The Journal of Oman Studies, v 6* (1983):

It would not be overstressing evidence to consider that in the late 7th century there was a considerable migration of Arabs to the East African coast, who came to settle rather than to trade and return home.

Malindi reached a peak of prosperity during the 16th century, because it was there that friendly relations were established between the Portuguese and the local dynasty. The Portuguese local headquarters remained there for 95 years until they moved to Mombasa and offered the Sultanate of Mombasa to their protege from Malindi. Thereafter, Malindi was ravaged by native Simba and Galla invasions and became moribund until the coastal empire of the Omani Sultanate of Zanzibar was established and it was resettled in the late 1830s as a plantation colony served by vast numbers of slaves. When the British enforced abolition of slavery at the end of the 19th century, Malindi slid yet again into obscurity until British settlers saw it as a pleasant seaside resort before World War II.

A cursory look around Malindi gave the impression of a detached suburb of Mombasa. There was a busy market, many dukas with Indian and Swahili names, a few rough little lodging houses, a substantial residential area of small houses, and packaged tourist hotels discreetly sheltering behind high walls and barriers of trees and bougainvillaea hedges. We drove to the municipal campsite next to the deserted Silversands Hotel which was gradually falling apart in sad decay. The campsite was the only one on the coast north of

Mombasa where young backpackers from Europe spend days of their tropic odysseys. The sun had been shining all the way up from Mombasa and the heavy storm we had experienced there seemed to have been an aberration, after all it was not supposed to be the rainy season. I looked around at the rows of tents parked at the edge of the beach on well-cropped grass and suggested that we might pitch our small tent. But while I was waiting at the office, purple clouds rapidly moved in on the monsoon wind and a shower came hissing down.

"It's raining," I said to Jonathon. He nodded gloomily.

The short round manager with an Indian face smiled at me. "The rains are most peculiar this year, they have not stopped when they should. We have a banda free. That would be better for you."

We took a banda; a hut the size of a large tent, almost fully occupied by two beds, but it had a thick macuti palm thatch roof and the inside was lined by fine plastic mesh to keep out the insects. It was clean and there was a small verandah with room for two chairs. Sitting there, resting a moment after unpacking our food and cooking gear, I felt snug and secure when another shower passed over and drenched the tents and washing hanging on lines strung between coconut palms. A French camping safari group that were travelling in a Bedford overland truck huddled miserably in the back of their vehicle under its tarpaulin roof.

Eric Axelson, *Portuguese in South-East Africa 1488-1600* (1973), on the first visit of the Portuguese to Malindi:

> The day after leaving Mombasa the Portuguese captured a coasting baggala which contained not only provisions but silver and gold. Gama obtained information from the prisoners as a result of which he anchored in the roadstead of Malindi, close to four vessels from India. The local Muslims committed no hostile act, for the aged sultan and the regent doubtless appreciated that they could use these powerful newcomers in their feud with Mombasa. The Portuguese were fortunate enough to obtain one of the most distinguished Indian ocean pilots of the day, ibn Majid, and on 24th April [1498] the squadron sailed for India borne on the south-west monsoon.

[It has been more recently established that Ibn Majid provided advice; he did not actually pilot da Gama's ships. The pilot who was engaged at Malindi was a Moslem Indian from Gujerat.]

Axelson writes, regarding the expedition of Cabral in 1500:

... King Manuel sent out a fleet of thirteen sail, under Pedro Alvares Cabral, to profit by the footing gained in Calicut, to further friendship with Malindi, to sign a treaty of peace with the sultan of Kilwa. ...

At Malindi ... the Portuguese found three vessels from the gulf of Cambay, each of one hundred tons burden. The sultan sent the Europeans refreshments including 'the best oranges in the world' which cured those who were suffering from scurvy. ... The sultan and the admiral met on the water, there was an exchange of presents, and friendship between Malindi and the Portuguese was further pledged.

There was a modern jetty sticking out from the waterfront at the centre of the town which was to aid the promotion of the local fishing industry and alongside it was a cold store and market where excellent and cheap fish could be bought after high tide when the fishing boats could come alongside the jetty. We walked out over the drying sand and old coral towards the deeper water where Portuguese, Indian and Arab ships anchored together peacefully nearly five centuries before.

The monsoon was blowing strongly and waves were breaking over the reef which lies offshore to the south-east of the jetty, and in the small harbour sport-fishing strikers, commercial motor boats, small sailing dhows and dug-out canoes were bobbing and swaying at their anchors. A handsome young man, slim with Arabic features despite his coal-black skin accosted us and chatted amiably. He was a Somali, he told us, although he had been born in Kenya after his father migrated to Nanyuki twenty-five years before to join the Somali trading community there. He was brought up in Nanyuki but had come to Malindi because he felt drawn to the sea. His family were from Mogadiscio where they had always been traders with the ocean dhows, but when the trade had died in the 1950s, his father decided to emigrate. He and Jonathon talked while I was absorbed in this chance meeting and what it told me about the continuation of old tradition. It is more difficult for people to move about Africa to-day, with passports and work-permits, but they still do so. Movement about the continent has always been more common than Europeans have often thought, believing that tribal barriers and long distances made Africans simple tillers of the soil ignorant of the world beyond the nearest mountain or river.

"Do you want to see the old town?" our new friend asked, then sensing my hesitation he smiled:

"I don't want money, I just want you to understand our town." He led us into a maze of alleyways through simple, square wattle and daub houses with macuti roofs and a few more substantial buildings of cement block and corrugated iron. Children followed us and people smil?d after he spoke to them, explaining what we were doing. He reassured bystanders when we wanted to take photographs. I was wondering how to reward him, when I suddenly remembered that we still needed stools and asked about them.

"That is easy. I have a friend who makes any kind of furniture. Come." I followed him to a shed filled with the fresh sweet smell of piles of aromatic shavings and sawdust and met two quiet serious men who listened to the translated requirements. They were proper furniture-makers of course and were not interested in the kind of stools I had seen in Mombasa; they would build me proper stools. They needed the money in advance and we arranged that I would fetch the stools the next afternoon, meeting the Somali at the fish jetty.

"Do you think you'll ever see your money or the stools?" asked Jonathon. "We'll never find that shop amongst all those houses."

"Oh, I think so," I said. "Let it be a test if you like."

The next morning, just after dawn when I was up lighting the Primus stove for tea, the young Somali came through the campsite hunting for me.

"We forgot yesterday afternoon. To-day is a holiday and my friends must close their shop. So they worked in the night to make the stools. Come, they are ready." They were well-made square stools, finished with craftsmanship.

Later, in town we booked seats on the next day's flight by twin-engined Piper Cherokee that flies from Malindi to Lamu. On the way back I drove down the track leading to the coral promontory where Vasco da Gama's padrão stands. We parked under thickly spreading flame trees and walked to the shore alongside the wall surrounding a luxurious private villa. A gleaming cream Rolls-Royce was standing in a carport. "I don't believe that has moved since I was here two years ago," I said. "That's the massive continuity of wealth, if you like."

Da Gama erected his padrão, or cross bearing the arms of Portugal, on his return from India in 1499, but it was removed by objecting Moslems. Later Portuguese erected a replica and that survived, being set in concrete by a British Naval captain to preserve it both for the sake of sentiment and as a seamark which was its original purpose. The waves were breaking over the coral rocks as we walked out on the exposed point to where the white-painted memorial stood. Jonathon was fascinated by the waves breaking over the rocks with white thunder while I stood by the padrão seeing the Portuguese and Indian ships, and the many Arab dhows, that anchored in the shelter.

Two men in ragged clothes, probably in their forties, came to join me. They had pleasantly ugly faces with broad foreheads and their skin was the particular black that made me think they were from Central Africa.

They watched me shyly until I smiled and walked over. "*Jambo*," I greeted them and went through the usual ritual of where we were from and what we were doing. They were from Kisumu and were looking for work. People from Kisumu seemed to be haunting me. One said his name was Robert and every year they came to Malindi to work as waiters or in the kitchens of the big hotels that catered to the European package tourists. "I speak English quite well," he told me and I nodded. "But I speak a little German, French and Italian. Those are the people who come to Malindi now, especially Italian. We believe in friendships with all people in the world, so that is why we come here. Not just for the money, but because of meeting people from all over. We are Christians and we love all people."

I paused on the way back to where Jonathon was watching the waves. The two men were standing, arms folded, by the padrão looking out to sea as if watching for the returning fleet of the strange White men.

CHAPTER THIRTEEN : THE PURALAON ISLANDS

The Periplus of the Erythraean Sea (c100 AD) :

> Then the Lesser and Greater Strands, of another six courses, and after them in succession the courses of Azania, the first called Sarapion's, then that of Nikon, after which there are several rivers and a series of other roadsteads separated by several stations and courses of a day, seven in all, as far as the PURALAON ISLANDS and what is called The Channel, from which a little to the south-west, after two courses of a night and day along the Ausineitic coast, the island of Menouthias is encountered, ...

I was concerned about our car filled with camping gear so when we went to Malindi Airport to catch the plane to Lamu I was glad to see a battered sign pointing to a shack which said: 'Airport Police'. There were two tall, slim Kamba policemen who greeted me with smiles and an invitation to come into their little room. I explained my problem.

"You are very good to report what you are doing. That is what we are for. If people do not cooperate with us, then we are unable to assist. Now that we know your car will be here for days, we will watch it carefully." They walked back with me and looked over the vehicle. "It will be alright."

They both studied me with knowing grins. "Of course, you can help us when you return and all is well." I wondered how much appropriate 'help' should be, but that could wait.

In the simple airport building a man in overalls looked at our tickets and added our bags to a pile on a wheelbarrow. "You are checked in now!" he declaimed, and laughed at my expression. "Here at Malindi we are very quick, not like Nairobi."

One of our policemen was acting as the security check as we went out the door, his battered SLR gun leaning against the wall. He was looking in handbags and held me back with a detaining hand until Jonathon and the other passengers were at a discreet distance. "You have many films for your camera, my friend," he said. "You can spare one?" I picked one out and gave it to him,

"Of course," I said with a forced smile. "Of course, my good friend."

The sky was clear but for a bunch of rain clouds moving up the coast from Mombasa which our plane easily outdistanced so I could look down, absorbed, at the coast-line. One advantage of small propeller planes is that you fly below 10,000 feet and fly less than two hundred miles an hour; perfect for sightseeing. If ever some entrepreneur starts dirigible flights from London to Cape Town I will queue for days to get on. Close to Malindi, the Galana River snaked to the sea and I pointed it out to Jonathon, speaking in his ear over the noise of engines: "The traders' route I told you about on its banks in Tsavo." He nodded. Thereafter, the coast curved gently forming a long shallow bay until the delta of the Tana River was reached.

This was another of the few great rivers of eastern Africa, rising thousands of feet up in the Mount Kenya massif. Diogenes, the Greek trader quoted by Ptolemy as the first European reporting the equatorial snow-capped Mountains of the Moon is believed to have travelled up the Pangani River to see Kilimanjaro. He could as easily have travelled up the Tana or Galana to see Mount Kenya. The system of the mouths of the Tana and the Galana and the complex Lamu archipelago was one of the principal reasons for the early and long-lasting Arab, Persian and Turkish contact with Malindi and the area which the *Periplus* named the Puralaon Islands.

Although the Tana does not make direct contact with Lamu or the other islands to-day, it was clear from the air that the archipelago with its several twisting channels and waterways that approach the delta was perfectly sited to provide locations for a dozen settlements of different petty chieftainships and sheikdoms, secure from the mainland but with sheltered access by small craft to the Tana River. In any case, who knows exactly where the Tana delta had been one or two thousand years ago. From the air it was clear how flat the sandy coast was with rivers and creeks meandering in huge S-bends across the landscape and inland as far as the hazy horizon. I felt tremendous excitement watching from my flying platform, seeing it all fit into place in my imagination. 'The Channel' mentioned in the *Periplus* was

140

obviously the inland waterway to-day perhaps more than a hundred miles in length, through the islands and reefs. If the Tana River delta channels had linked up with the Lamu islands, 'The Channel' could have wound along for over a hundred and fifty miles, providing sheltered coastal waterways linking two major strategic rivers and several secure island bases, whatever the state of the monsoon, creating an enviable base for ocean traders.

We landed on a rough coral-rock strip on Manda Island, immediately north of Lamu Island and separated from it by a creek maybe a kilometre wide. A corrugated iron roofed shelter was all that composed the airport at this end of the journey, and beside it a small crowd of porters and touts was waiting, calling out and waving. A tall young man with huge eyes and a gollywog hairstyle quietly took my bag and talked to me as we walked out on the jetty to a ferry that was waiting.

"Yes, Sir. I know what you want. A small lodging for yourself and your son. One room with two beds, very comfortable and quiet with shower bath and lounging room. I know of two such places which have vacancies, so don't worry. Costing only about sixty shillings per day. You pay one day in advance, each day. You give me a small tip. And then I can arrange excursions for you. ..."

"What is your name?" I asked to stem the flood of his patter.

"Oh yes, Sir," his face lit in a delightful grin and he clapped his hands. "Yes. My name is Borbo." We shook hands solemnly and clambered down into the ferry.

He was true to his word and took us to an old house, called *Sumuki* (Fish in Swahili), where there were four rooms opening off a tiny interior courtyard on the first floor. Neither the floor nor any wall were level or flat, the doors and windows were made of old hardwood and did not fit well. The bathroom contained a huge tank, which was storage and not for bathing. It was filled by the young house-boy hauling buckets from the public tap outside every morning when it was working for a few hours. He then hauled it to barrels on the flat roof which fed the shower and flushing toilet. In the tank a large fish lived to feed on mosquitoes and other insect larvae. I asked the boy if it had a name and he said that it was 'Mr. Fish'. Our room, with a drawing of a swordfish on the door, was about six feet by ten and had an unglazed window with bars across it which looked down an alley to the sparkling blue water of the creek and the green line of the mangroves on Manda Island opposite. The walls of the open, interior court were still covered with maps, faded old press photographs of J.F.Kennedy, Bob Dillon and the Rolling Stones, cuttings from magazines from the 1960s and early '70s and some strange drawings by the 'hippies' of those years. Lamu had been one of the more important dream-destinations then. Samaki was a folk-museum and I wondered if any of its guests ever came back in respectable later life on a pilgrimage to their idealistic and carefree youth.

"I wonder what weird and wonderful things went on in these rooms fifteen years ago?" Jonathon mused, looking at the drawings and pictures. "Plenty of hash, LSD, local rum, a hot climate so no clothes. Everybody freaked out. I think I was born into the wrong generation..."

I laughed. "Maybe it would have been more fun two hundred years ago with a more noble and delicate debauchery. You should read Michener's *The Drifters*. His characters weren't very happy."

Lamu is a central compact mass of solid houses in Swahili and Omani tradition, like our Samaki lodgings, and wattle and daub African huts in the surroundings. It is not a big town, it looked minute from our circling plane, and its longest axis, along the straight waterfront, is less than a mile. So it is a town that can be walked around completely in an hour. We strolled the waterfront and met Borbo chatting with some companions, enjoying the cool of approaching sundown.

"Sit down, my friend," he invited, and we joined them. He gave us a quick rundown of information. Lamu was 'dry' but there was a licensed hotel three kilometres away at the north-east point at an old village called Shela where there had been a battle between the people of Pate and Lamu and Pate had been repulsed. There were several good restaurants in town, he named them and described their specialities, and there was a tourist hotel near the museum but one had to pay a sort of club 'membership' fee to drink there. He was available to guide me and arrange excursions.

"I'm interested in historical places," I told him. "I would like to go to Pate, and I want to see where dhows are built in the old ways. Maybe like they still build them in parts of Oman or Dhubai. Is this possible?" He agreed to find out about Pate the next day and he would take us to Matondoni where dhows were built.

I was interested in Borbo for he was a well-spoken and sparkling young man. I had noticed that he had addressed other tourists in French and I complimented him on this.

142

"I learned my not-good French when I travelled in West Africa," he said.

"West Africa?" I was astonished for he seemed to be in his mid-twenties and Kenyans of that age have little opportunity to travel. "Were you a sponsored student?" I asked.

"No. I am from Lamu and I decided I should learn about other parts of Africa before I settled. I received some money, so I travelled to Uganda, Zaïre, Cameroon, many places. In Algeria I was tired so I took a plane to Germany then later I returned home."

"How did you go? On buses and hitch-hiking?"

"On trucks and buses. Yes, and lifts if possible. I was young, only nineteen, so I didn't care how I travelled or where I went." At my urging he described his routes and a couple of adventures. The story was restrained and low-key.

"So you went through Isiro?" I smiled, recalling my own memories of a town in the Zaïre rainforest. "Do you remember ...?"

It was dark when Jonathon and I wandered on to the Sindbad Restaurant, one of the several recommended by Borbo. "I can't believe all this," said Jonathon. "Sitting on a quay wall in Lamu talking about Zaïre bars and the Sahara desert with a Black guy who runs about renting cheap rooms to tourists....."

I smiled. Africa is always surprising. And so was the Sindbad Restaurant, a rough shed of a building with bougainvillaea tangling the supports of the open verandah. Paul Simon's *Gracelands* and reggae music played cracklingly over small speakers fed by a cassette player, delicious iced fruit juice appeared at the table as we studied the scruffy, hand-written menu. We ordered grilled crayfish, chips and salads from the young proprietor who waited, weaving to the music and singing quietly.

The crayfish were huge and carefully grilled with a light butter and lime sauce. The chips could not be faulted by any English connoisseur, the salad was a pile of sliced onions, tomatoes, shaved carrots and lettuce. What was missing was a bottle of iced white wine, but the crayfish was delicious and it all cost an astounding sixty shillings [£2.50] each. I slept content on my coir matting bed, after drifting for a while listening to Jonathon's quiet breathing beside me and the shuffle of sandals and an occasional call in the street below.

In the morning I was woken by the sun and the noise of the house-boy hauling his buckets of water to the tank with 'Mr Fish' and the barrels on the roof. Appreciating this interminable chore, we were carefully abstemious with our washing, but most of Samaki's more transient guests were not. We became the oldest inhabitants after the first couple of days and when others who stayed a night or two ran the shower for many minutes the house-boy and I would exchange rueful smiles and he would roll his eyes. Lack of domestic water was the major blot on the good life in Lamu.

Borbo met us as arranged for coffee after our breakfast of french toast and sausages at the Kenya Soft Drinks restaurant nearby and I endeavoured to plan our days ahead. The problem with visiting Pate was the spring tides which made the channels difficult to navigate and the dhow-ferry could not run a regular schedule for one week out of every two. It would leave for Pate and maybe not return for two or more days if the timing of low water did not suit the captain. We should try to fix our programme first, then see if the ferry fitted. The priority was to arrange overnight accommodation, and to that end we had to meet a man called 'Bushbaby'.

We went in search of him and eventually tracked him down in a fine old merchant's house with a tall elaborately-carved, brass-fastened door and high ceilinged rooms furnished with inlaid wood tables, colourful Somali camel-hair rugs and shiny plastic-covered chairs. We were offered small cups of coffee; it was all very Arabic. 'Bushbaby' was a plump young man who spoke with an exaggerated British accent and called me 'Montgomery' in an old-fashioned way. He was pleasant enough with his pompous air, which amused rather than offended me for he was half my age. We got to know each other well in the next days, because Lamu is a small place, and I countered his drawling manners with teasing and leg-pulling and this suited us both well. 'Bushbaby' was trying to put together an organised and sophisticated private tourist operation and he had the right ideas, but was not organised himself. He told me several times that he knew this and longed for a trusted European partner with whom he could create a little empire: he knew local politics and how to get liquor and trading licenses and who to bribe and "suck up to". He needed somebody to organise and administer. There was a financial killing to be made in property development. I was satisfied that he was absolutely right, the Lamu archipelago was prime tourist country, it had all the natural advantages of mysterious indigenous history and several cultures, superb beaches on the eastern side, the rich ambience of the town itself, reasonable communications, intelligent people with a millennium of trading experience. Twenty years before I would have been sorely tempted, but 'Bushbaby' would have been a difficult and erratic partner. When he or others eventually found partners I

144

could only hope that the inevitable development would be restrained and tasteful, but after viewing what had happened to the coast around Mombasa I was pessimistic.

He could arrange for me to rent an apartment on Pate for any length of time, there were excellent servants available in a refurbished Swahili mansion of character that he managed for an absentee landlord. He would arrange for food and liquor to delivered. I became dazzled by his descriptions, I felt like a visiting Turkish Pasha, or Ibn Batuta travelling in the 14th century. I said I would let him know.

I had an introduction to the Curator of the Lamu Museum, but he was on vacation. This was disappointing, but I met a charming fellow who was the education officer and got to know him well too. He was an older man and a Swahili aristocrat. His father had been a member of the Sultan of Zanzibar's Council of Ministers before the Tanzanian revolution forced him to retire to an estate on the Comores Islands. I found him self-conscious about his breeding, but he was kind and helpful to me and we enjoyed each other's company. He was open on controversial subjects and local East African academic politics. His ambition was to be sponsored to enable him to do a PhD. at a British or American university. His interest was Swahili history, which created the bond between us, but he did not wish his research to be prescribed by professors for whom he had no respect and the university at Dar-es-Salaam required theses to be written in Swahili. So he lived in restless obscurity in Lamu.

The museum was put at my disposal and I spent several hours there. I was particularly excited by the scale models of the various types of dhow that had visited there or were built locally over the centuries. There were faded old photographs to show that the perfect models were not romantic reconstructions but accurate illustrations. There were three local types, apart from the range of trans-oceanic visitors from the Yemen, Persian Gulf and India. The *mtwepe* was a large vessel, capable of ocean voyaging, with sharp bow and stern and a simple square sail hoisted on a single mast. It was the direct descendant of the sewn ships of south Arabia of two thousand years ago, when planks were attached to the ships's frame and to each other not by nails or wooden fastenings but by hand-spun coconut fibre rope.

The traditional mtwepe, interestingly, did not have dolphins or birds for a figurehead but sported a large stylised camel's head. They were not 'ships-of-the-desert' but 'camels-of-the-sea'; clear suggestion that the first people to build them, Sabaeans about three thousand years ago probably, were desert dwellers and overland caravan traders who took to the ocean. What excited me particularly was the fact that mtwepes were still being built in Lamu in the early 20th Century, as the old photographs showed. That was almost unbelievable cultural continuity over two thousand years or more. On the other shore of the Ocean, my son had seen derelict sewn vessels at Taqa in Oman six months previous to my visit to Lamu. I excitedly studied the finely-crafted models for an hour or more.

The second type of East African indigenous vessel was the *jahazi*, a smaller open-decked ship suitable for the coastal trade. It carried a lateen sail on a long yard on the single mast and along its sides tightly woven macuti matting was mounted as protection against spray. The third type was the *mashua*, a fast boat used for offshore fishing, ferrying light cargoes or transporting people between islands and the mainland along the coast within the protection of the barrier reefs. Mtwepes had disappeared from the scene in the 1930s and that craftsmanship was undoubtedly lost now after two millennia, but jahazis were still common in the Lamu archipelago and further south around Zanzibar and Pemba. There were mashuas to be seen everywhere. When I was on Mocambique Island in the 1970s, I had seen two types of coastal vessels, similar to the jahazi and mashua, but subtly different in style; they had slimmer lines, sharper bows and were probably faster sailors. They had less of a pure Arab influence and more of a European, Portuguese design. The larger ones, the equivalent of the jahazi, had two masts and in those days their sails were painted with the traditional Portuguese cross, just as da Gama's ships were.

I asked 'Bushbaby' about the coastal carriage of goods by jahazi and he assured me that it was still a major activity. "But only in the favourable monsoon. For half the year when the sea is too rough the jahazis are too small to sail on the open sea and we don't have big dhows any longer. So, then Lamu is cut off except by road. Usually, at that time, we have heavy rains and the road across the Tana flood-plain is closed so Lamu can be isolated for weeks."

"How do you mean 'isolated'?"

"Completely cut off. The shops run out of sugar and flour, there are no cigarettes or tinned food. People get very anxious and nervous. That's one of the problems of starting a proper tourist industry. You can't fly in all those kind of things in light aircraft."

"But surely just because the jahazis can't sail that does not mean that bigger, modern ships can't come to Lamu."

"Of course not. The Kenya Navy sends its corvette with supplies for the army and the police, but it won't carry commercial goods."

"But there must be coasting steamers," I persisted. "The merchants of Lamu and Pate could combine and fill a coaster using a good shipping-agent. It would be good for tourism too, much more interesting for tourists to sail up from Mombasa overnight than spend twelve hours in a bus on those bad roads."

He touched my hand. "You see what I was talking about the other day, Montgomery. We don't have that kind of thinking in Kenya now. There is no coasting steamer, nobody can organise these things. I don't think there is a commercial coasting steamer based anywhere in East Africa."

"Extraordinary," I said almost to myself.

"I agree," he said triumphantly. "In my father's day there was a regular service, but it was organised by Europeans in Mombasa and those days were finished long ago. Now everything comes by truck overland, it costs much more and the service is erratic in the extreme. Never mind goods, when the big rains come and the sea is rough, ordinary people without money for aeroplanes can't travel, no matter what the emergency."

I remembered a delightful week spent sailing on a thousand-ton Portuguese coaster from Nacala in Northern Mozambique to Lourenzo Marques, fully loaded and carrying deck passengers, in 1972. I remembered sailing on a tough little South African coaster from Walvis Bay in south-west Africa around the Cape of Good Hope in 1970, against a great gale that was a re-living of da Gama's epic voyage as far as Natal. I also remembered examining and photographing five rusting coasters beached together in a rotting row in Dar-es-Salaam in 1985. The Swahili people were descended from races of great seafarers with three thousand years of maritime history. What had gone so terribly wrong since Independence in East Africa?

After a day, Borbo came to me with bad news. The Pate dhow had left and would not be returning for many days, as he had predicted. The moon was such that the tides were high at morning and evening which was useless since they needed high water at midday to pass over the reefs in daylight. I could get there, but I would have to hire a fast sport-fishing boat.

"How much?" I asked.

Borbo's eyes would not meet mine. "About six thousand shillings."

I sighed. "I'm not going to Pate then. Damn! Damn!"

"Come and drink coffee," he said. "There are other things to do."

We walked along the waterfront to Shela that evening to have a beer or two at the tourist hotel on the ocean beach. Mashuas were returning from the sea with fresh fish for the restaurants of the town, sailing fast with the wind behind them, trailing sparkling white wakes across the blue water. It was a lovely evening and the southerly monsoon breeze was balm. The village of Shela had an old mosque perched up above a small anchorage sheltered by the corner of the island and clustered about were a number of rough old houses and a few modern luxury villas built in a vaguely 'Swahili' style. I presumed that Shela lay outside of the planning zone regulating modern construction in Lamu town. I was glad to be there then and not ten years later when time-share holiday apartments might burgeon. The hotel clung to the steep dune on the ocean beach and was reasonably unobtrusive. Steps climbed to a narrow terrace and closed verandah, both of which were crowded with tourists and local visitors. This was the only officially open public drinking place in the whole Lamu Archipelago.

It took a little while to get warm beers from the hard working waiter and I did not like the atmosphere. Several of the locals were staring glassily into space and others argued loudly. White tourists yelled and guffawed. "Some 'hooray-henrys' here," observed Jonathon. "Pissed out of their little minds."

"We'll just have this beer. It's a pity; it's a lovely evening."

"It's fantastic! Just look at that beach, going on and on...."

As we wandered slowly back past Shela there was a hail from a large jahazi standing off the beach. "Lamu?" the captain called. He wore only a *kikoyi* (Swahili lungi) and turban and I felt quite confused for a moment. He was a fisherman at Quilon or Kovalum Beach. Jonathon nudged me, "Don't you want to sail back?" We scrambled aboard and I still felt bemused and psychically so close to India as we slipped up the channel in the soft air of sundown.

After dinner of sailfish and fried rice, the owner of our favourite Sindbad restaurant suggested that we might like to have a few beers at the police compound. Foreign tourists and respectable locals from up-country were welcome there. After the frustrations of the afternoon it seemed a good idea, so we followed his directions. The compound lay on the crest of the hill above the town within a tall security fence. We hesitated at the gate but the watchman waved us in

148

with a bored hand. A row of barracks and small rectangular family quarters lined two sides of a quadrangle. At the far end, a large open-sided building stood beside an old giant of a fig tree with scattered chairs. Light poured from the open building and there was the pounding of 'boogie' music. We went across to it.

A scrum of beer-drinking men hung around a heavily barred hatch from which half-litre bottles of warm Tusker beer were dispensed. The 'boogie' blared and a couple of men staggered together in a corner. There were no women. Along the low walls men were sitting alone or talking quietly together away from the noisy yelling and drunken laughter by the bar hatch. I got a couple of beers and we sat on the wall too, watching the scene. Our neighbour on the wall raised his hand slowly and gave me a wobbly smile. Nobody spoke to us. What a dismal drinking den, I thought.

Out of the scrum, two young White men in baggy shorts and designer sweatshirts emerged talking loudly with an older Black man, dressed in slacks and shirt with tie. They seemed an unlikely trio. When they settled near us, I was forced to listen to pieces of their conversation. They were discussing the Rhodesian war of independence in knowledgeable detail. One of the younger men, who was the talker, spoke loudly with a 'public school' accent and as they drank he became more dogmatic. Jonathon fetched another beer and the trio got yet another round. The 'public school' voice became offensively aggressive as he explained exhaustively why the Selous Scouts were almost as good as the SAS and the Black man's responses became monosyllabic.

"Dear oh dear," I said. "This is not much fun."

"The beer's warm and flat too," Jonathon said.

We returned to Samaki, but the evening of disturbance by others was not yet over. A French couple had the next room and their loud voices penetrated the thin wall. They seemed to wrangle interminably about whether to return to Mombasa or stay in Malindi for a while. *"Je suis fatigue de camping,"* the girl kept complaining. Just as I was drifting off to sleep their bed began a rhythmic thumping.

"Oh God!" Jonathon groaned. "I hope they really leave to-morrow."

149

Borbo, on the right, and friends on the Lamu waterfront.

CHAPTER FOURTEEN : SWAHILI DAYS

We sailed to Manda Island in a *mashua* named *Kudura* with a thin aristocratic captain, serious and withdrawn as many captains are, wearing a wispy beard and long, tousled hair. He had a crew of two to tend the sails and the passengers. It was a day's expedition to the Takwa ruins and an undefined 'picnic' on the Indian Ocean beach and there were two other tourists, English VSOs working in Nigeria. Unlike the Peace Corps volunteers, British VSOs tend to be older and have professional training. The man was a remedial teacher from Benue State and the girl was an occupational therapist from a hospital near Kano in the north. They were good company and we chatted about Nigeria, which I knew well from early post-colonial days.

"You'd see a lot of changes," the man said after a while. "Where I am, the district used to be a big exporter of palm-oil and palm-kernels. Now they don't even bother to harvest the fruit and the trees are old and dying. There's very little cash economy and when we left three weeks ago the rains were late and people were beginning to go short of food."

I was appalled. "I can hardly believe it. I know the area you talk about. Not only oil-palm products for export, but vegetables, yams and cassava used to be sent from there to Onitsha market. It was a highly productive district."

"Not any more," he said seriously, shaking his head. "They've let agriculture go. The Civil War and hopeless mismanagement of petroleum industry wealth have destroyed that country. It's heartbreaking, and the eastern states are in the worst straights." Whenever I hear stories of Nigeria's failure I feel sick. For six years I worked there as a young man and my endeavours were devoted to trade in the bountiful surplus of the rich land.

Before landing to tour the Takwa ruins, we stopped to fish for our lunch, trailing hand lines over the side. The crew caught several respectable multi-coloured fish but my bait was nibbled away. I am no fisherman. Suddenly there was a squeal of shock and the VSO girl was staring white-faced at a fish hook completely imbedded in her hand. I asked for plyers to cut away the eye and pull the hook through, but there were none on board. "To the clinic at Shela," the captain decided and we raced back, a glorious sail with the wind strongly abeam. "*Kudura* is very fast," the captain said to me with a spontaneous grin of pleasure, the thrill of the emergency and the excuse to make best use of the good wind breaking his reserve. I grinned with equal pleasure back at him. After an hour the girl was back aboard and cheerful, the hook had been cleanly and painlessly removed and the small wound strapped up. We raced back on the return journey to Takwa, trailing a foamy white wake.

The Lamu Archipelago has been archaeologically explored by several professionals, notably Chittick and Kirkman, most recently by Horton, and the outlines of history established. It was unmistakably described in the *Periplus* (c100 AD) and obviously visited regularly in the centuries before and after then. The area was certainly colonised and settled by people from Oman in the 7th and 8th centuries AD, probably refugees from invasions of that part of the Persian Gulf at the instigation of the Caliph of Baghdad, Abd-al-Malik. Other historical references are in the early 9th century when there was another migration from Oman because of troubles there. From the 10th century the sultans and imams of Oman were in firm control for two centuries, but the history of southern Arabia at this time was complicated and as rulers and influence changed there, activity at Lamu and Malindi followed. However, towns were built, trade persevered and there was considerable cultural exchange. It was not only traders who came to East Africa; skilled craftsmen, adventurous settlers, prospectors, religious leaders, representatives of rulers came, and scholarly tourists like Ibn Batuta.

Every year for centuries fleets and individual expeditions sailed down from the Yemen, Oman and Hormuz to Lamu, Malindi, Zanzibar and Kilwa. But as settler families became established and generation followed generation, bonds with the homelands loosened and cultural and racial mixing with Africa occurred. The Shirazi and Arab colonists took Black concubines and then wives from the new mixed-race elite. The Swahili people were born and some would claim that the Lamu archipelago was the source of the purest Swahili culture. Pate was the principal early town, hence my desire to visit it. Other notable towns rose and fell in importance as centuries passed.

James Kirkman wrote (1983):

> The ruins of the town of Shanga, also on the ocean side of the island [Pate Island] have survived, and the site has been recently excavated. Sherds of the 10th century have been found but occupation was heaviest in the 13-14th century and ended in the 15th century. It was replaced by Siyu, founded in the late 15th or 16th century, three kilometres away on the other side of the island. Faza is also on the sheltered side of the island. There have been no excavations but sherds as early as the 12th century have been found. Manda has been extensively excavated. It was founded in the 9th century and was the most important town in the Lamu archipelago until the 13th century. ...

And so it went on. A story of ups and downs, jockeying for position between rival clans and petty rulers for five hundred years until the Portuguese came in the 16th century and maintained tenuous control until the free-for-all began again after the Omanis conquered Fort Jesus less than two hundred years later.

Much has been written and said about the 'savage' Portuguese hegemony on this coast. Much is nonsense and obvious anti-European or racist bias. It was Arabs and Persians who built defensive walled towns or settled islands off the coast, separate from the mass of Black Zenj, the infidel *kafirs* of the hinterland. Apart from the fortress of Jesus on Mombasa, constructed late in the period of Portuguese influence in the face of increasing trans-oceanic threats from the Dutch, Ali Bey the Turk, and resurgent Oman, the Portuguese did not build important fortifications in East Africa. Some writers to-day proclaim the particular tyranny of the Portuguese quoting their own historical records whereas illiterate Black Africans were unable to leave us protests about colonising Arabs and Persians.

Certain modern popularist historians, such as Ali Masrui and Basil Davidson, single out the Portuguese as wicked and tyrannical, whereas Ibn Batuta and his fellow medieval Arab travellers commented from firsthand experience on the perennial armed conflicts between the coastal Swahili city states and neighbouring indigenous native people. Swahili literature itself often saw the Portuguese as no more than another force competing with local colonial dynasties, Omanis, Turks or whoever, all of whom disrupted ordinary living from time to time as the long centuries rolled by. Finally, severe exploitation in the 19th century by Omani-Arab slave-economy feudalism was replaced by 20th century British paternalism.

The size and effect of the Portuguese presence in East Africa has probably been much exaggerated, and I suspect that this is racial bias. My own observation suggests that judging by architectural and religious heritage the Portuguese made a far greater impact on the massive civilisation of India than on the small medieval towns of Malindi and Mombasa where it is virtually invisible to-day.

In the Lamu archipelago there are remains of only two forts; Lamu built by the Sultanate of Oman in 1812, after a fierce battle at Shela between Lamu and Pate supported by the Sultan of Mombasa, and Siyu built in 1863 after several wars of conquest by the victorious Sultanate of Zanzibar. Lamu town reached the height of its prosperity in the 19th century as the principal port of the archipelago for the export of the wealth of vast plantations on the islands and mainland cultivated by slave labour. Tens of thousands of acres were served by tens of thousands of *watumwa wa shamba* (farm-slaves) brought mainly from the faraway Swahili-Arab depots of Ujiji on Lake Tanganyika and Nkhota Khota on Lake Malawi.

Most of the sparse non-official Portuguese settlers mixed amicably into Swahili society. The complex elitist society of the Spanish in South America or the British in India was not established because there were too few Portuguese in East Africa.

Genesta Hamilton, in a little known book, *In the Wake of da Gama* (1951), provides a picture which has a commonsense look of accuracy:

> In the country places the Portuguese had increased in number [17th century], and some of their women had joined them.
> They and the Arabs usually lived together in perfect friendliness. The Portuguese and Arab ladies - so alike with their long black hair, dark eyes, and honey coloured skins - visited each other freely, and enjoyed each other's company.
> ... When the white people went out they copied the rich Arabs by having slaves to walk behind them, carrying umbrellas. .... The streets of Lamu, Mombasa, Mozambique, and other sea-lapped, sun-kissed towns were a gay sight.

Takwa, which we visited in the fast sailing mashua, *Kudura*, was reached along a track through the mangroves from the head of a creek entered from the southern side of Manda Island. Takwa had

154

been excavated and the coral rock buildings were spread about in amongst coastal scrub trees and palms. We tied up to a rickety jetty and our captain led us along a path through the mangroves to the sandy shore and up to the walls of the ruined town. I studied the principal mosque with its distinctive pillar. The 'pillar mosque' is the only notable identifiable building in this 15th and 16th century town, but I enjoyed walking the remnants of the streets between the crumbling, grey coral-stone walls. The few acacias and bushes created a tranquil park. The name of the ruined town was interesting to me for Taqa was a powerful medieval trading port in southern Oman, it was there that my son had seen rotting sewn-ships in 1986, and the similarity of the names seemed to be more than casual coincidence.

The addition of pillars to mosques is a tradition of Swahili culture distinct from Arabia and is believed to be because burials of important people were commemorated in this way. Much has been written about these East African pillars, often described as phallic because of the obvious shape. It seems to me that they are a merging of Islamic and indigenous culture where African veneration of ancestors, particularly those of chiefs, was joined to the religious importance of mosques as places of worship and centres of communities. Worship of large phallic sculpture was not practised by Africans and if there is any evidence of its introduction to East Africa, it must have come from India. There was another pillar tomb at Takwa which I particularly admired, standing by itself surrounded by large acacia trees.

From Takwa we sailed back into the channel between Manda and Lamu islands and came to anchor off the beach opposite the village of Shela. The day was a tropical dream: the blue sky with the blinding silver ball of the sun lay heavy on our heads as we plunged into the clear waters and waded to the fine white coral sand of the beach. The captain rested in the shade while his mate and the boat-boy started a barbecue fire and we four tourists plunged about in the sea. The fish that had been caught earlier were scaled, gutted with a rough knife, then spitted on the spines of palm fronds plucked from a nearby tree. When we had tired of swimming and splashing about and sank into the shade of a low palm, we were greeted by the savoury smells of grilled fish, laid out on a carved wooden plate. We ate local unleavened bread and the fish with our hands, licking at the grease on our fingers, ate oranges and sipped fresh mango juice they had brought with them. The *Kudura* dipped at its coral rock anchor and I could see little fish sheltering in the shade beneath its hull. Distantly there was the soft roar of surf on the ocean side of the island.

There had been no suggestion that we were going to have a 'historical' picnic, packaged tourism of that sort had not reached Lamu, but that is exactly what it was for me. We experienced a perfect re-creation of a simple event of five centuries before, especially so because the behaviour of the *Kudura*'s crew was so relaxed and uncontrived. They enacted a timeless role without conscious effort; we joined with them exactly as we would have done were we sailing down the 'The Channel' from Pate to Malindi in the 15th century. (Or even in the first century for that matter.) We stopped to refresh, rest and have a meal and there was nothing I could see, apart from our European features, that could have been different.

Jonathon and I particularly liked the al fresco snack bar attached to Petley's Inn. It was intended to be a pleasant beer garden fronting the quay, but the hotel did not have a general liquor licence and so it served excellent coffee, barbecued kebabs, steaks, chips and good fruit juices; albeit at twice the price of the Kenya Soft Drinks establishment nearby. I suppose its situation right on the waterfront was justification for the high prices; although our other favourite, the Sindbad Restaurant, had as good a location and was much cheaper. Significantly, no locals patronised Petley's, it was definitely a place for foreign tourists. We were drinking coffee after a fine seafood dinner elsewhere when the evening crowd of new arrivals off the bus from Mombasa surged past from the ferry jetty. As they came, Jonathon and I looked at each other and exchanged the glances of old residents. It is amazing how tourists can acquire the emotions of typical villagers: we were the 'residents', they were the interlopers. Before I could make a remark about this, a bustle occurred beside us.

"Everybody halt! Stop here!" a stentorian voice with 'proper' English accent commanded. 'Bushbaby' had emerged from the front of Petley's Inn and he had obviously dined and wined well. "There's no accommodation on Lamu, and the food is bad. You may get sick. There's no water! Turn back! Return to-morrow!" The crowd of tired people, sweat-stained and with drained faces, came to a stop.

"Jesus!" I heard a totally exasperated American voice as a backpack was dropped to the ground. 'Bushbaby's' friends drew him away: "You are going mad, Bushybaby," I heard one say.

Jonathon was consumed by giggles and I had to laugh too. Confused and arguing, the new arrivals wandered on hesitantly.

We decided to pay the 'club fee' and have a couple of beers in Petley's Inn bar on the first floor beside an empty swimming pool. 'Bushbaby' was there surrounded by acolytes including two pretty white girls.

"Ahah! Montgomery," he greeted me. "And why did you not go to Pate to my super Swahili mansion?" He shook the two smiling girls he was holding. "You could have taken these with you. They are looking for adventure."

"The tide was all wrong, I told you that," I said, and he laughed, shaking the girls again. "Why didn't you tell me. I can arrange anything. Anything...." The girls giggled and we moved on.

Two middle-aged lady school-teachers from west London were drinking a pile of Tusker lagers standing on their table. We joined them and I was immediately sorry. Beneath the swishing coconut palms, beside 'Bushbaby's' jolly party and with large Black men from upcountry laughing and joking next to us, I was subjected to a rhetorical, trendy-liberal attack on Thatcherism: the 'savaging' of the economy, the desperate police state', the 'vicious attacks' on English society, 'swingeing cuts' and all. The cliches spouted against a background of African 'boogie' music and party noise from 'Bushbaby's' corner. I kept silent, trying to think instead of the simple perfection of the day on Manda Island, five hundred years in the past, while Jonathon defended individualism and subsequently became enmeshed in a discussion of sexual mores.

"We had a wonderful time at Ngorongoro," one of the women said. "There were lots of animals. And there was a game warden who talked about female circumcision. He said that about 70 per cent of East African women still do it."

"Yes. I did not believe it," her companion said. "But he called over a young woman standing by and she was willing to show us." She snorted. "How could that arrogant, dreadful man think we would be impressed. He was laughing and asked how our life had been without being circumcised. I told him that it had been very pleasurable, thank you very much, but I don't think he understood what I was talking about...."

I was going to make some silly remark about male circumcision but my mind drifted away, thinking of the often impossible task of explaining African culture. It is a vastly complex subject unsuited to facile, after-dinner conversation by passing tourists. Jonathon listened with a suitably serious face to a statement of the merits of multiple clitoral orgasms without male assistance.

The Kenyan novelist, Ngugi, wrote in *The River Between* (1965):

"Why! Are we fools?" She shook Nyambura. Father and mother are circumcised. Are they not Christians? Circumcision did not prevent them from being Christians. I too have embraced the white man's faith. However, I know it is beautiful, oh so beautiful to be initiated into womanhood. You learn the ways of the tribe. Yes, the white man's God does not quite satisfy me. I want, I need something more. My life and your life are here, in the hills, that you and I know."

Could our feminist companions from Europe understand those sentiments?

Borbo came one morning to take us to Matondoni, the dhow-building village. We were hastened to the waterfront and climbed aboard a big, commercial *jahazi*, loaded with building sand and sawn timber. We were asked to get down on the cargo while the crew hoisted the vast yard from which the much-repaired lateen sail hung. The gear creaked and the sail flapped heavily in the monsoon breeze. There was a flurry of work by the three-man crew as we were born off the quay and the sheets were hauled and adjusted. Suddenly, in the way of sailing vessels, there was quiet except for the slapping of waves on the bows. We were slipping fast past the deep green of the mangroves on the shores. I felt, deep in myself, that I was again lost in time. Lamu town itself with the absence of motor vehicles and many of the appurtenances of European civilisation had already conditioned me well.

Like the beach picnic, the simple voyage to Matondoni was exceptional; mainly because there was no pretence at all. But whereas the expedition in the *Kudura* had been an excursion the voyage in the cargo vessel had an even deeper reality and timelessness.

The captain was a fat middle-aged fellow with a creased face who wore a kikoyi and a turban-like cloth round his head. When I looked at him closely, I realised that he was the same man who had ferried us from Shela the evening we had escaped from the heavy drinking crowd at the hotel there. With a paler skin he could have been a Turkish pirate, which may be exactly what his great-great-grandfather had been. I saluted him, smiling, and he gave me a sudden, wide grin and called to Borbo.

"What did he say?" I asked. "He hopes you can enjoy his ship."
"No doubt about that," I replied. "I love it!" I thought how it would be

to sail on this jahazi from Lamu to Malindi, on to Mombasa, Pemba, Zanzibar, Kilwa and Mocambique Island, even down to Sofala and Inhambane. It would not be strange, such vessels had done it in the past.

I asked Borbo about it and his eyes lit up. "Yes, that would be wonderful! If we had enough money, this captain would do it. He is very experienced. I think he went to Zanzibar when he was young." It was a fine fantasy to have that morning with the tufty white fair-weather clouds, the blue of the water, the sigh and splash of the wake, the easy professional competence of the crew.

After two or three hours we reached Matondoni. I was disappointed, at first, although I was not sure what I had expected. There were no stone buildings, this was not an old Arab town. Square wattle-and-daub huts with macuti roofs squatted amongst old trees: coconuts, figs, tamarinds and mangoes. It was a Swahili village without trace of feudal Arabs. There were some modern buildings with cement block walls and corrugated iron roofs, but these were scattered and few enough yet to be unobtrusive. We came to anchor and waded ashore to a sandy beach and it was this spit of sand protruding to the waterfront through the mud and the mangroves that was the obvious reason for the village's existence. In the shade of some trees, three mashuas were being built and I was delighted to see rough, hand-wrought adzes in use and wood-drills spun by bow-strings.

My son had described exactly the same implements in the Oman, although there electric power tools were now more usual. But there was no electricity at Matondoni, and no store-bought tools. The shipwrights gravely acknowledged our greetings and went on with their work.

On the other side of the village, which spread further than I had thought from the waterside landing, we reached a subsidiary creek reaching inland with hard white sand on the one side and dense mangroves on the other. "Here is where the dhows are built," Borbo told me. There were none under construction, but there were two large, sea-going jahazis in for renovation and repair. They had been emptied and floated in on a spring tide and propped up by a tangle of mangrove pole scaffolding. Some men were clambering about caulking seams, and the master shipwright, an elderly man in white robe, sat in the shade of a tree. I wandered about trying for the best photograph, and I could easily visualise ships under construction as well as these being refurbished.

159

"I suppose they could still build new dhows here?" I asked Borbo.

"Of course," he said, somewhat offended. "They know the old ways."

"If I wanted one, what would it cost and how long would it take?"

He went over and consulted with the master for a while. "About a hundred thousand shillings for the hull," he told me and screwed up his face, calculating. "About six thousand American dollars. And it would take about two years because they have to find the correctly shaped woods and prepare everything well. When it is the raining season they don't work every day."

What a dream, I thought, how marvellous to do it!

We stopped in the village 'hotel', a larger house with rooms to let and a covered terrace at the back where we sat to drink Cokes. Flowering vines crept up the roof supports and the proprietor joked with Borbo. I bought a quaintly carved wooden spoon as a souvenir.

We walked back to Lamu town, across the centre of the island which is quite flat except for two or three old dune ridges that run in a straight line from north to south. It was hot and the pathway was heavy, sun-baked sand, churned by villagers' feet trekking back and forth to Lamu. Because of the sand, I had to take off my flip-flops and my bare feet became sore. We stopped for a rest in the shade of a wild fig tree and a pale-faced elderly man appeared on a donkey. He was dressed in a long, traditional striped cloth robe and wore a turban on his head, and I thought he would have illustrated a Bible scene very well. He studied our red European faces and my burning bare feet and gave me a sympathetic smile before exchanging greetings with Borbo.

In the days of the Sultans of Zanzibar, a hundred years before, Lamu like the other islands and tens of thousands of acres on the adjacent mainland, had been covered by coconut, spice and fruit plantations. Now the few surviving coconuts were neglected and most of the land was open, the sandy soil leached and covered by coarse grass and slowly spreading rough scrub. Trudging under the blazing afternoon sun, I thought about the universal problem of 'development' in Africa. Much is said and written to-day about colonialist exploitation with its many 'evils'.

Arab, Persian and Indian exploitation with organised agriculture in a slave-based feudal system on the East African coast had been established for a thousand years, off-and-on, and it had

160

helped to fuel wealth in Egypt, Arabia and India. It had created the mixed-race and mixed-culture Swahili people. Was it good or bad? It was nowadays usually portrayed as an indigenous African Civilisation and was therefore almost automatically 'good'. Of course, it was certainly not indigenously African in origin; it was as colonial as modern South African culture is a mix from several European and native African origins.

British suppression of slavery had brought it to an end here in the 'Puralaon Islands' of the Greeks. Walking across Lamu Island, seeing in microcosm the evidence of the decline of agriculture with no apparent effort or plan to revive it in a continent frequently starving and forced to import food from the West to survive, all my fears and conclusions were reinforced again. Lamu existed to-day on subsistence farming and fishing, tourism and rich absentee landowners buying old houses to create exclusive 'places in the sun'. Time-share and condominions were coming. And there would be freight planes flying in the whisky and marmalade, detergents and cigars during the heavy monsoon when there was no sugar or salt in the dukas.

On the last day Borbo gave me an intimate guided tour of Lamu town. Jonathon took it easy because he was suffering sunburn from the outing to Matondoni. We walked the narrow streets, just wide enough for two laden donkeys to pass, and I was introduced to a number of shopkeepers. Obviously there was some hope that I should buy gifts and souvenirs, but there was no pressure. In one dark shop, smelling of incense and the delicate aroma of carved sandalwood I admired a host of perfect dhow models almost to the same standard of perfection as those in the museum. There were dozens of them.

"They are all made here, on Lamu," the proprietor told me. "I can pack them and ship them to England or America." I was sorely tempted, but remembered my curio littered home; where I would put it? I was also shown an old *siwa*, an elaborately carved horn, embellished with inlaid ivory and brass. The siwa horns which were blown to announce the passage of a notable person or on a special occasion are claimed to be a heritage from really ancient Mesopotamians, Assyrians maybe. There is no way this claim can be proved one way or the other, but undoubtedly they are from old culture. I was also tempted by antique jewellery from the Middle-East and India and modern finely carved ivory and ebony.

161

On the outskirts of the Swahili suburb of wattle-and-daub huts, Borbo took me to the blacksmith's establishment. He and a young apprentice squatted beneath a corrugated iron shelter at work at his craft, making hoes and pangas from scrap metal. The method in use was universal in Africa: the boy tirelessly worked goatskin bellows directing a blast onto a mound of charcoal where iron was heated before being hammered on a crude anvil.

After climbing to the top of the hill behind the town to view the panorama and see a new mosque under construction we descended the narrow streets again, walking between the crowded two and three story 19th century mansions of rich Omani merchants and plantation landlords. Some still had finely carved doors in the plain facades at ground level and the first and second stories sprouted balconies with flowering plants decorating them.

"Do people still live in all of these?" I asked.

"Some, not all," Borbo said. "They are all preserved by law, but the insides can be rebuilt. Some are being modernised for rich people or for guest houses."

Round a corner came my Swahili friend from the museum leading about twenty Afro-American women dressed in bright Western fashions. Their hair was straightened and they were flashily made-up. My friend stopped to talk and the women swept by, chattering with their distinctive accents. "My American lady-tourists," he explained, then laughed: "They have come to find their roots. I'm trying very hard not to disappoint them!"

Sailing in the cargo *jahazi* from Lamu to Matondoni.

CHAPTER FIFTEEN : GEDI AND JUMBA LA MTWANA

Instead of waking to the first shafts of sunlight entering our little room and the noise of clanking as buckets were carried about the house, the light was dull and the noise was the steady splash of rain. We had been lucky at Lamu, there had been no rain for days, and now the weather had changed. I looked out at a thick, low-lying greyness overhead and the usually cheerful street busy with people striding up and down as soon as day broke was dreary with wet and a solitary umbrella was moving swiftly out of sight. It was time to move on.

I rushed to the booking office and found that there was space on the plane and we packed quickly and assembled at the jetty for the ferry across the creek to the airstrip on Manda Island. I was glad we were leaving on a dull miserable morning so that the pangs at parting from a place that had been magical in many ways should be stilled. A tropical town that is gay in fresh bright sunlight, or drowsy and somnolent in the heat of afternoon becomes gloomy and unfriendly in the heaviness of monsoon rainfall. The brief showers and bright intervals of an English spring or summer do not occur in the tropics. On the coast it either rains relentlessly or it does not. Inland, on the great open savannahs, there is another kind of wet weather; the towering columns of purple thunderstorms rising to 40,000 feet, lit by flashes of electric blue lightning and silhouetted against clear skies, but on the coast we were not to see that.

By the time we reached the landing strip we were thoroughly soaked and there was a sharp breeze that made us shiver in our shorts and thin cotton shirts. We had to wait half-an-hour for the plane to arrive and as we were trooping out to it, I heard a shout and there was Borbo who had come to tout for business from new arrivals. I held his hand and basked in the friendship of his huge grin.

When we had taken off and climbed to 6,000 feet, I was freezing in the cold of altitude. It was a rough flight, bucketing about and dodging into dark clouds where the rain hissed and sluiced over the perspex of the windows. The pilot circled Malindi for twenty minutes, waiting for a break in the rain, then put us down fast. It was muggy and damp and a hint of wan sunlight crept from seaward.

The policemen were waiting with grinning faces. *"Jambo!"* they greeted me. "Your car is safe." I had almost forgotten about cars. I gave them the expected present and checked our gear quickly, then we drove to the Silversands camp site along a road silvered with pools of water. Inevitably, both Jonathon and I came down with colds or 'flu that evening. Whatever collection of germs were circulating in our systems after days mixing with various tourists and locals in Lamu were given their opportunity by the change in weather and several hours of cold and shivering. I was coughing and sneezing with a bunged up head, Jonathon succumbed to diarrhoea that had him prostrate for a day. The rain continued off-and-on and I was glad that we were in a weatherproof banda again and not being miserable in a tiny tent.

The next day was brighter and I completed my sightseeing in Malindi. We visited the Portuguese chapel reputed to have been consecrated by St.Francis Xavier in 1542 when he landed at Malindi on his way to India. He buried two sailors there. Standing in the little churchyard with its few English graves from the early 20th century, I looked at the small whitewashed building with fresh flowers in a jam jar on its simple altar within and thought of Goa, its cathedrals and the tomb of this great early missionary who had travelled as far as the China Seas, and which I had missed because of the language riots earlier in the year. India seemed a century ago and a million miles away, despite the historical closeness. I thought once again of the Indian ships that da Gama met at Malindi in 1498, both people far from home and their familiar civilisations, meeting at a crossroads on the African shore, where Arabs had created a colonial outpost of a third civilisation. I thought of Naipaul's remark about the subjugation of Indian civilisation in these days to the technical mastery of the alien one from the West and the even more severe subjugation of Africa to that same force in the late 20th century.

In 1498 the minute pieces of three civilisations that met in Malindi had far greater apparent diversity of religion and culture, but maybe they were closer then in spirit than we are to each other to-day. To-day's ideals seem in disarray dominated by the Western media's often trivial and fleeting opinions. Common law and religion seem to have lost their values, mutual understanding to be abysmally low and differences in technology between peoples around the Indian Ocean to be accelerating towards a psychic horizon impossible to imagine. Despite the supposed deep antagonism between Roman Catholic Portuguese and Islamic Arab and Swahili, the medieval mosques and that little chapel were still there after five hundred years. Standards of respect and tolerance survived in past centuries but many gulfs between people are judged to-day by the deteriorating behaviour of the present. Would that chapel still exist and have fresh wild flowers in a jam jar on its altar in 2542? Sadly, I doubted that very much.

I looked at the dug-out fishing canoes sheltering with the mashuas behind the reef with da Gama's padrão at the end and thought of the conservative Christian fishermen and their boats of ancient design on the Malabar Coast at Benaulim and Quilon and Kovalum. In the depression of my head-cold I felt suddenly sad and sick of it all.

On the first morning that the weather looked to be settled and sunny, we went to Gedi. Jonathon had recovered and spent the night before at a disco with Irish medical students who were spending a happy beachcombing holiday at Malindi and he was probably reluctant to look at another set of ruins amongst overgrown bush. So Gedi took him by surprise. It is the largest medieval ruined colonial town on the Kenya coast, and the best known, for tourists are brought there on excursions from Mombasa and the Malindi hotels. Whereas there is little left of medieval Malindi apart from the Portuguese chapel, the padrão and the 15th century pillar tomb beside the Friday mosque, medieval Gedi was abandoned completely to the forest and not destroyed by modern occupation.

On my last visit, there had been no rain for some time and the extensive coral rock ruins seemed like a vast cathedral beneath the towering canopy of giant trees. The grounds were dry and cleared of all undergrowth. The wind sighed in the treetops and below them the ancient town, dusted by dried fallen leaves, slumbered in the shafts of sunlight moving about the ruins. That airiness and space was missing on this occasion and the leaden sky, pervading damp and encroaching greenery produced an oppressive atmosphere. But the expanse of grey ruins, the size of the Palace and the Great Mosque, one of seven identified, impressed Jonathon. While he wandered about, I rested in the audience court of the Palace and tried to visualise the sultan with his council, bright in ceremonial robes and silk headgear, lolling about, drinking coffee, discussing some important matter of state or judging some complicated commercial argument between competing merchants. The Palace was a complex of many small rooms surrounding several courtyards each having a particular purpose.

James Kirkman's tourist guide to the ruins is excellent. As an example of the sophistication of Gedi, here is one description:

> This [the audience court] is a rectangular court running in front of the main block of the Palace, with platforms on east, south and west sides. Originally there was a flight of steps.
> ...   In its final state, as seen to-day, there is a bench along the east end where the judges would sit, protected until midday from the sun by the wall behind them. .... Between the reception court and the audience court is a small apartment. It includes a lavatory, which is typical of the lavatories of Gedi, consisting of two small cubicles with a low partition wall between them. In one was a pit with a square hole and a urinal channel; in the other a washing bench with two cavities for bowls in an upper tier, and a divided seat used as a bidet in the lower.

We walked around the perimeter walls of the town which enclosed an area of about fifty acres. Constructing stone buildings was the privilege of colonial immigrants of standing and aristocratic Swahilis with descent from Persian or Omani families. Within the walls would also have been the wattle-and-daub houses, like those of to-day's Lamu or Malindi 'old town', for domestic slaves, trusted natives and Swahili of a lower order who were granted sites for town houses. Outside the walls there would have been more mud houses and the smallholdings, shambas, of the peasants who provided the fresh provisions for the townspeople. Further away were the fruit and spice plantations and the cereal fields tended by peasants and slaves supervised by overseers. To coincide with the Indian Ocean monsoon system governing the arrival of fleets of dhows and Indian vessels, African traders would come down the Galana River from the interior with ivory, animal skins, honey, rhinoceros horn and tortoiseshell and by custom some would go to Malindi, only ten miles away, and some would come to Gedi. The existence of the town walls shows that Gedi, being on the mainland and not offshore like most medieval towns, had need of secure protection from the natives.

166

Gedi was founded in the 13th/14th century either by people from Malindi who were in dispute with the local ruler, or a direct settlement by a new wave of immigrants from the Persian Gulf. Shirazis from southern Persia may have been the founders of Gedi. Or they may have been Shirazis who settled in Malindi and subsequently fell out with the hierarchy of Omani origin. Archaeology suggests the Persian connection, but cannot tell how it exactly happened, and by the time Gedi reached its peak of development in the 15th century, it had become just another Swahili town of mixed background ruled by an established dynasty.

The reason for its abandonment and the mystery of it being lost in the jungle has caused speculation. Suggestions have been made, for example, that the wells dried up or that access to the sea became difficult because of silting but I dismissed these. Kirkman has suggested that Gedi was sacked about 1530 by an army from Mombasa who went to war with Malindi in reprisal for Malindi's alliance with the Portuguese during the long-standing feud between the two. In 1586, the Turkish privateer, Ali Bey, arrived in the area to plunder the coast and stirred up a hornet's nest from Pate to Mombasa with some rulers welcoming him and subsequently being punished by Portuguese expeditions. Other rulers, close allies of the Portuguese, resisted him. Gedi, probably weakened by the Mombasa-Malindi war, was not mentioned in surviving Portuguese contemporary chronicles.

Coincidentally, an extraordinary army was moving up the coast from southern Africa. This was known as the Simba and the Portuguese reported them on the Zambezi River in 1570 at Tete, which was sacked, moving north. By 1589, the Simba were on the Kenya coast and became embroiled in a bloody battle for Mombasa between the Portuguese and the rebellious local sultan supported by Ali Bey. It was recorded that the Simba horde landed on Mombasa Island, massacred the Swahili population and indiscriminately fought both sides in the ongoing battle. In the chaos and misery, it was thought that the Simba must have consumed many of the dead and a legend arose that they 'ate their way up the coast' A combined force of Portuguese, the Sultan of Malindi's army and an allied local tribe finally destroyed the Simba near Malindi. In all this bloody turmoil, Gedi was extinguished. There was a rejuvenation for a while during which time the town was repaired and a new town wall with a much shorter perimeter was constructed, which shows that it never regained its former stature. Finally, as Kirkman has pointed out, all the smaller mainland towns were laid waste by warlike nomadic Galla tribesmen from Somalia in the 17th century after the protection of the Portuguese had been thrown out. Gedi was finally abandoned as the Galla moved in with overwhelming force.

Gedi's location has also been made into a mystery. There is no reason for that either. It was built where it is because of the existence of an ancient coral reef which provided abundant building material. It was also close to Mida Creek, a fine harbour, within easy slave-porterage distance, and the many hand-dug wells still to be seen, properly walled within, have water in them to-day.

Jonathon and I drove off from Gedi, armed with instructions from the helpful curator at the entrance gate, to find Mgangani which was a medieval village with a mosque on the shores of Mida Creek and which I believed to be the port for Gedi. The map showed a straight road southwards from Gedi to Mgangani and we followed it. It had been the old main road from Mombasa, surfaced in colonial time, but was in bad condition, potholed and scoured by many monsoons without subsequent attention. After three miles on the odometer we came to a swamp where the road was flooded and although we could have gone on with caution it seemed to me that we were crossing the head of Mida Creek, so we turned back. I spoke to some women by the way and asked for Mgangani and they recognised the name but gave answers that I could not understand, pointing vaguely about. "It's obvious that this whole small area is called that," I said to Jonathon. I was ready to leave, having at least proved that it was a practical distance from Gedi to Mida Creek, when a pleasant-faced man stopped us.

"*Jambo!*" he called out. "Can I help you, please."

"We are looking for the ruins at Mgangani, which may be on the shore of Mida Creek."

"Oh, yes. I know," he said smiling. "But you will not find them easily, because the path is overgrown. We would have to ask people here to guide us. But I know it is near that road junction." He pointed to a turn-off in the track a few hundred yards away.

"What about Mida Creek?" I asked.

"This road does not reach there because it is swampy. But if you wish to see the water, I will guide you."

He was an assistant chef at one of the package tour hotels in Malindi and on his way to see his grandfather at the family shamba near the shore. For the sake of a lift, he was prepared to go out of his way to guide us. At the junction he had pointed out, we turned off, and there was a battered sign lying on the ground with 'Mgangani' painted on it. "There is a small village school called by that name here," our friend explained. He chattered to us as we drove through coconut plantations and passed the occasional shamba homestead. A shamba was about seven acres in that area and if you were a local you could get a government loan to help you buy or develop. If you were from somewhere else, one would cost you about ?10,000 and you had to finance your own improvements. There was no free land available, and some families were splitting their shambas which is why he had sought a career in Malindi and had married a town girl. He loved the country life, however, and found every excuse to visit his grandfather.

Watching the mileage and studying the map when we stopped to admire his family homestead with children waving at us, I saw that we were approaching Mida Creek about halfway between the marsh at the westernmost end and the sea at Watamu. We drove on and suddenly came to the end of the track where wind-ruffled water showed between the trunks of two old mango trees. I parked the car on a low sandy ridge and we scrambled down to sea level where there was a landing place between the encircling arms of mangroves. In the distance there were islands on the wide blue of Mida Creek. Astonished by our sudden appearance, a half-dozen sweating men dressed only in kikoyis paused from loading their beached jahazi with bundles of cut mangrove poles, neatly tied with coconut fibre rope. "Wow," I breathed. We were once again transported in time.

"How long has this landing place been here?" I asked our friend. "For how long have dhows been coming here to load?"

He shrugged. "Since before I was a small boy. I remember in those days there was a small *duka* here, but it has gone now." He pointed to the old mango trees where there were some chunks of half-buried rubble lying. "Dhows have always come here." Even in Gedi's time, I thought.

From the inland shore of Mida Creek we drove round to Watamu, where there was a small beach resort at its entrance. The sun was shining strongly by then and the white coral sand of the beach was dazzling. The entrance to the creek was quite wide and would have been no problem to the passage of the large ocean-going dhows of the Persian Gulf. We called at a pleasant colonial style hotel for cold drinks and sat on their open verandah with its macuti roof and beams built from well-polished rough-cut timber. The wind sighed in the casuarinas and rippled the emerald and pale blues of the sea over the reef.

The next day we headed south towards Mombasa, carrying with us three chirpy Cockney girls whom Jonathon had found, together with their backpacks which strained the carrying capacity of the car. The weather was dull and rainy again. Why were we cursed with the wettest southerly monsoon for years? I felt nostalgic, almost sad, travelling in the grey morning as we passed through the Arabuko Sukoke Forest. This was the last remaining tract of coastal rainforest and the beautiful natural mix of high trees towered on either side of the narrow ribbon of glistening road. Further south there were regimented rows of sisal plants for miles which disappeared over the crests of the inland hills. Forest that had been evolving for millions of years had been felled.

I turned off into Kilifi town, a shabby colonial relic with Post Office, Police Station, D.C.'s bungalow, hospital and a straggle of market stalls and Indian *dukas*. It was laid according to British practice with space between the official, commercial and 'native' sections of the town. In recent years, the edges had blurred and the spread of trees helped, but the town plan was still clear. To surprise Jonathon and the girls I pulled into the grounds of the Kilifi Club which stands on the edge of the cliff with a fine view of Kilifi Creek and the Indian Ocean beyond. "Cool drinks, beers?" I said after parking under an old baobab.

The Kilifi Club had become a rough disco with an outdoor concrete dance-floor and a partly enclosed bar and verandah. But it still had an ambience of simple colonial days when the small European community gathered there. Its position on the cliff-edge was superb no matter who owned it now or what its purpose. The manager was there with two jaded bar-girls wearing stale make-up and crumpled satin dresses and judging from the confetti-like swath of cigarette ends and beer bottle tops littering the floor, the night before had just ended. The manager was drinking Tusker beer out of a litre bottle and he greeted us with laughter and shouts of welcome. One of the Cockney lasses put a coin in the juke-box and 'The Police' blasted the creek below, at 9.30 on a Sunday morning. It was fun. One of the bar-girls found a broom and began sweeping up the detritus with vigour. The manager exchanged joking insults with Jonathon and served us drinks. The three English girls began dancing on the concrete floor, brandishing beer bottles and the second bar-girl joined them.

"Staying here all day are we, Den?" Jonathon asked, grinning. "It could build up to be one of those great parties."

"If it weren't for the bloody rain, I'd say we should put up our tent and do just that," I replied.

Across the creek, on the opposite cliff top a couple of hundred yards away, there was a line of superior, old-established villas and the expensive Mnarani Club Hotel. Some of the characters from the Earl of Erroll murder scandal that rocked East African and London clubland society in the 1940s had lived or frequently visited there. Each villa had an established and manicured garden, some with private swimming pools, and I perched on the verandah wall with a Coke and gazed at them across the calm grey water pocked with the drips from the leaden sky. The relative of a friend owned one of them and he had taken Julius (our mutual Kamba friend from Nairobi) with him on a visit and they had walked over to the Mnarani Hotel for a beer. Julius had been refused entry to the bar by a haughty uniformed servant. Julius had been deeply hurt and Charlie angry, but that was their rule.

I told Julius that it would not happen in South Africa nowadays and he was not surprised. "I have heard that South Africa is much different now, but some things in our Kenya will never change," he said quietly. "As long as those kind of Europeans and Americans still come here." Below the hotel there was a smart jetty with a crane for landing marlin and sailfish and anchored off it were three superb ocean-going yachts, one of which was an old topsail schooner about ninety feet long and in immaculate condition. Feeling perverse, I was glad of the raucous noise of the rock and roll thundering from the old Kilifi Club which had become a friendly local bar.

After we crossed the creek on the ferry, I stopped to visit the ruins of Mnarani, a minor medieval town with the same history as Gedi, which had used the deep water of Kilifi Creek as its harbour. Its mosque and a tall pillar within a small complex of buildings stood on a projecting bluff up river from the ferry crossing, the luxury villas and the Mnarani Club Hotel. The cliff fell away on three sides providing some security but the Arab-Swahili people who had lived there and used the creek as shelter for their dhows were also ravaged and forced to flee by the Galla invasion in the 17th century. What was important to me at Mnarani was the unique inscriptions sculpted into the carved stone of the mosque walls, especially in the surrounds of the *mihrab*. These inscriptions had not been deciphered although they were Arabic in style.

The custodian was a lonely young man, glad to see us because his last visitors had been some days previous, who told me that from time to time experts came to examine the writing and photograph it. It seemed to me that there were two different scripts, one more flowery and ornate than the other, and the writing could not be dismissed as the work of some mischievous person because it appeared on a holy portion of the mosque. Had some long-forgotten Persian or Arab scholar attempted to design a Swahili script there? Maybe he had written it all down and compiled a grammar and it had been lost to a Simba swarm or invading Galla clan?

The girls suddenly realised that they had lost two days. When signing the visitor's book and checking the date with the young custodian, they discovered that they should already have arrived in Nairobi and were flying home at noon the next day. This was a real panic since they were flying on bucket-shop excursion tickets by Sudan Air and there would be no chance of refunds or re-issuing of tickets if they missed their flight. So we had to hurry away and I raced them to the outskirts of Mombasa and saw them onto a bus. They had two days of hard travelling ahead of them, overnight train from Mombasa to Nairobi, out to the airport somehow, flying to London via Khartoum and Cairo, then underground trains and buses to their homes.

"We were booked to spend a night in a posh hotel in Nairobi and get sorted and cleaned up," one of them wailed. "We haven't bathed for nearly a week and just look at my dirty, sweaty clothes ...."

Jonathon gave me a whimsical smile as we retraced our route to where we were going to sleep overnight: "Just think if you had agreed to party at the Kilifi Club, old Den. Those girls would have been really screwed up. They probably wouldn't have realised until they got to the hotel in Nairobi that their flight home was already gone."

Yes, indeed.

I had chosen to spend the next nights at Kanamai because there was one more significant ruined town to visit. Kanamai was a camping and conference centre on the coast owned by the National Christian Council of Kenya and comprised a church, a conference hall, a kitchen and dining room, several self-contained bungalows and dormitory blocks for men and women. A large hall was under construction by a local Swahili contractor and his men worked long hours despite the rain. The grounds were already flooded and when we drove up the heavens opened again. Apart from Malindi, there was no other secure campsite north of Mombasa, but since Kanamai was a couple of miles from the highway with no bar or shop, there were few tourists. We were given space in the dormitory which consisted of a cubicle with seven foot partition walls and wire netting over the top to discourage thieving.

The rain poured heavily all afternoon with brief breaks when the monsoon breeze blew coldly from the south east. I walked to the beach during one of the breaks and it was disappointing there; the reef was close to the sand and there was a lot of decaying seaweed strewn about and its astringent rotting smell was unpleasant.

After cooking our simple evening meal on the verandah of the dormitory on our trusty Primus stove, I felt shivery again and probably had a fever, but was reluctant to go to bed since I was sure to wake in the middle of the night and toss about. Jonathon was not feeling too good either and lay on his bed reading. So I was glad when a gentle Scandinavian couple turned up and wanted to chat. They were backpackers 'seeing Africa' in their summer vacation time like all the others, but they were different to the jolly young people we had encountered at Malindi. He was a male nurse in a small city near Stockholm and she was a teacher from some unpronounceable town within the Arctic Circle. Talking earnestly with his pale straggly beard jumping, he told me his gentle private philosophy and his simple expectations of life. He had travelled in South America and had done the obligatory 'hippy' pilgrimage to Katmandu, but this was his first visit to Africa and he found it confusing.

"I don't understand the African culture," he said in his lilting accent. "In India I know that I am travelling in a strange world; all those temples and Eastern writing everywhere, like a child's story. And in South America it is different again. I can't explain well. But Africa," he shook his head. "I can't find what I look for. Of course it is different..." he waved his hand at the warm blackness filled with the steady hiss of rain. "But what is the culture?"

"Africans did not build great permanent temples or cities, not in East Africa anyway. The ruined towns are of the Arabic civilisation." I tried to explain. "There is nothing physical to see, and the modern buildings are just cheap European imitations usually in poor taste with no style. Africans were illiterate, there is no history. It all takes time to discover, because the culture is an invisible way of life; an attitude, an inherited style with inherited religious and social rules that are not rigid and exact like our dogmas and legal codes. European missionaries and administrators thought that because

Africans seemed so vague that they were unprincipled savages and tried to impose order in our way with books and implacable laws. Because it is impossible to explain to a stranger in a strange language your whole complex culture and traditional law in a discussion sitting under a tree for an hour or two, Africans never really tried. How would you explain the whole of European Civilisation in conversation, even if you could, to some impatient Eskimo who showed that he thought you were inferior anyway? So, Africans were always thought to be secretive and evasive as well as unprincipled and ignorant. There were no books or engraved monuments to study, so our people mostly never bothered to try and understand."

He was nodding enthusiastically. "And that is why I don't understand..."

"Exactly. Don't try too hard, just travel and enjoy the people. They are friendly, tolerant and very kind. They like to have fun and love to laugh."

"But there is so much thieving and we are worried about being attacked, especially my girl-friend."

"That's because there are many people in the towns with no work and their traditional morality gets lost. So be careful, of course. But don't look too hard for 'culture', just try to absorb it like rice taking up boiling water in the pot."

He laughed. "You are a philosopher!"

"No," I disagreed, smiling. "But I have lived many years in Africa."

Next morning the sky still dripped, but we went out and a watery sun broke through later for a few hours. The ruins of Jumba la Mtwana lay close to Kanamai, just north of the entrance to Mtwapa Creek, conforming to the need to have a safe harbour nearby, and we drove over after a frugal breakfast. Jumba la Mtwana is Swahili roughly translated as 'The House of the Young Slave' and I have not found any adequate explanation for this name. Like other Arab-Swahili towns on this coast, it flourished in the 14th/15th centuries and declined because of warfare and depredations of the wandering Simba and invading Galla. It was not a large town, probably similar to Mnarani, but the ruins were well preserved as at Gedi and its particular charm lay in its location right on the ocean front.

The 'Mosque by the Sea' enchanted me. In the five hundred years since its abandonment the beach has probably not moved much for there is a barrier reef to seaward, and I admired the imagination that designed it to stand on a level shelf of land right beside the sand close to the freshness of the water. The *mihrab* facing Mecca to the northwards was well preserved in the standing walls with an arched doorway at its side. There was an ablution area with a cistern and foot scourers of rough coral. The distant thunder of the surf on the reef filled the air. Nearby the 'Mosque by the Sea' there was an important tomb with an inscription. Unlike the mysterious Mnarani writing, this inscription was carved in clear Arabic. It was taken from the Koran, translated and quoted by Dr Hamo Sassoon in his guide:

> Every soul shall taste death. You will simply be paid your wages in full on the Day of Resurrection. He who is removed from the fire and made to enter heaven, he it is who has won the victory. The earthly life is only delusion.

I am impressed, over and again, by similarity in the philosophy behind all civilised dogma; and saddened, as always, at the floods of blood that have flowed in national or racial conflicts blamed on the lofty cause of religion and 'true faith'.

A rain shower came on while we were in the 'Mosque by the Sea' and we sheltered with some friendly women with little stalls under a macuti roof and drank Coca Cola. When the rain blew over I walked back to the centre of the ruins from a different direction and found a new perspective I might not have otherwise seen. To my astonishment, I was looking at a miniature version of the double circular stone walls of the massive 'Temple' Ruin at Great Zimbabwe. There was the main, curved external wall and a curtain wall enclosing a house within, with just enough space for one or two people to walk through. I photographed it excitedly and dug into the guide book but there was no description of the building. The defensive walls of the town continued away from this 'Zimbabwean' wall. Obviously, there was no clear connection between Jumba la Mtwana and Great Zimbabwe. What excited me was that the close similarity showed the senselessness of statements like: 'Arabs always built square structures', and 'buildings with curved walls are exclusively African', and so on.

But, maybe that house on the northern edge of this small medieval town had been built by a Swahili trader who had visited Great Zimbabwe once and had copied the 'Temple' ruin? Why not?

Malindi - the St.Francis Xavier chapel, 1542

CHAPTER SIXTEEN : KWALE POTTERY

My next objective was the Shimba Hills and from Kanamai, we drove to Mombasa and parked behind the Manor Hotel to stock up with provisions at the Fort Supermarket next door. Strangely, although Kenya is unashamedly capitalist, the retail industry flourishes in an old-fashioned style. There are many so-called supermarkets but none are much more than large grocery shops with one or two check-out tills at one end of the floor. Even in socialist and impoverished Zambia I have seen more modern supermarkets though goods there are scarce. The Kenya supermarkets are almost all run by Indians and maybe that is the reason; they are family businesses managed traditionally under the keen eye of the owners. The Fort Supermarket was no exception. The small rectangular store was crammed with household goods, some displayed in their original packing cases, some in nooks and crannies, the alleyways as crooked and confusing as a medieval town.

Travelling light and quite fast down the coast we were now relying on canned meat and could find none except stewed goatmeat from some local cannery. I don't mind goat but I was curious and asked a lady in a gorgeous sari why this was so. "Tinned meat is very scarce in Kenya now," she told me. "It has been like that for some time. That goat stew is the last of our stock because it is not popular." She did not know why supplies had dried up.

We tried several other shops but apart from the same brand of goat stew, there were only imported American corned beef and European sausages and delicatessen at extraordinary prices. A modest range of Kenyan canned fruits and vegetables were available, so why not meat? "Maybe the only factory broke down and they can't fix it," suggested Jonathon and he was probably right. We were in Black

177

Africa and although Kenya gives an impression of efficiency it is a veneer that frequently crumples showing how thin that impression really is. We did find a bookshop, however, and I bought an excellent 1:250,000 scale Survey Department map of the coast that was out of stock in Nairobi.

Increasing population pressures, urban growth and the sad multiplication of corruption have created a savagely divided society where the 'real' Kenya becomes poorer and standards steadily deteriorate while the wealthy, the expatriate community, foreign agencies and corporate institutions and tourism increasingly rely on costly imports and the expensive services of specialist entrepreneurs who are usually Indians. Kenya drank deep of the heady wine of Western technology but cannot keep up with its constantly accelerating progress and is now in danger of being unable to maintain the standards of a decade or two ago. Whereas most African countries gave up the impossible task, except for narrow segments such as official communications or the military which are of particular convenience to a ruling hierarchy, Kenya still tries to be up-to-date.

The lack of tinned meat in Mombasa and elsewhere reminded me of the futility of African countries trying to become industrial societies within tight national boundaries. The proliferation of South African consumer goods in much of Africa, as far afield as the heart of the Congo basin, reminded me that it was sensible for Africa to open trading doors within the continent; that each country should do what it could achieve best with its human and natural resources and fling away notions of nationalism and protectionism together with useless concepts of vengeful ideological politics.

Rhetoric may sound grand when uttered by presidents but it is damaging and pathetic when related to the real state of their nations. The failure of the common East African railways, other services and technical resources set up by the British colonial authorities between Kenya, Uganda and Tanzania before independence, with the concept that they would later be integrated with those of other regional states like Malawi, Zambia and Zimbabwe, was an example constantly in my mind. The steady regression of Zimbabwe, in real *per capita* terms, with increasing corruption amongst politicians in the few short years since 'official' independence parallels the current Kenyan experience.

Nationalist politics, personal antipathies of political leaders and short-term conflicts between those Commonwealth countries, pledged to mutual assistance, had brought hardship to their masses.

178

The same Commonwealth politicians were attempting to destroy the degree of regional trade and cooperation that still existed in southern Africa in order to 'force Apartheid to its knees' which seemed to me to be the most deliberately destructive and damaging single political activity to occur in Africa in this century. After Apartheid had been 'brought to its knees', who would salvage the mess of a sub-continent of 80,000,000 people that had been reduced to ruin after a century of hard-won progress? Black Africa has proved incapable of maintaining standards from internal resources let alone salvage itself from disaster.

Certainly, the protagonists of the destruction of southern Africa would do nothing. They had already caused retrogression in their own lands in the name of Black nationalisms and outmoded ideologies. 'Commonwealth' had become the most cynical word in an African political vocabulary. Some brave lexicographer will one day have to list two meanings for this word precisely opposite to each other. These thoughts churned in my mind for the hundredth time and depressed me anew as we drove up to Kwale.

[This was written in 1989. Shortly afterwards, President F.W.de Clerk's white nationalist government dismantled Apartheid and South Africa then acquired a new 'democratic' constitution with Nelson Mandela as President. But violent crime, corruption and falling per capita standards became endemic.]

South west of Mombasa there is a range of mountains called the Shimba Hills. They rise to 1477 feet twelve miles from the sea near the colonial administrative town of Kwale and run parallel to the coast for about twenty miles between the valleys created by the Pemba River in the north and Ramisi River system in the south. This mountain range was once covered by rich rainforest, for high precipitation results from moist ocean air surging over the heights. Large patches of this magnificent forest remain between open grassland caused by felling and cultivation. Nowadays it is a National Reserve and the forest is slowly expanding again, providing a home for forest elephant, giraffe, buffalo and the rare roan and sable antelopes. I visited the Shimba Hills because it is a restful wilderness with a pleasant camp on a magnificent site on the edge of the escarpment. And because of the Kwale Early Iron-age pottery culture.

The air grew cooler as we climbed and white mist formed and reformed about the green peaks and trailed along the edge of the escarpment. Kwale township was laid out in the traditional colonial manner: a spacious official area, run down now, was separated from the huddle of shacks and simple dukas that comprised the township. We stopped at one of the dukas to see what we could buy. There was not even tinned goat stew and the bread delivery had not arrived from Mombasa. But, the market had ample fresh vegetables so we knew we could come in for replenishment if we needed them.

"We'll call on the warden of the Shimba Hills Reserve," I said to Jonathon. "I need to see the Iron-age archaeological site here. I'll explain it all when we are there and absorbing the atmosphere."

The Reserve headquarters comprised a couple of simple rectangular buildings with offices opening onto verandahs and a shed with dilapidated equipment in it. Rusting, abandoned vehicles stood about under some trees. Some women sat on the verandah of one of the office buildings talking to a game-guard in crumpled uniform.

"*Jambo!*" I greeted him. "Is it possible to see the Warden, or some assistant?"

"Why do you need him?" The guard was cautious; maybe I had a complaint.

"I want to ask about archaeological sites in the Reserve."

He gave me a friendly smile. "Of course, that is in order. Go in that door and ask the secretary." A minute later I had been ushered into an inner office and met a large man seated at a desk with papers scattered on it. Like his subordinate, he was cautious and unsmiling until I explained my need.

"Ah, yes. The Iron-age sites." He smiled and invited me to sit in a rickety chair. "I have heard of them, but I'm a relative newcomer. Let me call my technical officer." While we waited we chatted about the unseasonable monsoon rains. They were causing him problems in road maintenance and his resources were stretched. He had a road grader but it was frequently out of commission. "It is always a matter of spares." He sighed and shrugged his ample shoulders. "I can wait weeks for a simple thing. And although I have a mechanic on my staff, he is called away for other priorities."

"Are the archaeological sites inspected regularly?" I asked.

He was embarrassed and ignored my question. They were clearly not a priority. Instead he gave me other interesting information. "In the Reserve I know that there are places which were sacred to the people in past times. Deep inside the forest in these hills there were what we can call shrines in English where the priests would visit to make contact with the spirits of ancestors and pray to God. At certain times of the year it was necessary to go there for

180

ceremonies and at other times if there was trouble, like failure of the rains or disease epidemics, sacrifices could be made and the spirits would be asked for help."

"Do you know when they were used?"

"Until recently. The custom is similar to the Kikuyu in their homeland around Mount Kenya and this is similar country. They were Bantu farmers, you see, not cattle herders like the Masai, and they liked these hills with good rainfall. They cleared the forest and grew crops. To-day we are encouraging the forest to spread again and that is why it is a reserve."

His assistant came in then, a tall very black man, heavily built and with a round beaming face. He greeted me cheerfully after the explanations were made.

"Yes I know those Kwale Pottery sites you are looking for. They are not easy to find and there are no signposts to them. Indeed, there is nothing to see because no excavations have been made for some time. The people at Fort Jesus Museum know about them and have the exact references. You can go there and ask them."

"I would have liked to visit the exact sites," I said. "But what is important to me is to see more or less where they were, to get a feel for the country."

He smiled. "That is easy. You continue on the main road past the entrance to the Reserve, down the mountainside to the valley below. The sites were near to the waterworks which you can easily see: the Pemba River Waterworks."

I told Jonathon of my disappointment at not getting exact information. "The map shows Iron-age sites on the high ground, not in the valley," he said. "I've been studying it while you were in there." He showed me the detailed map we had found in the Mombasa bookshop and it was so, but the Waterworks were also marked. "After we're settled we can have a drive around." I said. "Without returning to Mombasa we're not going to get a proper answer and the important thing is to know that this is the correct area, and there seems no doubt about that."

He folded the map saying, "It's not like England is it? You'd think something important to their history would be properly looked after in a National Reserve?"

His remark restored my humour and I smiled at him, "No, it's not England."

There was space at the campsite for tents under dripping trees but we went for a rough banda beneath forest giants, perched on the edge of a cliff descending a thousand feet to the shifting green branches of the high canopy below. Through the humidity and the mist that formed and reformed we could catch the flash of white breakers on the coral reef of the coast ten miles away and 1400 feet below us. The banda was a single-roomed rondavel with macuti roofed verandah from which to admire the view. I sat immersed in the scene for a long time while Jonathon pottered about and got the Primus stove going for coffee. It was cool and the air was rich with the aroma of damp vegetation. Sipping our coffees, we heard a squeal and binoculars were instantly in use.

Directly below there was a small clearing where the glow of yellow sand showed through the rainforest and as I scanned across it I saw the grey shapes of elephants briefly. "Ah," I sighed. "We're back in Paradise again."

I told Jonathon about the wardens's advice that the Shimba Hills were a spiritual home of local Bantu farmers. Jomo Kenyatta in *Facing Mount Kenya*, (1938), describes the religious structure of the Kikuyu, typical East African Bantu agriculturalists:

> The creator lives in the sky. Ngai eikaraga matuine; but has temporary homes on earth, situated on mountains, where he may rest during his visits. ... Apart from the official abode of Mwene-Nyaga ['Possessor-of-Brightness', the name for God] at Kere-Nyaga [Mount Kenya] on the north, there are minor homes such as Kea-Njaha [the mountain of Big Rain, presumably the Shimbas] on the East; ...

"As I think I said before," I explained. "The farming Bantu people during the Iron-age mostly settled on high ground in eastern-central Africa where there is better rainfall and less parasitic disease. That is why in Kenya there is population crowding today and pressures on the land in what were the colonial 'White Highlands', surrounded by huge areas of dry thornbush like Tsavo Park at a lower altitude and with insufficient rainfall for successful agriculture.

"The coastal strip was also ideal, but for the difficulty in clearing the massive rainforests. Improved iron tools and population pressures changed that, which is why the later Iron-age people began making inroads into the forests. It's amazing to think of people living here within true tribal tradition while the Arab-Swahili trading towns were down there, not far away, with ships from India or Portugal calling."

"You think they were completely isolated?" Jonathon asked.

182

"No. They would have traded ivory and honey for cloth and iron artifacts. But they would have been wild people from the hills to the sophisticated town dwellers. In a reasonably stable society, there were no pressures to mix. Each enjoyed their own style and kept to it. There was some culture adaptions, but I would guess that whoever lived here in small cleared patches in this great forest and the valleys around were not very much affected. There was not much reason for either side to integrate."

"It's strange to think that we are camping in a sort of specially historic place, like Stonehenge," he said.

We went for a drive later. Most of the extended summit was flat plateau, seamed by shallow valleys of small streams that led to gorges that had eaten into the escarpment walls over millennia. Rugged stone cliffs broke through the forest where these gorges had been formed. The plateau had the look of well designed parkland at first; highveld grasses spread evenly over the land like an undulating sea washing the shores of large islands of impenetrable rainforest. The islands were exactly defined, there was no intermediate stage of scrub or scattered trees between grass and forest, the change was complete and abrupt.

I was strongly reminded of the Zomba Plateau in the middle of the Rift Valley in Malawi where the landscape is almost precisely similar and old forest clearing has been allowed to commence healing. Thinking further, I saw that there was clearly recognisable similarity with coastal highlands in Natal: although some trees were different, many were the same species and the same juxtaposition of grassland and rich forest like islands in a sea impressed me enormously. I was deeply and suddenly absorbed by these impressions of easy comparison between Shimba, Zomba and Natal not just because of yet another example of the massive continuity of African geography, but because of the particular archaeological importance of the place. I was quiet, filled with intellectual excitement, while Jonathon drove carefully along the muddy tracks.

We saw buffalo close by, resting and chewing the cud, and so relaxed that our stopping to photograph them from about ten yards did not cause more than a penetrating stare from their wicked black eyes. "You'd never think they were so dangerous," Jonathon remarked, breaking into my thoughts. I laughed. "Try running around with a lasso like a cowboy," I said.

Circumnavigating a large forest island about two miles across we rounded a corner and came face to face with a herd of roan antelope. Some of them were contentedly ruminating and although alert to us did not immediately spring up. "Amazingly at ease," I commented in a whisper. "They're so beautiful," Jonathon said quietly as he cocked his camera.

Back in the camp we found that another party had arrived in two battered Landcruisers. There were piles of gear about and two White men with American voices were working with three Kenyans sorting it in order. When we had settled with a couple of bottles of beer and our stove going with a pot of rice, one of the Americans came over and introduced himself. He was a large man with curly grizzled hair and a breezy manner and he wanted to know what the roads in the Reserve were like after all the rain.

"We've been around most of the area this afternoon and had no trouble," I told him.

"That's good. Mind if I sit a while?" He perched on the low wall surrounding the verandah. "It's been a heavy day and we're getting on each other's nerves." He laughed and wiped his face. "The drive through from the Amboseli was torture. Every time I come to East Africa I find that the dirt roads are worse. They used to grade them two or three times a year and it wasn't too bad, but I guess everything is sliding faster now and I don't think the road I was on has been graded for a couple of rainy seasons. Jesus! Those ruts and corrugations."

He was a Professor of Zoology from Chicago researching fruit-eating bats and the Shimba Hills was the sole habitat of a rare species that they hoped to trap. He told us about his work and talked about flying foxes that I knew from the Seychelles. "Well, the flying fox is all over the Indian Ocean, from tropical Western Australia, Malaysia to Madagascar and most islands like the Seychelles which you have seen. But there's a real mystery which we'll never solve. They have migrated across thousands of miles of ocean and are found on Pemba Island, twenty miles off the coast of Tanzania." He paused dramatically. "But there is no trace of flying foxes on the mainland of Africa. How do you explain that?"

I shook my head. "There's more things. ..."

"Ain't that the truth! Anyway what are you doing here?"

I told him about the Early Iron-age sites and the interesting link I could see between habitable highlands in Kenya, southern Tanzania, Malawi, Zimbabwe and the eastern parts of South Africa. I explained the Early Iron-age sites and my difficulty in locating them. "The warden said he was new here and did not know about them."

184

"That's the new Africa!" he said getting up. "Maybe the warden gets off his ass once a month to drive round his kingdom. Poor guy, he can probably just keep his head above the useless paper-work and is totally disillusioned. It's not like it was twenty years ago when I first came." He waved his big freckled hand at us. "Best of luck..."

Next morning the sun woke us, shining golden through fast evaporating mist. Over coffee I sat on the little verandah and gazed contentedly over the lowlands below. I heard the trumpeting of elephants and could swear that I heard the distinctive grunting of hippo: there had to be a pool in the river down there. Beyond the boundary of the reserve, the forest had been felled long ago and in the clearer air of this sunny morning I could see how the local people had carved the land into their shambas of a few acres of maize, cassava and vegetables. There were patches of indigenous trees but most were paw-paws, mangoes and coconut palms clustered about the simple homesteads. Wavering yellow lines showed where dirt tracks connected the scattered shambas with the main coastal highway. I could see the white surf line on the reef clearly and the ocean was a deep blue. On the horizon tufty fair-weather clouds were riding the monsoon.

The camp caretaker was a cheerful, friendly fellow and he came over to tell us where the best places were for viewing elephants. When I said that we wanted to see archaeological sites at the Waterworks, he confirmed the directions I received in the warden's office.

"If you are going outside, can you buy me cigarettes?" he asked. "Sure," I replied, assuming that I was also agreeing to pay for them. But he rushed off and returned with the exact change in small coins.

The road down the western escarpment to the Pemba River was muddy and rutted from the recent rains and it snaked through one of the gorges created by a stream from the plateau above. Vertical rocky cliffs stood out in places where erosion had laid the them bare. As we descended, the vegetation changed from the highveld grasses and the mysterious islands of dense rainforest to a more uniform mixture of scattered leafy trees and acacia thorn. There were succulents including giant euphorbias and a greater variety of grasses.

Approaching the river we passed a small shamba with traditional homestead of three or four thatched wattle-and-daub huts, an enclosure for the few goats and a calf or two and a raised grain store. A paw-paw tree and an old mango shaded the homestead. A naked girl-child ran out and waved to us, scattering chickens clucking over fallen grains in the cleanly swept compound. I stopped to look over this homestead and the child watched us with hand now nervously in her mouth. From the foreground I swept my eyes up the green slopes of the escarpment to the heights of the Shimba above. Excitement had my heart running faster.

"This is how Africa is different to the other continents," I said to Jonathon, who had been waiting for an explanation of my particular interest in this area. "Apart from Australia, where the Aboriginal people and their culture were almost wiped out by the White colonists, there is nowhere that there is such massive similarity and continuity of geography and population as there is in this huge zone, straddling the Equator, from Somalia in the north-east to the Cape in the south-west. It is more unchanging than America, because whereas the Americas also straddle the Equator, they are separated by the long, thin jungly strip of Central America. Africa is not like that."

I waved my arm around. "What I find so exciting is that standing here and looking about me at the landscape and at that shamba there I could be anywhere in a range of 2,500 miles between Mount Kenya and the coastal mountains of the Ciskei at the Cape of Good Hope. An expert botanist might tell where he was because of particular species of plants that would be signposts, and there are variations in the birds that would give me a clear indication, starlings would be a good example, but otherwise you could be here, the Rift Valley volcanoes of Malawi, the Vumba Mountains on the Zimbabwe-Mozambique border or the Tugela Heights in Natal. Unless you were a linguist and talked to the people of that shamba, you would find difficulty in deciding what tribal group they belonged to."

I looked at the homestead again, noting the goat trailing a piece of rope as it chewed at the leaves of a shrub, I saw some exotic poinsettia in flower (a reminder of European influence also common throughout Africa), I saw some enamel bowls and a clay pot by the three-stone fireplace, I saw the hollowed tree trunk used for pounding grain and I saw some lengths of printed cotton cast over a bush to dry and fluttering in the light breeze. The little naked girl with a string of coloured beads around her belly had retired but was still watching us from the safety of the open door of one of the huts. A small field of maize plants produced their particular rustling sound from leaves moving in the breeze. Laughing doves were calling and bulbuls were singing cheerfully. I saw two fork-tailed drongoes playing together and when I looked upwards I could see a pair of yellow-billed kites

186

soaring. Yes, I thought, I could be almost anywhere. But there was one difference, and the Kwale pottery was a possible key.

"Can you remember visiting Zululand when you were a lad and probably being taken to some tourist showplace of a Zulu kraal?" I asked Jonathon.

"Yes, of course. I've got vivid memories of that holiday."

"Can you remember what their huts looked like?"

He looked carefully at the homestead before us. "They weren't like these. They were round like a football cut in half and made entirely of grass thatch."

"Right!" I said. "All over Black Africa, from the central areas of South Africa right through to the other side of the Congo forests to the Sahel in Cameroon, Bantu people build round walled houses often with poles on the outside supporting the roof so that there is a verandah all around. The only real variations being decoration or the influence of local materials, the kind of trees, thatching grass, clay or whatever. Some build in stone, but the general style is the same.

"But the Zulu group of tribes in Natal built 'beehive-shaped' grass huts and the only other people in this huge zone who built 'beehive' huts in modern times were the so-called 'Hottentots', or more correctly today the Khoi, of the Cape and the peoples of the north-east like the Samburu of Kenya. But the Khoi are thought to be part of the Khoisan indigenous race before the Bantu migrations, the Samburu are Nilotic nomadic herders and the Zulu are classified as Bantu who are farmers. In between, for 2,000 miles, huts are like those you are looking at. It's something that I find extraordinarily important, but I've never come across any special academic overview of it.

"What is particularly exciting about this very place is that there was a style of pottery found here, different to other East African pottery, and dated about 200 AD. The only other places where a related style of pottery has been found is on the coastal zones of Mozambique and South Africa. And the dates are more-or-less the same, moving towards 400 AD. ... You get the point of all this?"

"That's why we came here?"

"Yes."

"You think there were people on this coast, who were mixed with the ancestors of the Samburu and who were different to the Bantu of central Africa, who went south as far as Natal in South Africa about 300 AD."

I nodded. "Maybe. Or later, about 800 AD. It makes sense to me, even though it is never as simple as that." And then I paused. He had said something out loud which I had been holding in my mind for a long time; mostly without being prepared to expose it even to myself. I felt inner excitement there, below the Shimba escarpment, in the hot sun.

"There is another clue, which is language," I said slowly, almost to myself. "The principal attribute that defines the Bantu people, apart from the fact that they are all farmers, have similar social structures and so on, is language. All Bantu languages have the same ancient root. As centuries have passed and people moved, languages changed, but it is natural to assume that if there are abrupt differences in language between people living close to each other, then one or another has moved into that area from a far distance, and by comparison it should be possible to trace their origins."

Jonathon nodded.

"The Nguni languages, of which Zulu is the more important, are unlike any around them and there are other cultural differences between the Nguni and their close neighbours, the Sotho-Tswana. There have got to be reasons. ... I think the Nguni languages are closer to kiSwahili than any other. I haven't yet found any professional or academic opinion, but it's my gut feeling that there is a language link right down the eastern African coast. Like the Kwale pottery."

Jonathon gave me a playful punch on the shoulder. "You're planning another book after this one, aren't you?"

I grinned. "Naturally. But, meantime I think that it's time we went to see Richard Wilding, the archaeologist, in Mombasa."

We drove further on and found the Waterworks. Behind a high security fence there was a long corrugated-iron shed with blackened exhaust pipes penetrating the roof. Big pipes controlled by a valve system emerged from a wide pond formed by a weir. It seemed deserted and the chain securing the gate was rusted and broken. We walked down to see if there was a worker there who might know about the actual dig sites. But there was nobody. We peered through a broken window at two large twelve cylinder diesel engines connected to high volume rotary pumps.

"Ruston-Hornsby," Jonathon said admiringly. "Beautiful engines, must be twenty years old, I suppose. No bloody good now...." The engines had been stripped down for repair and the bright metal of the interior parts was richly coated with red rust. The smell of tired old oil and dirty grease wafted to us. I looked around the grounds, at the disused driveway and the grass and weeds growing everywhere.

"This pumping station has been abandoned for a long time," I said.

"Ran out of spares," concluded Jonathon. "And too idle to do anything about it, so a whole water supply system dies."

"Africa ..." I murmured, looking up at the hills and thinking of Iron-age people who had no need of pumps or diesel engines. Women and girls walked down every morning to the river with their Kwale pottery containers, singing as they went. They were still doing it.

Jonathon sitting on the 'verandah' of our simple *banda* on the Shimba Hills.

189

The Pemba River behind the Shimba Hills - definitive site of Kwale pottery.

CHAPTER SEVENTEEN : BANTU MIGRANTS

It was time to look further at Indian Ocean traders and their effect on the indigenous people of eastern Africa. It was this aspect of my quest which had tickled at my imagination twenty years before and prompted me to undertake earlier journeys to Zimbabwe, Sofala and Moçambique Island. In Mombasa I contacted the archaeologist at Fort Jesus Museum, Richard Wilding, whose name I had obtained from Julius' brother who worked at the British Institute in Nairobi.

We were invited to Richard's beachfront home at Mtwapa near to the Jumba la Mtwana ruins for coffee and a long relaxed discussion. One of his main interests was the old civilisations and nomadic peoples of Ethiopia and the Sudan. What inspired me immediately was his easy overview of a history of Africa in relation to real peoples and the lands and environment as they were, which obviously came from many years of field experience over wide areas. Not for him were fashionable dogmas developed in the isolation of campuses in North America or Europe.

When we were settled on the verandah of his small bungalow with the distant roar of waves on the reef and had exchanged preliminary remarks to see where we stood on a number of issues, we tackled the matter of early Bantu migrations. One of the great mysteries of Africa is that Bantu-speaking Negro peoples have inhabited the southern half of the continent for a comparatively short period of about 1,700 years. Before then, the San-Bushman race are usually assumed to have been the only occupants of the savannahs while the related Pygmies lived within forested areas.

"Are we sure that there were great migrations?" my new friend mused. "And were they exclusively Bantu-speaking? Many people have taken for granted that there was some kind of wave advancing down Africa two millennia ago like the Asian Barbarians swamping

Europe. I don't see evidence for that. In the first place, there were too few to make waves and Africa is not so hospitable that the geography welcomes tidal waves flowing over the landscape. I reckon it was thin trickles following the best paths; some succeeded, others died out. It was never coordinated. Small groups wandered across Africa, farmers kept to farming country or starved; nomadic pastoralists followed good grass where it existed, like the wild game. They must usually have coexisted and there was no reason to clash. Africa is very big. And if there was a clash it would have been a minor skirmish with lots of sound and fury but little violence."

"And if there were no clashes or struggles for territory they were friendly to each other and traded. ..."

"They helped each other out, firstly because they were facing a vast and often dangerous environment and secondly because they had things for each other. Farmers needed animals for milk, ceremonial rituals and for barter or to buy brides. Nomadic pastoralists needed grains, metal and other artifacts. Metal working clans attached themselves to one or another farming group where there were raw materials, in a symbiotic arrangement. Recent examples suggest that religion was generally similar and the principles were universal but each group followed the culture formed by the environment of their origins.

"Pastoralists from Nubia had a rather different life-style to farmers from Lake Victoria and so on. Customary cultures were carried with them as they moved. As time went by there were amendments and changes where necessary and, where it was not necessary, they stuck to their cultural heritage. There is some evidence for the transference of elements of Sudanic languages to Africa south of the Congo. So, probably the movement was not exclusively Bantu-speaking either. We must remember that there is evidence of Cushitic-speaking pastoralists from Ethiopia in East Africa before the Bantu-speakers came. And those Cushitic-speaking pastoralists were probably also occasional neolithic agriculturalists where it suited, as they have been recently. We are sure that Cushitic-speakers were in Tanzania, but who knows how far south they trickled either before the movements of Bantu-speakers or together with them? Or later?"

"Hence the Khoi-Khoi people," I said, excited at what he was saying. "They could have been descendants of nomadic herders who trickled south and became closely associated with the San-Bushman because they had a greater kinship with hunter-gatherers than farmers. The Khoi maybe were a mixed race: genetically predominantly San-Bushman with most of their cultural style, but having acquired cattle and sheep from their Cushitic ancestors they also inherited appropriate culture including their clan structures, their hemispherical hide huts and so on. I remember the first time that I saw a Samburu village in Kenya and being instantly reminded of Khoi huts of the Nama tribe I had seen in the northern Cape Province of South Africa. Maybe the conclusions of 19th century South African historians like Theal, who thought that the Khoi had Hamitic origins, were right."

He expanded on his particular interest in the nomad pastoralists and while I listened and interjected occasionally I was so glad to be there. I had seldom had an opportunity to talk easily with someone with such breadth of knowledge of north-eastern Africa. It was his concept that Cushitic and other pastoralists diffused over eastern Africa before and contemporary with Bantu farmers that kept me excited. I was delighted by his conviction that rivers were the communications link between the East African coast and the watered highlands. I thought of sitting with Jonathon beside the Galana River and talking about traders moving up and down. Being particularly concerned with the nomads of Ethiopia he saw the Juba River which runs to the sea near Kismayo in Somalia as vital to trade and interaction in early times.

We talked of modern tribal people living quite close to each other, adhering to common ethics and with similar language roots, yet having some clearly distinct cultural differences proving substantially different ancestors. The Nguni tribes, including the Zulus, who live closely alongside the quite different Sotho-Tswanas in South Africa to-day occupy the furthest south point of Negro migration in Africa. It is the Nguni who I see maybe having strange ties to Nilotic pastoralists whilst being undeniably Bantu-speakers with a language close to kiSwahili. Philip Tobias of Witwatersrand University has shown that they have a high proportion of possibly exclusive San-Bushman genes running in their veins and the unique Khoisan 'clicks' in their language prove that Bushmen and Khoi clans had been absorbed over long periods of time. I remembered reading that studies have suggested that the Nguni have Aryan genetic inheritance, which would confirm biological mixing with Arab and Indian sea-traders which had importance to our discussion. Alas, they were not a subject Richard had studied in detail.

"O.K.," I said. "Now what triggered this movement, whatever we call it. Why did Negro peoples of a particular origin and similar

193

culture, whom we call Bantu, suddenly diffuse over half the continent?"

"What do you think?" Richard asked, smiling.

I took a deep breath. "I think that the principal reason, of many minor and regional ones, is that agriculture based on sorghums and millet was introduced from the Nile region across the Sahara as the desert expanded and people moved south and west. The Bantu core-tribe were Neolithic people living in the fertile highlands of Cameroon and eastern Nigeria and this hilly, well-watered country was a successful environment for cereals and so the inhabitants expanded economically and in numbers. They came to the Great Lakes around the north of the Congo forests in the first millennium BC and at some time they acquired iron technology from Nilotic people. Settled for some centuries they extended their iron and agricultural technology and became intensive farmers. The environment around Lake Victoria in particular was eminently suitable and it remains so to-day. They probably met new ideas from other nomadic Nilotic people. In time, they also met Indian Ocean trade through middlemen via Ethiopia or the river routes like the Tana and Galana.

"This introduced them to exotic, high-value tropical fruits and vegetables like bananas, yams, coconuts, mangoes, citrus, rice, sugar-cane and so on. This produce flourished in high rainfall areas like the east coast and around the Great Lakes, which further boosted their health, economy and numbers, so they had to move outwards, wherever the geography was suitable which was southwards, and to a lesser extent eastwards to the coast. This is basically the theory of Murdock and Darlington, if I remember rightly, but it makes absolute sense to me."

He nodded, encouraging me.

"I believe that there were three distinct southward 'streams': one to the west of the Congo rain-forest, one centrally from the Great Lakes and one along the east coast. There are well-defined central and western types of Early Iron-age pottery and there is the Kwale pottery of the Kenya coast, almost certainly linked to similar pottery in Mozambique and eastern South Africa at the same date, around the 3rd century AD. The central and coastal streams were surely separate because of the geography. To-day, there is the sparsely inhabited wide belt of dry bush that separates the two agricultural zones, the one down the Rift Valley escarpments and the other along the coast, and if modern agriculture cannot bridge the semi-deserts, why should thin streams of Early Iron-age farmers have even bothered to try?"

194

He interrupted: "There is lots of un-proven in your scenario. Such as how did the coastal stream move so fast and get there before the central stream? If I remember correctly, the Early Iron age in Central-southern Africa is dated about 5th-6th century and 3rd century on the east coast."

"I think it's just geography. Feeling their way down the centre from one attractively arable area to the next across areas of awful dry bush infested with tsetse fly was pretty slow and there was no incentive apart from gradual pressure from behind. But, the coast was one long continuity of familiar geography which they had already mastered, with no new problems or challenges. They zipped along! A hundred years or so to move 2,000 miles along a friendly tropical coastline is not really excessive."

He laughed. "I like your enthusiasm and from my work on similarities in domestic pottery you must be right. Go on."

"I know that it has been shown that Bantu-speaking people migrated, or diffused, through the western Congo, to-day's Zaïre and Gabon. But they would not have been able to carry cereal agriculture or cattle with them through the rain-forest and must have survived through adapting themselves to that environment. Basil Davidson believes that was the main route of migration, but it makes no sense at all to me. Davidson, I suspect, is trying to show a connection between a Zimbabwean 'civilisation' with the West African empire states, so maybe he has an axe to grind. Although people moved down the west coast they would have to have revived savannah agriculture when they reached Angola and Zambia and probably met central-stream farmers from the Great Lakes region. They would not have had cattle and probably no metals. I believe the main thrusts were the central and eastern routes. Your picture of small groups moving down the centre as dictated by local environments rather than in a wave makes absolute sense, but I see the trigger the way I describe it. And I see the coastal route as the simplest and naturally easiest, therefore the fastest."

"The coastal route may have been the easiest, and we have all agreed for a long time that it was important, but why should small numbers move so fast? What motivated them? Are you going back to a wave migration concept instead of diffusion? Are you suggesting that Cushitic-speakers from the north-east were using the sea route? It is an exciting idea, which many of us have mulled over for some decades, but there is no evidence. I do not believe that pre-Bantu-speakers were on coastal ships, and what would motivate them to settle far afield?"

"If there were Arab and Indian sea-traders in communication with them and also exploring southwards in a parallel movement by water it would have stimulated them. They all communicated with each other. Some migrants may have travelled by sea as crews, guides, slaves or client helpers. Information about new and pleasant coast lands was brought back not only to the origins of the sea-traders but also to the homelands of the local Africans. The sea-traders may have encouraged settlements."

"What about cattle?" he asked. "How did they get cattle, if they were farmers and maybe moved through unhealthy environments? The earliest Iron-age people that we are talking about maybe didn't have cattle. They were farmers with farmyard fowls and goats and sheep who had to keep to the green highlands or the wet coast lands. Herding vast numbers of cattle and breeding them carefully is the work of experienced nomadic pastoralists not fixed to the land. Modern ranchers may grow some maize and vegetables, modern grain farmers may have a milk cow or two and a chicken run, but the two are separate industries and have always been so. They are different methods of using different kinds of land.

"I can imagine stud animals travelling long distances down the coastline and can't imagine proving it! But, I cannot imagine whole herds tucked into the bottoms of *mtwepes*. Somehow, specialist cattle herding either developed as an independent survival pattern in the south, or that cultural baggage was carted overland along the coastal strip however well-supplied later by sea.

"I wish I could see pre-6th century non-Bantu-speakers settling the coast by maritime networks in collusion with Indian Ocean sailors. It is exciting to think of it, and from what we know of modern Cushitic-speaking pastoralists, they could have developed mixed farming if the opportunity arose: they could have been proto-Swahili. But the evidence is thin save for a few hints in the domestic pottery which I have noted with scant conviction. As the evidence sits at the moment, the development of the Swahili culture, while obviously strongly influenced by non-Bantu-speakers of the hinterland, took on its characteristic urban, mixed farming and Bantu-speaking modes at a time and in a way which suggests that Bantu-speaking immigrants had a critical role. I have even thought of the Early Iron-age and Central African Later Iron-age stylistic connections in the pottery as indications that the pots were made by suppressed craft castes of

196

Bantu-speakers, even slaves, trading into the Swahili towns. That would lead to consideration of a more strongly Cushitic-speaking and north-east African indigenous presence in the towns. But it is all little more than a straw in the wind! As I see it at the moment, as far back as there are scraps of evidence, the specialist pastoralism and coastal mixed farming and fishing are very different ways of surviving in different ecologies."

"Late Iron-age people in South Africa practised both," I pointed out. "The Nguni were particular Bantu farming types to whom cattle were an obsession, and, as we know, they are a powerful and successful ethnic group. But they are a particular case in a particular environment, so I mustn't confuse the argument. ... I have to admit that I always lazily assumed that southern Bantu with a cattle-cult picked up cattle from the Nilotics in the southern Sudan or Kenya, learned husbandry from them and somehow became herders as well as farmers. I suppose that is because I had a viewpoint based on knowledge of the modern Nguni of Natal. I assumed that cattle sort of diffused southwards with the people."

He laughed. "The old circular argument. The cattle were there when the Europeans arrived on the scene, so they had to come with the people that they found ... It doesn't work in this case."

I nodded. "You, in particular, have shown me the most likely way it happened. And I can't think of any objections to your thesis. I have often wondered about the cattle in South Africa. As you said, one problem is that they don't seem to have been there in the Early Iron-age up to maybe 500 to 700 AD and the other is the two species of cattle recorded by the first Europeans: the 'African' long-horned, humped type and the short-horned, straight-backed type of the coastal Nguni tribes. It's always the Nguni who stick out as exceptions which makes me continue to believe in separate eastern streams, maybe two or three very different ones over the past eighteen hundred years."

De Barros in 1552 describing Bartolomeo Dias' pioneer voyage to South Africa in 1488 wrote:

> ... we then steered to the northwards, and thus sighted land in a bay which we called Angra dos Vaqueiros [February 1488], because of the many cows seen there, watched by their [Khoi-Khoi] herdsmen.

I went on: "Anyway, cattle generally appear to have been important to the beginning of the strange jump from Early to Late Iron-age in east-southern Africa don't they? In southern Africa all sorts of strange things happened a thousand years ago or so: cattle, different pottery, stone building and larger settlements, then towns and precious metal mining. All over the place. Then the rise of the Zimbabwean Empire. This jump was surely stimulated by the expansion of Arab and Indian trading between Africa, the Mediterranean and all around the Indian Ocean rim, further exploited by the founding of coastal colonies after the expansion of Islam? According to Horton there seems clear correlation between activity in Egypt and activity in southern Africa about 1000 AD. Maybe cattle were the result of a second movement of people southwards, maybe in more than one stream, as a result of changes in north-east Africa. Your Cushitic nomads getting restless around 700 AD and being absorbed with their cattle and 'cattle cult' by the already well-established Bantu farmers in southern Africa?"

He nodded cautiously. "I hear what you say.... And there were definite changes up here in the north-east. The Aksum civilisation declined about then, and there may have been particularly bad droughts in the Horn of Africa. The Kenya coast with good forage and established maritime commerce would have been especially attractive at that time."

We talked on about our agreement that trade might be the key to southern African migrations, stimulating population growth by introducing new crops and techniques, handing on information and intelligence on other lands and how to exploit them. Assuming that we discard the idea of migrating waves carrying old established technology with them, exchange of goods and ideas had to be the stimuli for a gentle diffusion of people.

Richard told how more archaeological exploration was needed on the East African coast and hinterland where almost all effort and the limited funds available was being devoted to the ruined towns of the Swahili medieval period. Naturally, this effort was necessary, but it had the danger of creating an imbalance of importance in favour of the last thousand years and the towns. Indonesian influence was important and often overlooked. Arab, Indian, Persian and Egyptian traders were active on the East African coast and in contact with people organised enough to be worth trading with at zero AD,if not earlier.

198

"The *Periplus of the Erythraean Sea*," I murmured. "The odd Greek too."

"Exactly! And it surely wasn't simple hunter-gatherers who lived at Rhapta 2,000 years ago. There must have been Cushitic peoples on the coast who later were displaced or absorbed by Bantu-speakers of the Kwale pottery culture about 200 AD who came down from the Great Lakes. Maybe there were other peoples living on the coast at that time just as the Swahili and local Bantu coexisted in the medieval period. And to-day, for that matter. There are many what-ifs still on the Kenya coast. Nevertheless, the fact remained that Early Iron-age people who smelted metals and planted sorghums as well as living by hunting and gathering, did migrate as far as Natal by 250 AD, they were different to the central African stream. And there may have been cattle-keeping groups well south along the coast before then!"

We sat, smiling at each other and catching our mental breaths. The sun was setting and we moved inside and talked of everyday things for a while. When we were chatting about the ruins Jonathon and I had been visiting at Lamu, Malindi and southwards, my new friend interrupted me.

"There's an apocryphal story that would amuse you. When St. Francis Xavier was at Malindi, when he is said to have founded that chapel which interested you, he was sitting on the beach taking his ease and chatting with the local Moslem imam: exchanging professional talk and arguing theology. The imam was amazed to discover that St.Francis used cue cards in his sermons and thought it was a jolly good idea. It's a lovely picture of these two men, supposedly deadly opponents, hitting it off and discussing the tricks of their trade."

As we were about to leave, he asked: "Do you think the Portuguese set out to conquer East Africa and establish a slave economy?"

"That was hardly the main thrust," I replied without hesitation. "They wanted to trade with India and the Far East. Royal instructions to the first admirals were quite clear about entering into friendly relations with local rulers. After they discovered that the gold trade with Zimbabwe was drying up before they arrived on the scene, Africa was low priority. They had neither the numbers nor the commercial motivation to colonise in Africa. Dominance of the ocean trade was their objective. History tells what little impact they really had. My own eyes have shown me that they had greater cultural

199

impact on architecture along the Malabar Coast of highly civilised India than on eastern Africa. Once they found that the gold of Monomotapa in Zimbabwe was declining, it was a matter of survival, wasn't it? The Arabs and Swahilis dominated eastern African ocean trade for two millennia, frequently squabbling with each other and defending themselves from the natives, while the Portuguese had a meagre foothold on East Africa for a short two centuries and were gone by 1700. 16th and 17th century expeditions to find Zimbabwean gold and silver via the Zambezi route failed."

He nodded. "There's an awful amount of nonsense spoken about the tranquillity of the Swahili civilisation and the terrible impact of colonising Portuguese. It's fashionable."

Basil Davidson wrote in *The Story of Africa* (1984):

> Putting all the evidence together, the conclusion is that the 'ancestral Bantu' began to travel, by a gradual spread of pioneering peoples, out of this area of northwest Africa about 3,000 years ago. Two areas of secondary dispersal were gradually formed to the south of the rainforests of the Congo basin, and from these, perhaps around 500 BC, the spread continued in two directions: southward into Angola and Zambia, and eastward into East Africa, reaching what is now Kenya by about AD100. From there, 'Bantu' culture moved southward through Zimbabwe into South Africa, crossing the Limpopo River in about AD300.

Davidson's view may be a popular standard to-day, but by 1984 research in South Africa had developed knowledge considerably. Davidson always seems weak when he is writing about southern Africa. Southern African pre-history was oriented to the classical civilisations of the Indian Ocean through ocean and coastal trade, not to the introverted kingdoms of West Africa where expanding peoples fought for territory in a constricting geography under pressure from migrants from the growing Sahara Desert.

Jan Vansina wrote of the Western Stream in the *Journal of African History* (1984):

> Original expansion of Western Bantu speakers resulted in a very thin occupation of the area as people moved to use more favourable locales....... Population pressures probably had nothing to do with this search for an early farmer's Eldorado

200

.... [But] Once farmers acquired new crops.... the incentive for this [expansion] was certainly local population growth. .... Eastern Bantu speakers had had cereals ever since they left Cameroun. In the Great Lakes area they also mastered techniques for smelting iron and eventually they carried cereal agriculture, cattle keeping and metallurgy all through eastern and south-eastern Africa in the first centuries AD. From AD100 and 400 onwards their pottery and iron are found in portions of Zambia and Shaba [outhern Zaïre], previously settled by Western Bantu speakers.

Mark Horton in his article *The Swahili Corridor* recently wrote in regard to eastern African Swahili seatraders:

This unified, indigenous seafaring society (the existence of which has been recognised only in the past five years) may have come into existence as early as the first century AD.

Whilst agreeing with much of his thesis regarding the power and extent of coastal trade links far to the south, I wonder at his definition of the Swahili as indigenous as far back as the 1st century. I do not believe for a moment that Africans initiated ocean trade in eastern Africa. But I do believe that the rapid expansion of Early Iron-age people from Kenya down the coast to Natal was influenced by seatraders. In any case, historians have been exercised by extent of uniform Swahili society for considerably longer than the 1980s.

Richard Wilding summarised in regard to East Africa in his *The Shorefolk* (1987):

....There was a mixed population of hunting and gathering, pastoralists and agricultural communities, who developed complex symbiotic relationships, or diffused among each other. The language families were Nilotic, Khoisan, Cushitic and Bantu with the last two dominating the area almost completely. .... A long distance trade network existed right across the region, following river valleys in some cases, and connecting the foothills of the Ethiopian and east African hills with the coastline. The commodities were passed to the coast either along a chain of seasonal markets or with dry season surplus cattle.

It is interesting that Richard's description of the Early Iron-age period in East Africa, before the permanent settlements of Arabs,

201

Persians and Indians founded the Swahili people and civilisation is remarkably similar to the picture drawn by South African historians of the circumstances there before the expansion of European colonists. In the case of South Africa, there is trickle-trade between the several different Bantu tribal groups and symbiotic 'client' arrangements between Khoi, San and Bantu tribes varying with the vicissitudes of climate in fragile semi-desert lands.

To complete my small selection of quotes, here is Tim Maggs in his review, *Iron Age south of the Zambezi*, in *Southern African Prehistory and Paleoenvironments* (1984):

> The ecological pattern of Matola sites   (similar pottery to Kwale)   in Natal is significant in terms of the present evidence for very rapid initial expansion of the EIA (Early Iron-age)   down the east African coastline. Settlements scattered over some 3200 km from Kenya to southern Natal may be within 150 years of each other. Movement at anything approaching this speed would seem to require special economic circumstances, a condition supplied by the Natal ecological model and perhaps applicable to the coastline further north as well.

Jonathon and I drove back to Mombasa, absorbed and excited, for our different reasons. My mind was full of the turmoil of intellectual stimulation, instantly seeing jigsaws meshing and other ideas crumbling. Especially, I was so happy to have had the meeting there, where some of it happened, rather than in an office in Manchester, Oxford or Cape Town. It makes such an extraordinary difference to me.

NOTE : Dr Richard Wilding relinquished his post at the Fort Jesus Museum some time after I met him and was later killed in a car crash on the notorious Nairobi-Mombasa highway. Before that happened we had exchanged correspondence and were planning to meet in England. He published a detailed, but little-known important monograph, *The Shorefolk*, in 1987. I believe that Richard had insights which could have changed many opinions of eastern African pre-history and that his passing was a great loss to an understanding of Africa. Much of what he said to me that day has been proven to be on track by later archaeology researched by Prof. Felix Chami in Dar es Salaam. My own intuitive thinking developed further along those lines in the next years and is expanded in detail in my book, *A Beautiful Ivory Bangle*.

CHAPTER EIGHTEEN : "WE'VE FOUND PARADISE."

From the crest of the Shimba Hills we had looked down on Tiwi and Diani Beaches spread along the coast some twelve miles eastwards. I had reflected on how close to the coast lay the Early Iron-age settlement of Kwale, within the forest that reached inland until distance from the moist air of the ocean changed the geography to the vast stretches of dry scrub bush that separated the coastal farmers from those in the Highlands and around the Lakes. I wished to spend time on those beaches for hedonistic pleasure but principally in order to let my thoughts roam free for a while, contemplating the role that the East African littoral has played in the evolution of mankind.

Twenty-two years before I had lived with a friend in a rough beach-cottage at Bamburi for three months, just north of Mombasa, where to-day there is a miriad of hotels, holiday apartments and cottage-complexes. In those days, the beaches were clean, we left the doors of our cottage unlocked and would not see another person for days at a time. An iguana lived in the wild garden of frangipani and rough grass lawn, there was a bright green snake in the loo and a pair of African pied crows learned to lift the lid off the rubbish bin. A very tall coconut palm acted as a beacon when we walked along the empty beach. I spent hours watching the translucent crabs at the tide's edge fossicking for seaweed or a local fisherman passing by in his mashua. We would walk along the beach to the old Whitesands Hotel for a beer in the evening and sit on creaking cane chairs on its wooden verandah and watch an unblemished scene.

The Whitesands was now a huge concrete block with barbed wire to keep out the besieging 'beachy-boys', petty thieves and touts.

The pied crows who mate for life and have family territories have been driven away by flocks of Indian pariah crows, the crabs have more plastic and trash to deal with than seaweed and I am sure that there are no iguanas. In 1985, the tall palm still stood forlornly amongst rising blocks of holiday flats, but by 1987 the palm was gone and the concrete apartments were occupied and their walls were already streaked with mould. Tourists are warned not to stray onto the coral sands in the moonlight because of lurking muggers. As the population increases and if unemployment continues to rise, which seems inevitable, the beach resorts will increasingly become fortresses within which affluent Western tourists cower. The social cancer of mass tourism in the third world is easy to study on the Kenya coast. I find it terribly sad.

I could not tolerate the degradation of tourism-infested resorts and approached Tiwi Beach with real trepidation. I had warned Jonathon, so we were both tense as we studied the signposts at the turn-off from the main coast highway.

"Twiga Lodge," he read. "You said Julius recommended it."

"Yes," I said. "It will probably do, although it's sure to be crowded. ... Look. There are three cottage resorts."

"They're sure to be booked up too."

"Let's see."

The first was full and a pleasant White woman with colonial accent was pessimistic. The tide was in and waves were running over the reef and rushing onto the white sands below her pleasant little bungalows prettied by bougainvillaea. I sighed as I got into the car and started up. Jonathon wiped the sweat from his face; it was a very hot sunny day. The next, Sand Island Cottages, seemed rather ramshackle from the road. There were a couple of abandoned old motor vehicles parked under the tall sighing casuarinas. I walked about, looking for an office.

"Hi!" a deeply-tanned American with a beard and faded swimming shorts greeted me. "Looking for the manager? I saw her over there. Go through that gap in the hedge."

Through the hedge I came upon a lawn that swept to the beach and a line of bungalows of various sizes, ages and styles. It was cared for but with that indefinable atmosphere of relaxed and casual pleasure that I was seeking. There were no formal flowerbeds and no planned layouts. It had obviously matured over a period of decades. A family was lying about in the shade of a casuarina and there were people swimming on a large sandbank spreading toward the reef. I suddenly wanted that place very badly indeed.

The manager was an attractive Indian woman in her early thirties and I found her in what must have been the original homestead of the property. The large main lounge was roughly furnished with sagging settees and odd chairs and on the walls there were faded photographs of men with fishing rods and rows of fish, laughing family groups lined up in dated swim-suits and amateur water-colours of fish and birds. A library of novels and battered reference books from the 1930s and 40s stood against one wall. Two vast deep-freezes containing home-frozen fresh fruit-juices from the last harvest, locally caught fish and crayfish, buckets of broken ice and joints of meat hummed beside a desk littered with papers and ledgers.

"Sorry about the chaos," she said, smiling. "That's the way we are at Sand Island; it's comfortable. Do you want accommodation?"

"Yes, just two of us. Anything will do."

She frowned and started to scrabble amongst the papers while I held my breath. "For how long?" she asked as she paged through a ledger. I said, "Some days, whatever you have." The paging went on.

"Well, you're lucky. I've got a small bungalow, a bedsitter with kitchenette and shower. Some people from up-country didn't turn up. You could have it for a week, if that suits?"

The little cottage was cramped with two beds, a table and two chairs, gas stove, battered refrigerator and sink. Behind a partition wall was the shower and toilet. A primitive solar-heater on the roof provided near-boiling water. The windows were slatted shutters with faded chintz curtains. But there was also a verandah almost as large as the room with long, old-fashioned lounging chairs with holes in the arms for drinks. From the verandah we looked down the lawn for thirty yards to the white beach, the sand island and the coral reef. Two arms of jagged old coral rock projecting into the sea a couple of hundred yards to the north and south cut us off from the rest of the world. Coconut palms rimmed the beach, casuarinas sighed and sang behind us and a few wild-looking bougainvillaea provided colour. A tall thin, very black man was cutting the grass with a 'slasher'.

"Wow!" I said. "I don't believe it. We've moved back thirty years in time." I slumped into a long chair and breathed the salt air and aroma of cut grass.

"I'm not moving for days," said Jonathon, slumping next to me. "I never knew what paradise was until now. We've found paradise!"

"We've got to buy food."

"Beer too, there's a fridge. After that. ..."

It was paradise there and we only ventured out to buy provisions, visit a medieval mosque still in use at the mouth of the nearby Mwachema River, drink a cold beer at Twiga Lodge nearby and have a look at the package-tour hotels at Diani Beach. I spent many hours at Sand Island sitting on the verandah watching the changing scene of the sky, sea and reef before me.

Heavy showers returned on several days so that purple clouds moved in on the steady southerly monsoon winds with their blue-grey veils of rain suspended from them. The temperature would drop to about 75 ºF and at the height of the storm I would be driven indoors by the cold spray from the heavens. The shower would pass and I could go out again and watch the purple mass replaced for a while by a pale grey or silver sky and the air was rich with the smell of sweet water and laved vegetation. Other days, bright puffy cumulus clouds rode the winds for hours and the intense heat of the near vertical sun at midday was like a dragon's scorching breath. As the sky changed, so the colour of the sea altered from battleship gloom to bright lead etched with silver edges, to brilliant blues and greens.

The rise and fall of the tide altered the colour of the reef so that at the height of a rain squall it might range from pale olive to dark green, and from brilliant emerald to aquamarine when the sun shone. The colour of the coconut palm fronds changed too in the light and as they were drenched or dried. Sounds were never the same either, affected by the degree of humidity in the air, whether the monsoon was lighter or stronger, as the palm fronds thrashed or rattled, as the waves were high or low according to tide. To an instant view it may have appeared a simple, even boring, land and sea-scape. But in a period of days it was a fascinating spectacle of marching colour and sound. Added to all the variations of weather, there were the grand changes of sunrise and sunset. I could have done nothing but stay at that place for weeks if only to see that same view infinitely varying.

Of course, I was not immobile. I walked on the sand island and the reef when the tide was low; I swam in the limpid water when it was higher. Especially when the tide was coming in over the sun-heated coral reef and sand, the sea was warm even to my sunburned skin. When it was ebbing, the water was cool and refreshing.

We ate well from fresh food we could buy either at a 'European' delicatessen run by a large German woman or in the small market in Tiwi village. We could buy fresh fish from men who scoured the reef at low tide. We often threw out tomatoes or pineapple that had begun to go soft, so rich was the bounty. I made the finest fresh goat's meat curry ever one day; simmering it all afternoon with coconut milk and peanut oil, onions and okra, lime juice and chopped pineapple, garlic and ginger root, green peppers, cloves, coriander, turmeric and cumin seeds. We ate it with boiled rice, raw bananas, paw-paw and tomatoes. Everything was freshly grown around there. What bounty!

We made friends with two attractive girls, Sarah and Vicky, cheerful and intelligent fourth-year veterinary students from Cambridge University who were at Dan Trench's campsite, sleeping in a loft over an old out-building, and we 'boogied' together until very late one night at the Tradewinds Hotel at Diani Beach.

I talked one morning to William, the tall 'garden boy', who described himself that way without irony pr emphasis though even in South Africa such colonial mannerisms are usually discarded. He owned a five acre shamba up north near the Uganda border and it was enough to support his family in food and clothing. But he had a twenty year old daughter who showed good promise and he wanted to send her to the polytechnic at Eldoret, so he was cutting grass at Sand Island with a 'slasher'.

"It is shameful work for a farmer," he told me. "But what can I do? There is only one chance for my daughter and she must have it."

"What do you earn here?"

He spat on the grass between his feet. "Four hundred shillingies [about £15.00] a month. It is less than the rent of that big cottage there for one day." He pointed at a nearby bungalow occupied by two visiting English families. And about the price of a simple plastic toy advertised on Saturday morning TV at home, I thought sourly. He wiped the sweat from his face and gazed at the grass still to be labouriously cut with the 'slasher'. "I am eating some *posho* [maize porridge] and whatever vegetables I find cheap, and that is all. I have had no sugar for a week."

"You speak English very well," I said. "can't you get a better job?"

"I attended high school, so I am educated. But there is no work for an older man like me. There is very little work for all the young people coming out of school now. That is why I am like a slave."

"These low wages and bad conditions; are they because the management here takes advantage?"

He shook his head. "No. That Indian woman is kind enough. It is the same all over Kenya. At least here it is quiet and safe, and beautiful. Not like Nairobi. If I had more money I would love this place. ..."

He would take a break and drink sweet tea or Coke with me in the middle of the morning or afternoon. He was a fine man and interesting to chat with idly while he rested his body and restored his self-respect. The Indian manageress said to me one day: "I see you drink tea with William at your banda. It's alright, and he's very unfortunate. But, some of the other guests might think it's a bit much..." I replied: "Too bad." She shrugged and gave me a smile.

With all that time to laze and watch I thought a lot. Of course, I thought about the Indian Ocean traders, especially as there were the triangular lateen sail shapes of *mashuas* moving up and down just beyond the reef at dawn and dusk. But that was my time of thinking much further back, much further back than Phoenicians sailing round Africa on the instructions of Pharaoh Necco or the Greeks who followed the *Periplus* in Sabaean sewn-ships. I thought about the first creatures on earth who could talk and habitually used tools for everyday tasks: about primates whose pelvises evolved until they usually walked upright on two legs, who lost their fur, evolved language and copulated face to face and learned to make love. I thought about the origin of my own species.

In the late 1960s two popularists of evolution and behaviour took the world by storm. Robert Ardrey launched himself with *African Genesis* and Desmond Morris with *The Naked Ape*. They both wrote later books, and there were others who were attracted to the same fashionable trend, but Ardrey was the heavy-weight. Perhaps in common with millions of others, I suddenly understood exactly who I was. *I WAS AN APE!* It was an extraordinary revelation. I looked at my fellow humans and saw them as apes; extraordinary apes who had created an extravagant, highly-disciplined, artificial world, but nonetheless apes. I lost my vague innocent acceptance of a romantic notion of being a different kind of creature, somehow separated from animal life, and gained a passionate and exciting awareness of my personal integration with all life on this Earth and thence into the totality of the Universe.

Together with this new awareness came the acceptance that our Western Civilisation and material progress was not something to be automatically proud of. Our seemingly endless and instinctive striving for new-improved technology was often counter-productive.

Both socialist and capitalist industrial and agricultural systems have failed badly. Somewhere there had to be a new enlightenment that must emerge if our special ape species is to survive and improve the quality of all life on our planet. Intellectual thrashings of the last two decades had solved nothing, but at least they had stirred emotions and arguments, which is a beginning. The ecology is bound to occupy more political energy in the 1990s than at any time in the past.

Richard Leakey, a master of prehistoric African archaeology, wrote the following in *Origins* (1977):

> By searching our long-buried past for an understanding of what we are, we may discover some insight into our future. There is much more than bones and stones buried in those fossil-bearing sediments; they are vital clues to human biology. Through an exploration of the forces that nurtured the birth of the hunting and gathering way of life perhaps three million years ago, and through studying the question of why such a long-established mode of existence was superseded, beginning some 10,000 years ago, by a sedentary agricultural society, we can hope for some insight into modern society, and with it some guide to our future.

The sentiments Leakey expresses are not unique, but he says it as well as anybody else. William Shakespeare wrote it with poetic brevity - "What is past is prologue."

Ardrey and Morris reflected opinions of the 1960s, and times and knowledge have advanced. Ardrey's later book, *The Hunting Hypothesis* (1976), probably summed up one of the dominant theories at that time and is still sometimes seen as the explanation for our evolution beyond that of our close cousins, the gorillas and chimpanzees. But most of these propositions from the 1960s and 70s are now discarded and some can be seen to be quite ludicrous. I do not believe that there is much serious acceptance today that forest apes could only survive in a declining habitat by hunting on the savannahs and becoming human, which is *The Hunting Hypothesis*. There are far too many examples from life to throw those concepts out. For instance, no successful predator would evolve to two legs from four. Successful predators creep close to the ground up to their prey, then attack with great swiftness. Wolves, African hunting dogs, lions and hyenas all hunt in packs or in close coordination with their fellows. All of them communicate and cooperate quite successfully without having to develop huge brains and complex language. None of the

African predators, nor their prey, nor other primates, have found it necessary to discard fur and hair to increase their cooling capacity, the usual explanation for our nakedness commonly put forward. (Ardrey also suggested that loss of fur was necessary to increase sexual attraction in the female so that male hunters would share the meat!) Contrarily, fur is most important to protect tropical animals against flying insects. Baboons, the savannah monkeys, are highly integrated socially, their children take quite a long time to mature and they run fast on four legs. They communicate as efficiently as is necessary, use their hands to grub for food and eat it, and have plenty of fur. They are survivors all over Africa from the Cape to the Mediterranean. Behaviourally, humans are closer to baboons in many ways than to our closer genetic cousins, the great apes, whose dwindling numbers barely survive in the dwindling rainforests.

The core of the 'Hunting Hypothesis' which occupied scientists and motivated much of Ardrey's writing is the proposition that because man developed primarily as a hunter, aggression and the potential for warfare and attendant inter-species slaughter and murder became part of his genetic heritage. But, the study of apes, modern human nomads and, in particular, the San-Bushmen of southern Africa show that aggression commonly leading to bloodshed is not a trait of other apes nor of primitive modern man. Warfare and the disturbed social aggression of to-day is the product of territorial activity directly linked to the demarcation of land for agriculture and the rise of civilisation with its rigid legal systems, at odds with the infinitely fine variations and gradual merging of all natural social structures. War and killing began when people could not escape the excruciating tensions raised by fixed territory necessary to agriculture, the construction of permanent towns and the pressures on the boundaries of these domains caused by harvest failures, population growth and changes forced by demagogues.

The compulsion to view all problems in 'black-and-white' rather than infinite shades of grey, which results in endless confrontations at all levels of society usually leading to contempt and too often to violence, is a product of civilisation. There is an extraordinarily important reason for us to understand the true path of the origins of our species. People must understand which are our inherited genetic behavioural imperatives and which are the intellectually devised traits of civilised system that endanger us and our planet. By changing our society we can still take off on a happier and successful path to survival. Particularly, we must shed any excuse that we are aggressive killers and despoilers because of instincts developed 5,000,000 years ago in Africa. We still have the power to apply solutions.

Even though the 'Hunting Hypothesis' may be dead, Ardrey, Morris and others performed the valuable service of providing a stimulus for ordinary people to become involved in the story of our origins. To-day, scientific research is largely devoted to expanding the study of behaviour in areas where scientists are on firm ground. Our knowledge and understanding of modern baboons, chimps, gorillas and primitive man is being extended. Richard Dawkins shows in *The Blind Watchmaker*(1986) how it is possible for natural selection to produce genetic changes, within a period of only thousands of years, in quite sudden jumps with long plateaus in between. But, lacking any fossil trail that leads to knowledge of where and how the jump from ape to upright, talking, naked human occurred, that particular research is presently quiescent.

In 1972, in response to Ardrey and Morris, a book was published which proposed an alternative solution to the then current 'Hunting Hypothesis'. Elaine Morgan followed ideas suggested in 1960 by Sir Alister Hardy, a zoologist with early training as a marine biologist, and she expanded his alternative viewpoint in a popular style. *The Descent of Woman* was written by Elaine Morgan as an often angry rebuttal of male-dominant concepts, and her book contains some outmoded feminist protests. However, whilst properly protesting the male chauvinism of the early hunter, she also put forward the first popular description of the idea of an Aquatic Ape which satisfactorily answers some of the difficult questions regarding human evolution. In 1982, Elaine Morgan published *The Aquatic Ape* as a more mature exploration of this hypothesis and Lyall Watson devoted a chapter of *Earthworks* (1986) to the subject. Detailed arguments are available from them, and Desmond Morris in his later book, *Manwatching* (1977), lists fifteen persuasive reasons why the Aquatic Ape theory should be considered seriously.

Spending days at Tiwi Beach, on the East African coast where it may have happened, I thought deeply about Elaine Morgan's thesis and revised it in my mind. The alternative scenario to a savannah evolution directly to a hunting-gathering hominid, goes roughly like this. At the time of the retreat of the forests and the growth of grass and dry scrubland in the eastern and southern parts of Africa, *Ramapithecus* apes, our remote ancestors, were faced with problems of adapting to the changing environment. Those apes who lived where

211

the forests remained evolved to become modern chimpanzees and gorillas. Those who lived where savannahs were emerging naturally sought environments similar to that of the declining forests. They moved along the valleys of the eastern flowing rivers with their riverine vegetation which led to the Indian Ocean and became constricted in the humid littoral zone along the tropical coastline where there was always some forest no matter how dry and inhospitable the interior became. Becoming geographically constricted, they met the challenge by exploiting this habitat to its limits. Their existing ape intelligence as an advanced primate was stimulated by this situation and evolution by natural selection worked fast, as Richard Dawkins has shown it can. Powerful evolutionary jumps were triggered. Spending much of their time in and around the islands, coral reefs, estuaries and shallow bays of the eastern African shores, they adapted to a semi-aquatic life which produced the physical and psychic changes which made them human.

They shed their fur, which is a hindrance in the sea; their pelvises changed so that they could swim in streamlined fashion and stand upright in shallow water; their hands developed to gather shellfish from off the reef and use tools to prepare them for eating; they learned to call with specific language to communicate in the dangerous and complex ocean side environment where grunts and facial signals were inadequate. To handle language and efficient hands, they developed a bigger brain. Bigger brains and increased intellectual capacity led to a more complex society which exercised and expanded their minds in an exponential upward spiral of development. From gathering shellfish on the reefs the males were led to greater adventurousness in catching larger fish with resulting sexual polarity in food collection. Catches of fish, too large for individuals to consume, led to sharing of food surpluses, diet changes and accelerated the spiral of cooperation in a communal society and the complex communication that follows.

Having adapted to semi-aquatic life on the shores of the ocean and advanced their mental and physical abilities further than any other land animal, they later used their new abilities and powers of adaption to become masters of suitable parts of the interior lands. The food collecting habits of the seashore led naturally to the hunting and gathering lifestyle. Global climate changes created a wetter environment and river valleys led to suitable and attractive habitats around the lakes of the Great Rift Valleys of Africa. It is in those places that remains of early man have been found and the fossil searching continues.

When the Ice-age fluctuations added further stimulus to evolution, our ancestors spread into and mastered other continents, and the varied races of the *Homo* line resulted.

The 'Aquatic Ape' hypothesis is certainly more attractive than that of a 'Hunting Ape' if for no other reason than that we modern humans have always loved water and all people instinctively take great pleasure from bathing and swimming. It is intuitively a realistic and practical path. The massive despoiling of coastlines by tourism today is proof enough of our addiction to the seaside holiday, the warmer the better. Our upright nakedness and large brain are genetic in origin. Our familiarity with swimming and water has been shown to be instinctive from birth. And, we do not hunt by instinct otherwise we would have been incapable of domesticating a great range of lower animals. Hunting is a behaviour trait, learned after the 'aquatic ape' left the seaside, and is not a genetic imperative.

People may consider the great changes of losing fur, vertical stance, early tool-making and even the evolution of language and creative intellect from a distance. That all happened several million years ago and may be just a scientific curiosity. But sex is something we all know about, and therefore there has been considerable attention paid to the sexual differences between man and other animals. The 'Hunting Hypothesis' explained our 'sexiness' by suggesting that our great preoccupation with sex and the physical differences in the way we perform compared to other land mammals, resulted from the need to have strong male-female bonds and family structures to nurture slow maturing children and encourage males to share meat. But the great flaw in the 'Hunting Hypothesis' is that we did not have to be hunters to survive, we did not become hunters by genetic imperative. Therefore, there have to be other reasons for our sexual uniqueness, and again the solution appears simple. Undoubtedly, as our communicating abilities were extended, there was psychic in addition to physical pleasure by watching the partner's face while enjoying sex. That must have been an important factor in the spiral of increased social complexity and evolution of language. But a change to preferred face-to-face copulation would not occur for that reason alone. The simple answer seems to be that it was more natural to mate in the shallow waters of the tropical seaside. Animals always mate when they are at their most active, and the 'Aquatic Apes', especially the males, spent much of their days scavenging on and around the reefs and beaches. It is difficult for two apes to copulate crouching in moving seawater with the male behind: it is much easier face-to-face, hanging on to each other.

Very early fossil remains of our ancestors have been found from South Africa, in the vicinity of the Limpopo River, to valleys and lake shores in Tanzania, Kenya and Ethiopia. Limited resources have prevented further exploration in southern and eastern African river valleys and no serious effort has been devoted to looking for remains of 'Aquatic Apes' along the lines of ancient reefs of the Indian Ocean shore, and until they do so and succeed, we will probably never know with certainty where the great 'jump' occurred from ape to man. Indeed, maybe most littoral habitats are submerged in the oceans.

Lyall Watson in *Earthworks* (1986) wrote:

> We are not going to find webbed footprints on an ancient beach, but I predict that the context of the find, the evidently marine ecology, will confirm Alister Hardy's feeling that somewhere between the ancient apes and modern man lies a revolutionary being that can only be known as Homo Aquaticus.

Sitting at Tiwi Beach, gazing at the Indian Ocean, I ran through the arguments in my head several times. I examined many points of detail not mentioned here. I thought about the vast savannah plains of Tsavo that we had visited a month previously. I thought about the view from Shimba and the remains of the coastal forests that we had seen and driven through. I remembered my several travels on other expeditions through the two branches of the Great Rift Valley in central Africa with their chains of lakes. I thought about the potential disaster of civilisation and our desperate need to return to a simpler, non-aggressive society whilst continuing to advance our knowledge and culture and I wondered how we could evolve a system of logic that did not include the destructively combative 'black-and-white' approach to society. Especially, I thought about the Indian Ocean, so much more important to mankind than any of the other oceans.

One morning towards the end of our stay at Tiwi Beach, I was sitting on the verandah as usual after breakfast nursing a mug of coffee. The tide was flowing and water was deepening over the reef. The thunder and roar of the waves breaking on the outer bastion was growing. A holidaying English family was coming home from an early morning exploration to their breakfast, picking their way carefully over the old coral, the children trailing behind the adults and chattering. "Here come the aquatic apes," I smiled to myself.

Following the holiday makers were two dark figures, stopping here and there, moving confidently onwards, then pausing again. They were two local men whom I had seen many times and I idly followed them with my eyes, until a thought burst into my mind that astonished me with its simple and absolute obviousness. Those men went out onto the reef every day and on their return, they passed by our cottages peddling fresh fish and shellfish. I knew them by sight and they always greeted me whether I bought or not. Why had I not seen it? They were aquatic men; there for any doubter to examine. It was not necessary to theorise at Tiwi Beach, intuitive observation provided me with proof.

I watched while they emerged from the sea and strolled up the lawn. Each young man was clad in a brief kikoyi cloth wrapped around his waist and they were burned obsidian black by the sun. Their curly Negro hair glistened with moisture. From a string around their waists was slung a handmade tool, a simple metal spike with a wooden handle that they used to pry shellfish from the rocks, and they carried a roughly barbed trident on the end of a long bamboo pole that they used to spear fish and octopus. A handmade sisal bag hung from their shoulders for shellfish and each had fish strung through their gills by a length of coconut frond. Remove the machine-woven cotton kikoyi and substitute bone, ivory or stone for iron and they were equipped as any aquatic man would have been for a million years, since that last great evolutionary jump.

"*Jambo!*" they called, grinning as they came close to me. "You need fish today?"

"*Jambo!*" I called back. "Not today, thank you, my friend. But tell me, do you come every day to the reef to get fish?"

"Most days, if the weather is good and the tide is right."

"And you can make enough money in this way?"

They looked at each other. "Sometimes we help the tourists with what they need. But from the sea we can live." The spokesman held up his fine string of fish. "My family will eat one, the others we sell."

My God! The aquatic men had an easy life in paradise. While some of them scoured the reef, just like these 20th century Kenyans, others would collect fruits and roots, and the rest of the clan would attend to children, prepare shellfish, make tools and keep watch. It was an excellent life on the tropical littoral, provided your needs were simple.

"What do you do with the fish and shellfish you can't sell here by the beach?" I asked the aquatic man before me.

"Well, we take a *matatu* kombi-taxi to Likoni market and we sell them there."

They were from the mists of time, but they were also here and now.

*

Jonathon and I went on an excursion from Tiwi Beach to Shimoni and Wasini Island. My immediate reason was because Shimoni is almost at the border between Kenya and Tanzania so I would be 'rounding-off' our coastal safari. The brochure we picked up advertised snorkelling over a live coral reef and that would be an experience for Jonathon.

It was one of the raining days to start and I was pessimistic about how it would all turn out. We drove through a vast sugar estate, the waving sea of rich green extending away to the foothills of the Shimba Hills where the clouds rested on the summit. An elderly sugar-mill with corrugated iron walls and a smoking chimney was surrounded by miserable workers' hovels. The rain came down in smoking tropical force, bouncing from the road in spume, thundering on the metal roof of the car, the wipers unable to sweep the windscreen clear. We crawled to the junction just past the mouth of the Ramisi River whose valley formed the southern end of the Shimbas and which we had looked down upon from the look-out.

The local road to Shimoni was untarred and the rainstorm had turned it into a ribbon of mud. It was not long before we reached a place where it was flooded and a Peugeot station-waggon was stationery in the middle of a small brown lake. "Dear oh dear," I sighed. "I guess this is the end of our trip. We're going to be late." We got out and went over to the driver, a well-dressed salesman, who was peering into the engine with his neat trousers rolled up his calves.

"*Jambo*," I greeted him. "You have a problem."

He smiled at me through spectacles spotted with raindrops. "What can I do? There is water in the engine. My car is not a ship..."

I grinned. "No, your car is not a ship."

"We can push it out of the way," said Jonathon. "We could try to get through."

216

Some sugar plantation workers were watching and we called them over. It wasn't difficult to push the car through and then by walking back and forth in the water I found a track that was not so deep and we got through. But we had lost half-an-hour. I raced the remaining distance, skidding on the bends with all four wheels sliding, plunging through shallow flooded sections in a burst of brown spray. My adrenalin was pumping and it was fun. Suddenly we were at Shimoni, halting in a drenched little market place overlooking a sullen grey channel with Wasini Island on the other side. A dhow with people in brightly coloured clothing was chugging away to the sea. "Jump out and wave and shout!" I told Jonathon. "I'll park the car."

I did not think there was much hope, but the dhow turned back for us. The sun was breaking through when we clambered aboard apologising to the captain and the other tourists, and the whole mood of the day changed.

The dhow was a big *jahazi*, like the one that took us to Matondoni, but rigged out for tourists. It was fully decked with rough benches to sit on and a slow-running diesel thumped below. They had kept the mast with its long yard and sail, but only used it for special parties. The other tourists were French, a pleasant group of three or four families. I chatted for a while with the middle-aged mate who was born on Lamu and had sailed in cargo dhows to Pemba and Zanzibar as a boy. He told me that the dhows used to sail up and down the coast in day-long jumps, stopping at Malindi, Kilifi, Mombasa, Shimoni and Tanga on the way to Zanzibar. So, if the weather was average, it took about a week from Lamu to Zanzibar. It was exactly as I had imagined it would have been.

Wasini Island was long and thin and the channel provided fine shelter in both monsoons, so I was not surprised that there was an old Arab settlement with medieval mosque on it. Coral cliffs, undercut by the waves, bounded it and there were no bathing beaches. As we cleared the entrance, long lazy ocean swells burst on a reef in the middle of the channel and I could imagine the diffidence of a navigator approaching without foreknowledge.

An archipelago of reefs and low coral islands spread seaward and we cruised amongst them. As the monsoon clouds blew away northwards and the sun blazed steadily, the sea changed from ominous green-grey to brilliant translucent blue and aquamarine as we moved over shallow patches. Dug-out canoes were out with their pilots fishing with handlines, waving as we passed. We dropped anchor at the furthest little island, Mpungutiyajuu, out of sight of the mainland and far enough from Wasini that it was a low line on the horizon. Away to the west, a misty lump showed where the foothills of the Usambara Mountains lay inside Tanzania. Alongside the Usambara range runs the valley of the Pangani River which rises at Kilimanjaro and which Diogenes the Greek trader may have travelled to become the first European to see snows on the Equator.

Most of our group plunged in using snorkels and ill-assorted flippers borrowed from a box hauled out from a locker. I stayed on board to savour the sudden quiet on our jahazi, afloat on the broad ocean, sheltering behind a circle of coral rock fifty yards across crowned by an incongruous burst of green where seabirds had sown the seeds of vegetation.

Southwards the character of the East African coast changed. The endlessly long straight white beaches, rimmed by an equally straight reef and breached by the few rivers that we had seen, suddenly changes to an indented coast with many offshore islands and a mass of irregular reefs. From where we bobbed at anchor, the immediate hinterland of an ancient shoreline had sunk and the flooding created a tropical marine wonderland. From Wasini the islands and reefs run offshore all the way past Moçambique Island down almost to the Zambezi River.

If it were not for the silt from the Zambezi which kills coral, the

reefs would proceed unbroken past Sofala as far as Durban in South Africa - the greatest tropical barrier reef that the world could ever see.

What an incredible paradise for *Homo aquaticus* !

*

William - the 'garden boy'.

218

CHAPTER NINETEEN : ZANZIBAR !

What an evocative word : Zanzibar. It has a fine ring to it. ZANZIBAR! It means the land of the Zenj, the Black People of Africa.

I was quite nervous about our expedition to Zanzibar because the United Republic of Tanzania was always difficult for tourists and was then in a state of mild ideological flux because Julius Nyerere had nominally retired from politics. He had been in undisputed power since independence and was the architect of the disastrous economic policy of 'African Socialism'. All socialist authoritarian regimes can be a problem to Western visitors and I knew from past experience that two decades of anti-Western propaganda with some anti-White racist undertones had created some effect on the normal kindness and easy friendliness of African people. One of the few places in Black Africa where I have been refused service in a hotel because of my skin colour had been in Dar-es-Salaam two years previously. I warned Jonathon to be patient and keep his cool.

I would have preferred to drive down the coast to Bagamoyo, twenty miles across the strait from Zanzibar Island, and famous as the land base from where Livingstone and Stanley, Speke and Grant, had set off on their epic explorations of 'Darkest Africa'. Bagamoyo was the port serving the Omani Sultanate of Zanzibar during the 18th and 19th centuries and from where the Arab and Swahili slave and ivory traders set off for their inland depots at Nkhota Nkhota on Lake Malawi and Ujiji ("Dr Livingstone, I presume?") on Lake Tanganyika. Bagamoyo means 'Lay Down your Hearts' because it was there that all hope was lost by the hundreds of thousands of slaves herded down to the Indian Ocean. Two years previously I had camped at Bagamoyo, by the sea, and had visited the White Fathers' mission where Livingstone's body had lain in the old chapel before being sent across to Zanzibar and shipped home to Westminster Abbey. From Bagamoyo we might have enjoyed a leisurely and romantic journey by jahazi across to Zanzibar, but it took up to two months to get a permit to take a private car into Tanzania from Kenya, and the chance of finding it intact on our return was remote. So we flew direct from Mombasa in a well-used Fokker Friendship of Kenya Airways.

Leaving the car and our gear with the friendly askari in the grounds of the Manor Hotel in whose safe my spare currency and travellers cheques rested securely, we were driven to Mombasa's Port Reitz Airport by a large taxi driver who told us how much we would enjoy Zanzibar. "Of course it is quiet there and people are very poor, but for Europeans there is much to see."

The airport was built for jumbo loads of packaged tourists and its vast echoing concrete and glass cavern shimmered in the noonday heat. After passing through the relaxed Kenya controls we drank a warm Coke and ate samousas in the near-empty concourse. There were no planes in sight until our Friendship whined in from Nairobi.

The plane was not full and I was able to shift from side to side during the flight to watch the coast and the offshore islands and reefs as we progressed. The Friendship flew at 17,000 feet, low enough to pick up details of the landscape. I identified Tiwi Beach and the Tradewinds Hotel with its blue swimming pool, and I followed the road up to Kwale and the Shimba Hills. The change in the coastline at Wasini Island was marked. The straight and featureless perfection of beach and parallel coral reef abruptly came to an end, the mainland swung away to the west in a series of curving gulfs and the brilliant emerald and aquamarine of the reefs filled the sea below us, studded here and there by the dark green of small islands. As my maps and naval charts told me, islands and reefs proliferate from there far south into Mocambique for a thousand miles. This unspoiled tropical wonderland is not as extensive as Australia's Great Barrier Reef, but the principal differences are human. The eastern African barrier reef and its many islands are steeped in two thousand years of the history of seatraders and fishermen. Ancient man evolved on its ancient shores. Movement of Early Iron-age Black people, influenced and stimulated by ocean migrants, had occurred along it. It was also unsullied by modern tourism.

The ironies were there. I was frustrated by the problems of travelling in Tanzania, (I would have loved to visit Kilwa, for instance), but I had to be glad of them because they kept my fellows out. In the future I feared that the economic realities of Africa must inevitably change it all unless extraordinary strength and foresight was brought to bear. There was still an opportunity to keep this great unspoiled tropical coast and islands free of the tasteless development that has damaged the Kenya coast probably beyond redemption. The examples of the Mediterranean were surely powerful enough to show how easy it is to shatter natural beauty. As the degradation of the Mediterranean is completed, the suddenly wealthy masses of Europe in the latter 20th century are moving in on Africa and the developers are there in advance. Kenya has proven the absolute truth of this. Elsewhere on the same continent, the rash of high-rise hotels, holiday apartments and villas that spread along the South African coastline, catering for only a few million people, is another terrible indictment of the lack of conscience of the affluent society of Western Civilisation. No doubt there are people in power in socialist Tanzania and Mocambique who intend to maintain purity and have an idea of allowing only simple, appropriate development in harmony with nature. But can they and their successors resist the pressures that the future must bring?

After passing the great gulf in the coast south west of Wasini, Pemba, the first of the three large islands off Tanzania, came in sight. From our height it looked magical: a hazy green expanse of land rested on the blue velvet of the great ocean. Deep bays edged with thin strips of white beach were rimmed by the aquamarine of coral reefs. Occasional white dots showed where dhows were sailing. On the island itself I could pick out one red streak of a dirt road and a small grey smudge of the main town, Chake Chake. Forty miles on was Zanzibar.

When the Portuguese were in East Africa, the Sultans of Zanzibar and Pemba were their allies and the Portuguese were often at war with the mutual enemy, Mombasa, on their behalf. After the great siege of Fort Jesus and the Omani conquest the local battles and skirmishes did not cease. Mombasa was always a maverick and the Masrui family who became the established rulers there broke away from the control of the Sultan of Oman. In Oman, there were dynastic problems and the Lamu Archipelago also broke away to become the fief of the Habhanis. Zanzibar remained loyal and there was intermittent warfare between these three. The Sultan of Oman sent forces to Zanzibar to keep this foothold secure in 1746 but bloodshed and insecurity, greater than in the two centuries of Portuguese hegemony, continued into the 19th century.

In 1806, Sayyid Said succeeded to the Sultanate in Oman and took an interest in his nominal African Empire. Unable to persuade the Masrui and Haha families to recognise his suzerainty, he sailed with a mercenary Baluchi army in 1828. Mombasa was taken and retaken in a series of seiges of Fort Jesus until peace was achieved by exiling the mischievous leaders of the Masrui family to Bandar Abbas in the Persian Gulf. Sultan Sayyid Said became fond of the fertile island of Zanzibar where he was always welcome and which was such a contrast to the dry rocks and desert hinterland of Muscat. He saw how greater was the potential of East Africa compared to Arabia and he shifted his capital to Zanzibar in 1832. It was this far-seeing colonial ruler who re-established the wealth of the Arab-dominated Swahili states of East Africa and saw the importance of trade with the interior.

He encouraged the exploitation of old routes to Lake Malawi and the Zambesi River to the south, and in the west to Lake Tanganyika and beyond to the Lualaba River, the headwaters of the great Congo. Zanzibar town became the fairest city in East Africa, finer than all of the medieval towns, with the possible exception of Kilwa which had sunk into obscurity in the 16th century. Later, Zanzibar and Oman were ruled separately and there were two Sultans, but they were of the same dynastic family. To-day, Sultan Qaboos Bin Said rules Oman and the last Sultan of Zanzibar was sent into exile by President Julius Nyerere after the incorporation of Zanzibar by Tanganyika to form Tanzania.

A history of Zanzibar and East Africa may have gone on to tell of the growth of a great Islamic-Arab dominated imperial state in East Africa, a rival to the Ottoman Empire which controlled Turkey, Syria, Palestine and Egypt. In the late 19th century, Hamed bin Mohammed el Marjebi (famous in Europe as Tippu Tib), a subject of the Sultan of Zanzibar, established a private empire as large as many European countries in Zaïre with his capital at Kisangani on the Congo. For some years he was even appointed by the Congo Free State of Leopold II of Belgium, to rule his own lands as the official Belgian representative and became enmeshed in European colonial wranglings for control of the upper Nile and Congo regions and the Great Lakes. He was a slaver and ivory trader but also an efficient coloniser creating order and prosperity under an undeniably ruthless regime. As a result, KiSwahili remains the lingua franca throughout much of eastern Zaïre. Christian Ethiopia could have been an island in a sea of Islam over the whole of North and East Africa until it surged down to the British colonies of South Africa. It is an interesting scenario.

However the Arab tradition of slavery brought it all to an end. The moral revolution in Europe, led to a large extent by Britain, was stimulated by the deeds and writings of men like Livingstone who became popular heroes. The material and martial powers that Europe had obtained from the Industrial Revolution provided the means to carry out a moral crusade to Africa. Livingstone and others promoted the concept of economic development of Africa as a goad to public opinion and an incentive for governments to act. But European society was sophisticated and complex in contrast to the simple and direct colonial objectives of the Ottoman and Arab princes. Europe had a whole spectrum of motives, from outright greed through enlightened self-interest, through liberal moralising to crusading fervour. Livingstone, Burton, Stanley and other travellers provided the tantalising aromas that excited appetites for African Empire in all the Western capitals including the United States. American commercial and diplomatic activity was considerable in East Africa. Men such as the indefatigable British consul in Zanzibar, Sir John Kirk, and the influential colonial official, Sir Bartle Frere, undermined the authority of the Sultan of Zanzibar until Britain finally took over all his lands as a protectorate, and therefore gained almost exactly the area of influence that the Portuguese wielded two centuries before. From these island and coastal bases Britain eventually established the colonies of Kenya and Uganda.

The British story was repeated in Germany, France, Belgium and Portugal. The formal division of Africa into zones of European influence and exploitation was decided at the now infamous Treaty of Berlin in 1885. Germany obtained Tanganyika and Portugal's centuries old claim to Moçambique was consolidated. The Belgian state took over Leopold's private Congo empire. Men like Tippu Tib faded away. Britain's authority over Kenya, Uganda and the interior of Central Africa was established. And it all started with Livingstone's implacable opposition to the slave-trade in eastern and central Africa.

Our plane swept in over the northern end of Zanzibar and I was astonished to note that it was devoid of trees. I had assumed that the whole island was a verdant mass of spice, fruit and coconut plantations. What I had still to discover was that firstly with the abolition of slavery in the late 19th century and then the socialist revolution of January 1964, the plantation economy had faltered and finally died. Travellers who visited Zanzibar in the 1940s and 50s always spoke of the powerful scent of cloves that greeted them as their ships approached. Much of the island to-day is covered by poor grassland with scattered secondary bush, decayed plantations of aged trees and small shambas.

223

Eighteen hundred years ago the *Periplus* described Zanzibar:

... after two courses of a night and day along the Ausineitic Coast, the island of Menouthias is encountered, about 3000 stades [30miles] from the mainland, low and covered with trees, in which are rivers and many kinds of bird, and mountain tortoises. Of wild beasts there are none except crocodiles; but they hurt no man. There are in it small boats sewn and made from one piece of wood, which are used for fishing and catching marine tortoises. In this island they catch them [fish] with a local form of basket trap instead of nets stretched across the mouth of openings along the foreshore.

Men still use dug-out canoes and catch fish with traps along this coast, but the indigenous trees have mostly gone and the crocodiles which hurt no man are absent.

The airport building was small and the thirty or so passengers from our plane created milling chaos. Jonathon and I were the only foreign tourists and a bright young man took charge of us, found forms to be filled in and piloted us past the lackadaisical officials. He told me that he worked for the Government tourist bureau and when I asked him about hotels and excursions to historic places he handed me over to another slim and handsome man with marked Arabic features, whom I assumed was a colleague, and we were rushed out of the building with our bags to a battered old Peugeot 404 station-waggon. There, we stopped to catch our breaths.

"My name is Abdul," the neat and handsome man introduced himself. He had a clipped moustache and large liquid eyes that were smiling reassuringly. He spoke with an educated British accent. "I'm sorry to hurry you, but we are a private tour company and I wished to take you quickly away from there." Aha, the official was a friend doing him a favour, or maybe there was a 'kick-back'. "If you agree, we can take care of you completely: hotel, tours, whatever you need. How long are you here on Zanzibar?" I liked him instantly and agreed.

The only tourists to arrive on that flight, one of only two a week, we had particular attention from the struggling private tour company and our visit was made memorable by Abdul. He was professional and proud and I felt that he was constantly on the verge of apologising for the shocking roads, the poverty of the peasants, his sad old vehicle and the extraordinary hotel where we eventually stayed. As our visit progressed, he relaxed and smiled, even told a few jokes, but he was correct and formal at the beginning.

224

We drove fast into town through twisting narrow alleys between old two and three story Arab houses that reminded me immediately of Lamu. But Lamu had been a provincial town and Zanzibar the capital of the Omani empire. Zanzibar's old town was extensive and carried the patina of wealth in excess of anything Lamu or Mombasa had experienced.

There were no advertising signs and we found no shops open. "Is it a holiday?" Jonathon asked peering at the empty streets. I shook my head. I knew it was the heavy blight of socialism that we were observing, and I hated the drear atmosphere. The immediate comparison with the extravagant bustle of Mombasa gave Zanzibar the ambience of an old tomb. We stopped in a cul-de-sac where there was an official tourist guesthouse. It was a fine example of a 19th century merchant's home, but there were no rooms free. I caught a glimpse of a polished wooden stairway and the blink of brass ornaments in the light of a wrought iron lamp. "It's a pity about that," said Abdul. "You would enjoy it and the food is excellent and traditional. There are only a few rooms and it is usually full." He sighed. "We will go to the Bwawani Hotel.

"Will they have room?" I asked anxiously. The sun was lowering.

He looked over his shoulder, smiling faintly. "Oh yes. You will see."

The driver, a bright impish youth with a pale skin like a Chinese, flashed a grin at me as he heaved the old car through the alleys and back onto a modern street. "It is there," he said pointing ahead along a narrow causeway. We drew up with a screech of worn brakes beside a long squalid concrete building with black streaks of mould on its facade. It was splendidly isolated on a spit of land between the sea and a swamp of waving reeds separating the spit from the mainland. I looked at the swamp and thought of insects.

The Bwawani Hotel is reputed to have been designed by the first Governor of Zanzibar after the revolution, presumably after a visit to Moscow because it would have suited a Siberian industrial city. It had some interesting features. It was designed for a cold climate with large fixed windows and no air-conditioning. No kitchen had been provided so a catering block was added later. A dull concrete monster cowered in the grounds incorporating a cracked and empty swimming pool and tasteless lounging area littered with rubbish and broken furniture. A monumental statue brooded gloomily over the unkempt lawns and forgotten flower beds. Inside, the lobby smelled of damp and decay and the unsuitably thick carpet was scuffed and stained by water. Torn wallpaper drooped from mouldy walls. But there were smiles from the uniformed receptionist and five porters and clerks who greeted us with efficient courtesy.

"Welcome to our country," the receptionist said. "Do you want a suite or two separate rooms?"

"One room will do. Can we stay until the 28th?"

He gave me a half-smile. "You can stay all year if you wish."

"I don't believe all this," said Jonathon when we were alone, striding around the suite and checking the balcony overlooking the waving reeds of the swamp and the shanty town beyond. "I've never stayed in a hotel like this before."

"It's in a terrible state."

"I can see that," he agreed. "But we're in Africa...." I smiled at that as he went into the bathroom exclaiming at the size of it and testing the water. "No hot but plenty of cold. How much is it costing if you don't mind me asking? Can you afford it?"

"Twenty-five dollars a day, bed and breakfast, for the two of us."

He gestured. "Christ! I don't believe it."

We went up to the penthouse leisure complex after a simple but elaborately served dinner in an echoing barn of a dining room. A visiting Indian family was playing ping-pong in the bare games room and the children's shrieks bounced off the concrete walls. In the next-door bar three waiters and the barman were watching an especially crudely violent American video on an old TV with the colour flickering on and off. Vicious close combat with sprays of blood and endless screaming and gunfire had the men entranced.

I ordered a local rum liqueur that Abdul had recommended.

"I'm sorry, Sir. But that is not available here in the hotel bar. They have it in the public bar by the restaurant. We have Scotch whisky, Russian vodka, Bacardi, Martini?"

"Have you cold beer?" asked Jonathon.

"We have Heineken beer from Holland," he said, pulling one out of the rattling refrigerator. "But there is no beer at the other bar."

"How does this work?" asked Jonathon after taking a grateful gulp of his beer. "I thought the country was bust."

I explained. "We are paying our account in dollars. Locals aren't allowed in here where there are imported goods. We have to pay for all tourist services in foreign currency, including Abdul's tours. That's why Tanzania doesn't like foreigners drifting around using local facilities and inevitably changing money on the black market. Overland travellers are usually a particularly hard time at the borders."

"Of course! It's just like that hotel in Moscow."

The next morning we woke to rain, but it cleared and the sun came out while we ate a respectable English breakfast. Abdul's Peugeot station-waggon was waiting for us, its battered and faded paintwork freshly washed and the interior well brushed and dusted. Abdul and the cheeky young driver greeted us warmly. We were to sightsee in the town.

Our first stop was the municipal market, built by the British in the 1920s. As always, the delights of an African market excited me: the colour, the bustle of purposeful people, the cheerful calls and grinning faces, the bounty of the world on display. Jonathon was entranced by tropical produce such as paw-paws, coconuts, lychees, avocados, jackfruits, yams, plantains, limes and mountains of giant pineapples. I was glad to see some of the traditional spices and piles of tamarind seed-pods like giant runner beans. It was an excellent market with plenty of traditional vegetables like tomatoes, onions, garlic, cabbages, carrots and pumpkins on sale. Goat and sheep carcasses were strung up in the butchery section and chunks were carved off at the customer's instruction. The fishmarket smelled cleanly of the sea and we saw marlin, grouper, tunny, stingrays, sharks, squid, octopus, kingfish, snappers and piles of various shellfish. What bounty! We were told that fresh-produce market-traders were allowed to operate in the private enterprise sector. "Otherwise we might all be starving...."

The Anglican Cathedral, an impressive Victorian church that would grace any English provincial town, reposed in a quiet compound. I was assured that Christianity was tolerated after the revolution and a mission school and clinic had been allowed to keep running. The church itself was in good order and I was reminded of St. Mary's in Madras. There were polished brass plaques on the walls and memorial stained glass in the windows. Before the altar there was a marked area on the floor.

"Here was the centre of the slave-market," Abdul spoke quietly at my shoulder. "After the British stopped slave-trading, the church was built." He pointed to the floor. "On that place was the whipping-tree. Slaves were whipped to test their strength and quietness in front of all the buyers...."

A simple wooden cross was fixed to the wall near the altar. It had been made from a portion of the *mpundu* tree under which

Livingstone's heart and liver had been buried by his faithful retainers where he died in 1873, at Chitambo's place south of Lake Bangweulu in Zambia. They embalmed the remains and carried them with his papers to Bagamoyo, to his own people, fifteen hundred miles in eight months. The Africans abhorred the idea of carrying the corpse because the spirit could not be released until proper ceremony was carried out and it would travel with them. The burial of the heart and liver at Chitambo's was a way of propitiation. The staunchness of the friendship of those men is always an emotional story to me.

I read the several plaques on the walls. One was a memorial to Staff-Commander the Hon Richard Orlando Beaconsfield Bridgeman DSO, RN who was killed in a seaplane over the Rufiji Delta in World War I. Jonathon was behind me: "Marvellous! What was he doing here in those days, I wonder?"

"Searching for a German heavy cruiser that bombarded Zanzibar and ravaged the Indian Ocean. Did you know that British forces under the command of the South African, General Smuts, were chasing von Lettouw Vorbeck's German army in East Africa and it was still going on in November 1918?"

Jonathon shook his head. "They didn't teach us that kind of history at school."

Nearby, in the centre of a small park was the white-washed museum which looked like a small circular mosque. It was being redecorated but the friendly curator, who reminded me of my friend at the museum in Lamu, let us in. The exhibits still carried the faded typewritten notices and descriptions from the colonial regime of more than twenty year ago. There were many priceless manuscripts and mementoes of the days of the great explorers. Porcelain, coins, weapons, and fine craftware from the Arab coastal colonies lay in glass cases. There were earlier items dug up in medieval sites and I was told that there were many chests of historical treasure in storage. Coins minted at Kilwa with gold from Great Zimbabwe before the 15th century fascinated me. There were Indian coins, Persian and Chinese ceramics, old glass beads.

We walked through the old town to the waterfront. It was called the 'Stone Town', because only the Arab and Swahili elite were permitted to build in stone. It was a warren of tall shuttered buildings and twisting alleyways just wide enough for people and donkeys. Some of the houses still had the magnificent carved doorways for which Zanzibar had been famous. I reflected yet again that Zanzibar had been a city of great wealth a hundred years before. The dullness and emptiness of it as we wandered along saddened me and I tried to picture those alleys and townhouses as travellers had described them from Livingstone's day onwards. A few people who were lounging about were talking quietly and lapsed into silence as we passed. I felt uncomfortable as unsmiling eyes followed us. Where was laughter and purpose? I would almost have welcomed the beggars and persistent hawkers of Bombay and Madurai.

On the waterfront we emerged beside the old British Consulate, made famous in many explorers' journals. It was a dilapidated building, a depot for the state trading cooperative, but still there.

A plaque was stuck on the wall: *This building was the British Consulate from 1841-1874 where at different times lived Speke, Burton, Grant and Kirk. David Livingstone stayed here and in this house his body rested on its long journey home.*

I stood for a while looking at the ugly old building, a warehouse really, where the ground floors had been used to store goods for British traders and the upper floors were the residency. Overlooking the harbour there was still a trellised verandah, and there those men would have sat in cane chairs, taking their ease and discussing their plans. I noticed that Stanley's name was not included on the plaque. He had a furious row with Kirk, the consul, accusing him of neglecting Livingstone, causing him hardship and even premature death. Stanley was *persona non grata* at the consulate. I imagined the stiff Victorian figures in their white cotton duck clothes, mosquito boots and solar topees passing through the door before me, going in to talk so seriously of trivial matters while they took tea or gin and quinine, and puffed on their pipes or cheroots.

In 1985 I had travelled in Central Africa and my arrival at the southern shore of Lake Victoria was a particularly powerful experience. I wrote in *The Reflected Face of Africa:*

> Historically, here was where John Hanning Speke on 3rd August 1858 first set eyes on the great Nyanza, the inland sea, that Arab traders had told him about and which he decided, intuitively, was the source of the Nile .... We parked a few yards from the gently breaking waves and I watched the sun set in a red-gold ball across the waters. We pitched our tents in the afterglow as the hills turned to sharp black silhouettes and the nearly full moon rose as we ate our dinner. As I drifted off to sleep, my imagination heard the little waves washing in a sibilant chorus: 'Speke Gulf, Speke Gulf, Speke

229

Gulf...' What exulting thoughts did Speke think as he slept for the first time on that same shore 128 years before?

Further along lay the great dark bulk of the Omani fortress, built by Sultan Sayyid Said, dominating the Zanzibar waterfront. It was as large as Fort Jesus, maybe larger, the high walls enclosing a vast quadrangle with circular towers dominating the corners. We climbed one of them and surveyed the harbour, looking across the pale blue of the sea towards the coast of Africa just over the horizon. The triangular sails of *jahazis* moved beyond an offshore islet. I had seen similar sails on Lake Victoria two years before.

Abdul told us that the fort had been built on the site of the original Portuguese church of the early 16th century, and that stone from the church was incorporated in the walls. So there was some continuity of half a millennium there. I asked him if there was any clue about the original town of the Shirazis who had settled five hundred year before the Portuguese and with whom they had been allies. He did not know but it had to have been thereabouts.

Next to the Omani fort was the simply elegant three-storied construction of the modern Sultan's palace, built by British colonial engineers in imperial Indian style. White-painted, it stood tall with an impressive facade and a clock-tower in the centre. The three floors were surrounded by wide verandahs supported by closely spaced slim columns. I thought that the palace admirably dominated the waterfront. It achieved a fine balance, light and airy, yet peacefully confident next to the brooding mass of the old coral stone fortress.

Standing there I felt I was at one of the historical vortexes of the Indian Ocean. Livingstone walked where I was walking, and Sayyid Said, and before them there were d'Almeida and Cabral, and before them Ibn Batuta, and before him. .... I looked at the coarse grass around my dusty flipflops.

They had walked *HERE*.

CHAPTER TWENTY: SPICES AND SLAVES

On that great open space of rough grass with the outlines of old formal flowerbeds and scattered with a few trees before the red stone fort and the airy white Sultan's palace, Jonathon and I had fruit drinks at a refreshment kiosk while my imagination kept running free. Further along from the Palace there was an ornate building in reasonable repair that had been lifted from India. Abdul explained that it had been built by Hindus. The sense of the unity of the Indian Ocean was strong and the vortex of trade and communication over many centuries that I was pursuing, filled me. On that waterfront, viewing those three particular monumental buildings, it was all so clear and obvious: Arab, Indian and European symbols standing on an African island surrounded by the Indian Ocean.

From the majestic waterfront Abdul took us into the port. He knew the customs officials who waved him through with a laugh and a joking remark. Time had stood still and I was filled with excitement. The trappings of British administration were there: the custom house, old trees giving shade, the uniformed guards, a weigh-bridge for trucks at the barrier, a public toilet, solid warehouses with corrugated iron roofs, massive stone copings on the quay walls, a sailing ship anchor encrusted with tar and set in concrete. In the port and beached on the mudbank beyond were about thirty dhows!

"My God, Jonathon! Look at this," I called and he grinned as I rushed forward cranking the film wind on my camera.

Men were loading and off-loading the *jahazis* by hand, carrying sacks of produce on their backs, and sailors were lounging in the shade. Abdul and the young driver settled to a languid chat with some acquaintances. I wandered about and Jonathon sat on a bollard. The midday sun beat down and fair weather cumulus clouds drifted across the sky on the monsoon. I could smell the pungency of copra and the thin sweet aroma of spices. The calls of the working men were easy and sing-song. Here survived spare remnants of the machinery of the Indian Ocean trade, in greater abundance than I had seen on all my travels in eastern Africa over twenty years. It was a shadow of the greatness of years past when *boums* from Oman sailed in and *thonis* from the Malabar Coast arrived with fine cottons of India and silks from China.

I felt a psychic thread joining me to Cochin and Goa; I sensed the memory circuits in my brain meshing as I recalled the sights, sounds and thoughts I experienced on my journey in India only some short months ago. I had a sudden mental picture that I had not visualised for a long time: a gaunt yellow cliff standing above a wind-thrashed sea under a hazy blue-white sky, Cape Gardefui or Ras Asir, the north-east point of Africa, the gateway to the Red Sea. I had stood on the deck of a Messageries Maritime liner, SS *La Bourdonais*, in 1965 to watch our passage.

I reflected on the connection between the quays on which I walked, through the jahazis in front of me, to Bagamoyo where I had camped by the beach, along the endless safari trails of Africa into the far interiors. The Portuguese had found Arabs, Swahilis and Indians far up the Zambezi at Tete in the 16th century. Livingstone had met Swahili traders on the borders of Zambia and Angola in the 1850s. I have read a restaurant menu in Swahili in a town in northern Zaïre, on the banks of the Epulu River in the Ituri Forest. I was suddenly so excited there in the port of Zanzibar!

Wandering slowly through more of the old Stone Town I was stopped by an old Arab with pale face and wispy white hair. He was not a beggar and was squatting comfortably in the shade, dressed in his long gown of fine cloth with an ivory topped walking-stick in his hand. A handsomely embroidered cap sat on his head. Despite his lack of teeth, he spoke very well and his old eyes were sharp.

"Are you English or American, Sir?" he asked.

"English."

He nodded, looking me over. "I used to meet very many English ladies and gentlemen. I was official tour guide before, when the Sultan was still our ruler. I would take the people from the liners and mailships who came ashore on launches. British-India Line, Union-Castle Line, Holland-Africa Line. I knew all the ships in those days. Of course they have not come for many years now."

While he reminisced, partly to himself, I remembered that my parents had come ashore on Zanzibar from the *Bloemfontein Castle* in 1952 when travelling between London and Durban. It would be a strange quirk of fate if this old man had been their guide. I like to believe that it was exactly so.

"You look so well, but you must be an old man?" I asked him.

He cackled delightedly. "Ho yes! I am very old. I remember the German battleship sending bombs onto Zanzibar." He nodded, eyes twinkling, mouth chewing on empty gums. "That was in the Great War. I remember the Prince of Wales when he came; the one who became King Edward after King George."

I asked if I could photograph him and he cackled again. "Yes, you can do that, but you remember how we professional guides always used to be. ...?" His wizened hand came out and I poured loose change into it.

Before returning to the hotel, Abdul took us to see the house where Livingstone had lived for some time readying himself for his final great expedition in 1866. It was a simple, square house standing alone off the coastal road to the north. It was well looked after because it was the offices of the Tanzanian state tourist organisation, which seemed appropriate enough. In front of the house lay Funguni Creek where the tide was far out so that there were a few *jahazis* and several *mashuas* either lying on their beam-ends or propped up by mangrove poles with men at work careening them.

"This is the traditional place of dhow building," Abdul told me. I stood in front of Livingstone's house looking out, and that thread of time and distance, linked through the traditional seagoing ships of this ocean, was bright and strong again. I felt the particular link from there to my son's visit to Sur in the Oman and our journey to Matondoni on Lamu Island.

In the evening at the hotel there were a group of about ten British tourists who were on a package to the Serengeti and Ngorongoro Crater Game Parks and had flown in from Arusha to see Zanzibar. At the lower bar the women in the party were served 'Bloody Marys' and Cinzano and lemonades and there was joking amongst them because the safari lodges on the mainland had not had stocks. "Now for a nice cold beer," one of the men said and Jonathon nudged me. There was quite a row when they discovered that beer was only served in the penthouse bar.

A young American with a rather beautiful full red-brown beard was at dinner and I got into conversation with him later. He had been on Pemba Island for a few days and had to spend a week or more because the plane had broken down.

"I ran out of local currency and there was no way to change dollars," he told me. He was a graduate student in Bantu languages from UCLA and was doing a thesis on Swahili. I listened with interest especially when he told me that he had been in South Africa for four years, but when I asked him about similarities between Swahili and the Nguni language group he changed the subject.

"Typical bullshitter," Jonathon explained to me. "I bet he's never been to South Africa."

The next day we were taken on a tour of the interior. We drove through the shantytown that sprawled to the westward. "What do all the people who live here do?" I asked Abdul. "Of course they all work in offices in the city," he replied in a neutral voice without turning round to look at me, but I noticed the glance that the driver gave him. I wondered what they really did, then reminded myself that Zanzibar was no different to any other modern African city with 70% of the population living in shanty townships and scratching a living somehow.

We were to call at a number of small shambas along the dreadfully potholed road up the centre of the island to see examples of various spice and fruit trees. Our car travelled almost at walking pace, clattering and lurching, the driver constantly working the gear lever. The shambas were similar to those along the Kenya coast, but simpler and poorer. Sheltered by trees, there was typically a small two roomed mud house with macuti thatch roof, a screened toilet space behind and a small enclosure where the chickens were put at night. Some had a goat or two, but not many. There must have been cattle on the island, but I don't recall seeing any. Abdul told me that the average size of peasants' shambas on Zanzibar was three acres; not much land on which to raise a family. (The shambas around Gedi had been 7 acres). The people themselves were dour and did not smile or greet us. Many were short in stature and I thought their faces were ugly.

I suddenly realised a simple truth about the peasants of Zanzibar. They were all descendants of slaves brought there from the interior. Their great-great-grandfathers and mothers had come from as far apart as the Zambezi and the Congo, from the savannahs of Malawi to the forests of Burundi. They had no common tribal culture, no common native language, no traditions to hold them together, no old dynasties of chiefs or elders, no history or legend. No past of which to be proud. No individual past either, for I doubted that many had much idea from where their ancestors had come.

In Nigeria I had lived among people some of whom were doubtless descended from slaves. In Brazil the same had occurred, but there, as in the United States or the Caribbean, there was the racial marker to make it clear: anybody with Negro features or hair had to have an ancestor who had been transported from Africa to an alien land. In Egypt and other Arab lands this is also so. But in eastern Africa I had never been really conscious of slavery outside the pages of books until that day on Zanzibar. I had been to places like Nkhota-Khota on Lake Malawi where hundreds of thousands of slaves had been penned before being sent down in 'coffles' to Bagamoyo, but I had not been among a population who were *all* doubtless descended from slaves transported from far lands. It had a sudden and most powerful impact on me.

I became aware of what it meant to be rootless with great clarity that day on Zanzibar. Voluntary refugees retain their roots. Usually, no matter how dire their material circumstances, they remain in clan or communal groups and some elders survive to pass on proud tribal traditions and their own laws, however temporarily degraded, are retained. Descendants of slaves torn from their families and distributed wholesale like mixed seeds strewn on the ground lose these essentials to humanity.

I learned that there were strange rituals of witchcraft on Zanzibar, like the Voodoo of the Caribbean, the Makonde of Bahia in Brazil or the Juju of coastal West Africa. When tribal traditions are lost and the law is imposed by alien slave-owners, then in seeking for something to unite each other in their disaster the lowest common denominator of their racial heritage is used on which to create a culture. Corrupted religion in which fear and vicious ritual dominate may be the only way to form bonds in their degraded group within a foreign society in a distant land. I suddenly felt that I understood these matters better.

I felt something of the tragic mystique of the American Negro. I thought of the truths in the joking reference to the American Negro women on Lamu who had "come to find their roots". I thought that future historians may view the South African Apartheid ideology of 'separate development' of 'tribal homeland states' as a very valuable socio-anthropological system in the post-colonial era of that region, which had repressive political effects for a relatively short period.

When we stopped, I wanted to photograph the road and the typical forest on its verge. A man was walking along it and I waited until he was a good hundred yards away because he had looked nervously at my camera as he passed by. At the faint sound of the shutter he dropped to the ground as if shot and then scrambled embarrassedly away. That troubled me and I could not forget it. Why was he so frightened?

Abdul had regular shambas that he called at on his tour where good examples of the various spice and fruit plants could be seen. We saw common oranges and limes, mangoes and coconuts, manioc and cassava, yams, passionfruit and pineapples, bananas and avocados, cocoa bushes, sugar-cane and oil palms. Some shambas had little patches of 'European' vegetables like tomato, onion and garlic. We also saw pepper, cinnamon, nutmeg, coriander, cloves, cardamom, ginger, lemon grass, turmeric, star fruit and tamarind trees. Most had come from India and the East at some time in the last 2,000 years and I was delighted to see them all in the course of a few hours. None we saw were in plantations, secondary growth and natural wastage over the years had taken their toll since the land holdings of the days of the Sultan's regime had been broken up. Abdul told me that there were state-managed plantations on Pemba Island. I could see where coconut plantations had been because some of the palms were still alive and the headless boles of others stood like a forest of ships' masts. It was something like the abandoned coconut groves of Lamu. But the bushes and small trees of spices and other fruits seemed to have dissolved into an anonymous mass of jungle. Each shamba had a few flourishing trees or plants which the peasant farmer looked after, harvested in season and then sold the produce either in the market or to the government depots.

Abdul took us to the simple copra processing establishment of a middle-aged Arab who bought raw coconut flesh from his neighbours, smoke-dried it on metal grills over fire-pits, constantly tended. When cured, the copra was collected by battered government trucks. It was all typical peasant agriculture. The people were living a rough, bare existence. Efficient plantations with labourers housed in compounds were long gone and the general economy suffered, impoverishing the state as a whole. Would enlightened development occur in the lifetimes of those people, perhaps a happy amalgam of both systems? Who could say and the future seemed dark.

We visited an agricultural experimental station where new varieties of tropical oranges were growing and we were shown short-boled coconut palms which were easy to harvest. We stopped off the road in the shade of a rubber plantation.

"Do you know what these trees are?" Abdul asked.

I grinned. "Rubber, of course. Many years ago I was an expert in rubber in Nigeria." I walked into the plantation which was well tended, the aisles cleared of weeds and encroaching scrub. The trees seemed about ten years old and tapping had been going on for a while, but it was obviously intermittent. Many trees had not been tapped for some time. On others where cups to catch the bleeding white latex sap of the tree were hanging, the latex had not been collected and had dried and solidified into dirty yellow lumps. I pointed this out to Abdul and he made a face. "So maybe our officials are wasting our precious money again. Why don't they collect the rubber?"

I shrugged. "Maybe they haven't set up a processing plant. It's quite complicated: you need filters, special coagulating tanks, rollers, a controlled smoke-curing house. There's quite a lot of know-how needed. Maybe this is just an experiment into growing the trees....."

"What good are trees growing here if they are not used?" he asked with disgust. I shrugged again, guessing that it was bureaucratic ennui at fault. It was the first time that Abdul had shown emotion about the failing socialist regime.

Nearby were the ruins of an elaborate Persian bath-house that a Sultan had built for his bride, the daughter of a Shah of Iran. Inside, there were elaborate decorations in faded gilt and peeling plaster on the mouldy walls and the series of baths and changing rooms gave some idea of how this little pocket of exotic luxury had been. Earlier, we also visited the ruins of the Marahubi Palace, built for the Sultan's harem of concubines. Each girl had her own boudoir with bath and toilet supplied with running water. There had been elaborate gardens running down to the sea and old trees stood around. A large circular cistern showed where the girls were encouraged to bathe naked and parade on a low wall for the Sultan's selection. The young driver giggled and watched my reaction with a sideways look while Abdul explained these delights of royal privilege.

Late in the afternoon we drove along an overgrown track near the north-west coast to visit the Magapwani slave-pits. I was not sure what to expect and was horrified with what we were shown. Amongst the thick scrub and tangled growth where we stopped, there was a grey stone roof at ground level covering a rectangular chamber about forty feet long by twelve wide. The roof was in two parts with an entrance to the chamber in the centre. We peered into this black hole about ten feet deep which had coral stone walls but no steps down into it. "The slaves were put in there for some time to wait for the dhows to take them to Mombasa and Malindi or Egypt and Arabia,"

Abdul explained. "Sometimes, the dhow was not ready, that is why they waited here. There were other places like this."

"Why here?" I asked. We were about twelve miles from Zanzibar town. "Why did the dhows not take them from the port?"

"It was the custom in those days."

I was puzzled until an explanation came to me while studying the awful chamber. In size it was more-or-less that of the hold of an ocean-going *boum*. While waiting for a dhow to come, the slaves would be safe in the pit, but it would also have been a good taming period. They would get used to the cramped and fouled confinement in a safe and isolated place before being put aboard. Those who could not stand the pit or died could be replaced. I was reminded of the pens in which captured wild animals are kept before being shipped off to zoos in crates by aeroplane. That is exactly what the pit at Magapwani was: a taming pen.

The blue of the sea flickered through the scrub and Abdul led us along a path for about thirty yards to where we could scramble down a narrow defile to a small secluded beach, protected by the arms of steep coral cliffs. The sun was lowering and it was a beautiful little beach.

"This is where the dhows came to load the slaves," Abdul said. And because of the safe landing, the pit had been located close by.

After a ten minute drive from the pit and its tiny harbour, we stopped by the sea again next to a taxi and an old pick-up truck. Music, calls and laughter of men and women came up from a wide white-sand beach fringed with coconuts. Three confident young French tourists were swimming and there was a party of local Swahili girls and a tall thin Black man. A cassette player was playing rock music. The French men were teasing the girls who giggled and splashed them. It was clear from the lack of tracks through the overgrown road that we had been the only tourists to visit the slave-pit for some weeks so I asked Abdul about the beach.

"This is a well-known beach for swimming. The British used to come here at the week-ends before independence." He pointed to a fine colonial style villa with wide verandahs that stood on a rise about a half mile away in a grove of trees. "That now belongs to our army where the officers have a resthouse."

I sat quietly enjoying the scene which was out of any tourist advertisement. Jonathon chatted to our young driver and Abdul joined the Frenchmen's taxi man. The sun slowly sank into the sea turning sky and water yellow and orange and finally red. Almost as if at some remote film director's command, a mashua with sail set came out from behind a nearby headland and sailed directly into the sunset.

Flying back from Zanzibar to Mombasa, we could not see the coast. The monsoon brought thick clouds that day and our Fokker Friendship seemed to be bouncing along over the top of them. I realised that the invisibility of the coast was a kind of symbol in its way. I had finished my exploration of the East African coastal sites of the Indian Ocean trading system for that year.

Kilwa was the only major medieval town that I still wanted to visit but it was difficult to get at without hiring a private plane which was beyond my resources. I wanted to go there because Kilwa was the Sultanate that controlled the gold trade with Zimbabwe through the entrepot of Sofala in medieval centuries. The *Africa Pilot* (1980) has this description:

> Kilwa Kisiwani, a village which in 1959 consisted only of grass-roofed huts, is situated on the NW extremity of Kilwa Kisiwani island. A baobab tree, about 14m high and painted black and white, stands in an open space one mile E of the village....... Between Kilwa Kisiwani village and Ras Ruvura are the extensive ruins of the ancient settlement of Quiloa. The most noticeable of these is an old Arab castle, consisting of a high keep-like tower, which stands on the shore at the NW extremity of the island [8°55'S, 9°30'E]. Castle Islet, which is thickly covered with mangroves, is situated at the extremity of the coastal reef 2½ cables NW of the castle. In the morning, both the castle and Castle Islet are good marks and may be seen at about 10 miles.

The 'high keep-like tower' is not that ancient. It was built by the Omani Sultans of Zanzibar in the last century. The remaining medieval ruins of the days of the great southern African gold trade consist most notably of the Great Mosque and an octagonal bathing pool of the palace of Husuni Kubwa.

Ibn Batuta (14th century) wrote:

.... and then pursued our journey to Kulwa, which is a large town on the coast. The majority of the inhabitants are Zanj [Negro], jet-black in colour, and with tattoo-marks on their faces. I was told by a merchant that the town of Sufala lies a fortnight's journey from Kulwa, and that gold dust is brought to Sufala from Yufi in the country of the Limis, which is a month's journey distant from it. Kulwa is a very fine and substantially built town, and all its buildings are of wood. Its inhabitants are constantly engaged in military expeditions, for their country is contiguous to the heathen Zanj. The Sultan at the time of my visit was Abu'l-Muzaffer Hasan, who was noted for his gifts and generosity.....

I had to be content with those descriptions and my imagination.

*

NOTE In October 2000 I eventually reached Kilwa with two old friends and safari companions, travelling in a Toyota Landruiser pick-up and lodging in a guesthouse in Kilwa Masoko. We visited all the ruins and modern towns of the district including an extensive examination of Kilwa Kisiwani island. I was well briefed by Neville Chittick's exhaustive descriptions in two volumes, *Kilwa*, published by the British Institute in Eastern Africa in 1974. As I have done in so many places, I was pacing the paths that Ibn Batuta had trod more than six centuries before. (The story is in my book, *Mud, Seas & Sands*.)

Jahazi dhows in Zanzibar old harbour, 1987. Still in general use at that time.

240

CHAPTER TWENTY ONE : "WHERE ARE ALL THE ANIMALS?"

I wanted Jonathon to see Kilimanjaro, the highest mountain in Africa, so I diverted into Tsavo West Park on the way back to Nairobi from Mombasa. That was the principal reason, but we did not really need any excuse to spend a few more days in the great wilderness of the central bush-country plains of Kenya.

The green of the coastal belt was gone when we had climbed the first escarpment ten miles inland from the blue of deepwater Kilindini Harbour. "Say good-bye to coconut palms," I said.

"Shut up!" replied Jonathon with mock anger.

The grey of dry acacia scrub stretched away to the west punctuated by the mauve bulks of baobabs. It seemed to have been years since we had driven the other way towards the coast, still excited by the extraordinary herd of elephants at Aruba.

We stopped to fill up with petrol at Voi and eat samousas and drink cold Coke. Just a couple of miles away was our first camp where the lone bull elephant had terrorised us and we could pick out the cluster of buildings on the mountain where we had sat on the terrace of the Voi Lodge and Jonathon had first gazed at the vastness of the plains. We did not talk so much on this return journey. At the Tsavo Gate the guard was asleep when we drove up and he was in bad humour and surly. We argued for fifteen minutes about the correct fee for our entry: he started off by wanting to charge us eight hundred odd shillings [over ?30] and in the end I never got a receipt because he said they were finished. I had a twinge of foreboding about this unpleasant incident and kept having a feeling that we should stay at the coast another few days, but put it down to gloom at the ending of our safari.

We headed for Ngulia Lodge near to which there was a safari camp that the guide book said had simple and cheap bandas, and on the way saw little game. There was a lone klipspringer antelope on a rocky hillock, a giraffe and a pair of zebra by a dry river and a lone elephant. The road from the Tsavo Gate to Ngulia was quite good and little used but when we got close to the Lodge we joined the regular package tour route and hundreds of kombis had created corrugations and soft sand patches. I was tired and depressed when we reached the Ngulia Camp but its location on the side of a mountain overlooking a small artificial water-hole and the spread of a broad valley took the breath away.

I was admiring the view when the caretaker joined me. He was an engaging little man, middle-aged and cheerful, dressed smartly. As a lad he had been a domestic servant in Mombasa and he spoke a sort of colloquial 'colonial' English and often came to chat to me. I supposed he found life very boring with hardly any private tourists in the Park.

"*Jambo!*" I greeted him. "We want to stay with you. Have you got a banda for us?"

"I hope so," he said smiling. "I am sure it will be alright, but I have no communications. Sometimes they suddenly make bookings in Nairobi and I never know about them until the evening when the safari company brings people in matatus."

"How can this be?" I asked. "Do you have no radio?"

He shrugged. "We used to have one, of course. But for some years now it has been broken and never repaired. I can show you." He pointed to a mast that trailed a piece of broken aerial wire. "But, don't worry. I will give you a banda. Nobody has come for many days."

"And if a party comes we can camp, I suppose?"

"You are free to camp anywhere here. Please don't worry, you must go and be easy. The banda has a fridge and there is plenty water."

He and his assistant helped us with our gear and quickly swept out the simple room. It was perched on the edge of a rugged cliff in an irregular line of six sited wherever there was space amongst giant boulders and broken ground. A verandah had chairs and we sat there for a while after we had been left alone. A small herd of waterbuck arrived to drink at the pool directly below us and through binoculars we watched some buffalo. Later, Jonathon saw a dozen elephant and that night, after dinner, they came to drink in the moonlight. The whooshing of water in their trunks and the crashing of their bulk through the bushes was loud twenty yards away. No human visitors arrived to disturb our wilderness.

The next morning the sky was clear and we hurried to drive over to Kilaguni Lodge to see Kilimanjaro. In between, there was a high volcanic ridge and we drove down the valley to the south of it, startling the small herd of elephants from the previous night when we rounded a bend. They were frightened and trumpeted loudly, milling around with their ears wide and flapping. I backed up fast, then we were able to get some fine close-up photographs. The road was very bad over the ridge past the black lava rocks of the Chiemu Crater where rainstorms had caused washaways which had not been repaired, and at one point I had to reverse cautiously down to the bottom of a steep rise and try again, our wheels spinning and sending up clouds of red dust. But we were rewarded at the top. Kilimanjaro stood up clear and majestic. Its summit was rimmed by snow and its foot lay in purple haze far along the level plain below us. We stopped and got out to photograph and watch it all. A faint breeze cooled the sweat on our bodies. In all that huge wilderness before us nothing moved in the vision provided by the binoculars.

We went down to Kilaguni Lodge where we had sandwiches and cold Cokes on the verandah while seven kombi loads of package tourists slogged their way through an indifferent four course lunch in the stifling, enclosed dining-room. There was an obligatory artificial water-hole a quarter of a mile from the lodge surrounded by bare red earth where concentrations of game had killed the grass and dust rose from a small herd of zebra that were drinking and milling around. Jonathon complained at the general lack of animals while I thought of the other occasions that I had been at that Lodge. The most recent was two years previously on my grand safari the length of Africa and I had sat there with my good friend, Ted, and we had watched the zebras (the same little herd?) and talked of Africa.

In the afternoon we visited Mzima Springs to see the hippos grunting in the pure water before returning to Ngulia via the magnificent look-out at Roaring Rocks. From there we could look across two open plains: thirty miles northwards to the grey mass of the volcanic Chyulu Hills and southwards to the 6,000 feet high Ngulias behind which our camp sheltered. Apart from the hippos, the zebras, vervet monkeys and baboons, and the few elephants we had frightened in the morning, we saw no game the whole day. Back on the verandah of our banda, watching the colours of the valley change with dusk, Jonathon read to me from a small guide book he had bought at Kilaguni Lodge:

Jonathon read from the brochure : " 'Tsavo is most important as the stronghold of the elephant, and many thousands are found there, the latest count revealed over 18,000. There is also the largest rhino population of the world there.' That's nonsense isn't it? And here it says: 'A recent study and survey resulted in an estimate of between 6,000 and 8,000 black rhino in Tsavo.' I read somewhere else that there are less than 200 rhino in East Africa now after all the poaching."

"When was that guide published?" I asked.

He paged around then said, "1971. That shows you doesn't it? They still sell this old guide so tourists won't know the truth. I wonder what the tour guides tell them when they don't see any game? It's terrible. I thought Kenya was supposed to be so good at conservation, and seeing all those ellies at Aruba was amazing."

"What we saw at Aruba was exceptional and I'm afraid may be a symptom of the disease. I thought at the time that maybe they are now so aware of being slaughtered by poachers that they gather like that from time to time in some kind of extraordinary group paranoia. As if they are compelled by some psychic force to meet and reassure themselves that they are still part of a larger group. There's no doubt about the massive poaching and there have been scandals involving the political elite that couldn't be hushed up. Anyway, how many game guards or poaching patrols have you seen either here or in Tsavo East?"

He thought a moment. "None at all. The only other vehicles we've seen are the tourist kombis and they just race through breaking all speed limits from one water-hole to the next."

"That's right."

The next morning I asked our friendly caretaker about poaching. "Oh yes, there are many poachers. Sometimes I see them passing down there and they even wave to me. We used to hear them shooting, but there are not so many animals here now. They don't come if there is nothing to shoot."

"'And where have all the poachers gone?'" I murmured to myself in disgust.

"They wave to you?" Jonathon asked, amazed.

He laughed. "Of course! They know we have no radio for years now. So what can we do?"

In the afternoon we went over to the Ngulia Lodge, two miles away around the corner of our wide valley. It was an excrescence of a building to construct in a wilderness area: a vast dark bulk standing up square, unrelieved and 'modern', on the skyline at the edge of the great Ndawe Escarpment. I stopped the car to look at it, shaking my head. "That is maybe the worst thing I've seen in Africa," I said.

"Haven't you been here before, Den?"

"It's new since my first long exploration here twenty years ago and last time we stayed around Kilaguni."

I wondered how any architect could have designed such an incredibly bad building for such a beautiful site in a game reserve. As a hospital or school in a city it would have been criticised; in Tsavo it was horrendous. There was no excuse at all because the rocky hillocks along the crest of the 2,000 foot high cliffs of the Ndawe Escarpment were ideal for a low-profile, rambling design. A plaque at the entrance proclaimed that the designers were a Nairobi company of architects.

There were seats at the very edge of the Ndawe Escarpment and from there we had a view which exceeded that from the Voi Lodge. The Teita Hills sheltering Voi were in full view, thirty miles away, and we could see beyond them to the low, level escarpment that marked the track of the Galana River.

"If we had a compass and knew exactly where to look we could probably pick out Aruba," I said to Jonathon. We watched one small family of elephants below us, meandering slowly through the bush. An old bull who trailed them stopped for half an hour and we could see with the binoculars that he was leaning against a tree, sleeping. We thought we saw some buffalo at a distance. That was all.

Staring, entranced, at maybe 5,000 square miles of landscape, I thought about the early man-apes and the migrations of Bantu peoples in recent time. What we were looking at was as inhospitable as any desert in the dry season. As I had reasoned many times before, the only clear passageways between the richly watered highlands around the Great Lakes and the coast were the few perennial rivers like the Galana. Man can survive in that dry acacia wilderness before us all the year round only with extreme difficulty and in small numbers, living close to springs at the foot of mountains or precarious waterholes in the river beds, sharing space with the great cats and hunting dogs. It was a landscape not dissimilar to the Great Kalahari Desert where small, well-separated bands of San-Bushmen have learned to survive, and similar tough nomads prowled the Sahara before it lost its vegetation. Looking at that view, I could understand how Ardrey had been so enthusiastic about his 'hunting hypothesis'. But he had missed the point of the rivers leading from the interior forests to the sea. He may have sat at Ngulia, at the edge of the Ndawe Escarpment, and believed absolutely in his propositions, but he did not understand the significance of that distant ridge where water and trees formed a road to the coastal forest and coral reefs, a natural second home for erstwhile forest apes under stress of climatic change.

Staring at the dry vastness, I could also consolidate in my mind the thoughts about Bantu migrations following my discussions with my friend, Richard, at Mtwapa. It was impossible for there not to be a clear division between the people who developed an Iron-age agricultural economy in the interior highlands and those who lived along the coast and in the coastal hills like the Shimbas. There were ways to communicate up and down the rivers and a few adventurous Arabs, Indians and the occasional Greek may have done so 2,000 years ago, exploring the interior and contacting the early farmers and herders. But it was a journey not to be undertaken lightly, and certainly not when encumbered by children and domestic animals. You would move en masse if you had to, in order to survive, but not otherwise. Explorers and experienced trading caravans were geared to this landscape, not wandering clans of farmers.

"Where are all the animals?" Jonathon kept muttering to himself, staring endlessly through the binoculars.

Later we sat on the Lodge terrace and drank a couple of beers as the sun went down. Three elephants came up to drink at the concreted 'water-hole' and Jonathon was particularly disgusted by a hotel servant bringing out bruised oranges and mouldy bananas to throw to them. One elephant came up to the terrace and the tourists drinking there squealed with delight as its trunk came over the wall sniffing for snacks. One lady, egged on by her companions and watched by grinning waiters, held out a sandwich and the delicate trunk lifted it gently away. The crowd clapped.

"We're in a fucking zoo!" Jonathon exploded.

That evening the eastern horizon was lit by a swath of red and gold as a grass fire swept steadily by. We were up in the middle of the night and could see bright flashes through the binoculars as flames exploded as they engulfed clumps of dry thornbushes.

The next day we left our banda after a fine farewell from the caretaker and his assistant. We passed through the smouldering path of the great fire on the way to the main gate at Mtito Andei where I

246

turned off to the Park Headquarters on a whim. "I want to see what it's like," I said. "And if there's anybody to talk to we can ask about the congregation of elephants at Aruba."

It was a sad experience. The staff quarters showed signs of becoming a suburban slum. The buildings were shabby and the workshop area was dirty with spilled oil and littered with years of discarded broken parts and surrounded by cannibalised vehicles without wheels or with their guts exposed. There were abandoned road-scrapers, trucks and jeeps of various makes. An office block with grimy windows had a radio mast over it and I wondered if that was in good working order. There were no people in sight and nobody came out to see who we were. A dust-devil swirled past and red dust, grass and leaves were lifted high to float everywhere. That was the headquarters of the world-famous Tsavo Park system. I was glad that it was hidden from the main road behind a low hill.

"Oh my God!" I exclaimed when we drove off. "Now you know why we didn't see patrols and why the roads are so neglected. The government must be milking these game reserves of every penny they can and putting nothing back at all. Can you imagine trying to be the Warden of this place: you would either give up in shame or take to the bottle."

"I get the feeling that it's just one great big con-trick," said Jonathon. "Tourists come and are pushed around from one lodge to the other where they have water-holes close by for photographs. They go to Mzima Springs and look at 'Kili' and that takes up a day. The lodges are very expensive and are let out to commercial hotel companies at a high rent I suppose. Remember how much the sandwiches cost at Kilaguni? There're hardly any people like us around who really look at what's going on and travel independently. You can remember what it was like twenty years ago and tell me stories about it. But how many others know what the truth is?"

"I guess there are those in Kenya who do, but they keep their mouths shut. Anyway, what do they have to compare against? In East Africa, this is the standard, so if it all deteriorates slowly, little by little, until it's beyond repair who can really know what is happening? The old timers who built up these game reserves have gone. They are still publishing guide-books that are hopelessly out of date quoting the status of fifteen and twenty years ago, and the tourists buy them and take them home to show their friends. The glossy photography books in Nairobi bookshops are produced by professionals from selected portfolios of pictures taken over years of game watching. The only

247

standards they have to compare against are the game parks of South Africa, which are run extremely well with big budgets and with many thousands of well-informed and critical private visitors as well as foreign package tourists."

"But South Africa doesn't exist," Jonathon interrupted me. "Africa stops at the Limpopo River, you silly old wally!"

I grunted. For many people he was right of course.

From the *National Geographic*, October 1988:

In many African countries elephant population estimates in past years have been largely guesswork. But careful surveys in East Africa by elephant expert Dr. Ian Douglas-Hamilton demonstrate the drastic reduction of the animals. From 1973 to 1987, numbers in Kenya have dropped from 130,570 to 19,749. Uganda's elephant population - greatly affected by continued unrest - has gone from 17,620 to 1,855. In Tanzania the decrease from 1977 to 1987 was 184,872 to 87,088.

From the London *Daily Telegraph*, April 16, 1989:

Four British holiday makers in Kenya described yesterday how they narrowly escaped death when bandits peppered their safari minibus with rifle fire. The two couples, both on a £550 two-week packaged holiday, dived for cover as bullets flew past them in Tsavo National Park in southern Kenya on Wednesday. But a bullet penetrated the left arm of a West German woman sitting in a bus in front, and then went through her chest and her right leg. ... The gunmen were believed to be Somali poachers.

Elephant in the
Shimba Hills Reserve.

CHAPTER TWENTY TWO : "FOUR OF US TOGETHER."

In Nairobi, we stopped a couple of nights at Madame Roche's overlanders' camping rendezvous where travellers from all over Africa have a break to pick up mail, repair their vehicles, get visas or wait for money to arrive before going on to Zaïre or Zambia. Those travellers do not like cities, as a rule, especially Nairobi, and Madame Roche and her garden camp-site is famous to many thousands of them. I spent some time with my Kamba friend, Julius, and arranged to meet him again before we finally left.

Jonathon located our veterinary student friends from Kiwi Beach at the Youth Hostel and we had steak and chips with them at the Grosvenor Hotel nearby, sitting out by the dank swimming pool under a moon. They were fine, attractive girls, full of intelligent humour, and were having an interesting time attached to a local vet with a lucrative private practice involving flying around the Highlands checking on wealthy clients' horses and prize cattle.

"You should see some of those old settler homes and some of the old settlers in them," Sarah said. "They make *Out of Africa* look like middle-class suburbia. I had no idea these people still survived."

I wanted to visit the Hyrax Hill archaeological site and to show Jonathon the famous Nakuru flamingoes, so we set off for the Great Rift Valley, travelling across the rich agricultural land of the Highlands which reach 8,000 feet at the escarpment edge. The whole of that part of Kenya is high and damp, the result of much volcanic activity in past millions of years and the particular convulsions that formed Africa's Rift Valleys. A new motorway had been built as far as Naivasha in recent years and from it there are fine views into the Valley itself and the volcanoes like 9,000 foot Longonot that rise from its floor. I had enjoyed camping at the fishing club on the shore of

Lake Naivasha in 1965, so when I read in the guide book that there were still camping facilities there, it was not difficult to decide where to spend the night.

But something had happened to the fishing club that I remembered. Instead of grassy lawns reaching to a neat waterside with a jetty for boats there was a black mud beach, smelly from waterbirds' droppings, and a tangle of reeds and thorn scrub along the foreshore. Was it the same place, gone badly to seed, or was it another property to where the club had moved? But there were fine old fever trees with their distinctive yellow-green trunks to give shade and we rented a tiny wooden banda with a bit of a verandah for little money and the young caretaker sold us some neatly chopped firewood. There was a variety of birds on the water or by it: pelicans, cormorants, darters, squacco herons, a purple heron, coots, jacanas and several other waders. Superb starlings hopped around the banda looking for scraps with their cheeky bright eyes. Amongst the high branches of the fever trees an oriole with a particularly liquid call sounded. I have only heard that call in the Kenya and Zaïre Rift Valleys and it is so rich and strong that it seems to come from all around. In the evening, sitting by the fire with a beer, we heard crashing sounds and a hippo ran from the reeds through the camp.

On the way to Nakuru I stopped at Gilgil where there had been a training depot for Empire troops in World War II before the campaign to liberate Italian Abyssinia and Eritrea. I wanted to see the Commonwealth War Graves cemetery which we found signposted and in an immaculate state of tidiness. The visitors' book had been signed by many modern Kenyan soldiers and although there were some jeering remarks about British imperialism, most were on the theme of respecting their brothers-in-arms who had died to help Africa. There were British graves from several famous regiments and corps, a lone Australian, White settlers of the Kenya Regiment, Black Kenyans and Malawians of the King's African Rifles and a group from the South African Air Force. Jonathon pointed to one of the latter, a flight-sergeant with a typically Irish Catholic name, and I stared at it. In 1941 that particular grave would have provoked no comment but in the 1980s it was loaded with sharp ironies. There, under the vertical tropical sunlight on a Kenyan hillside lay the body of a South African of Irish Catholic descent who had died to liberate Ethiopia from European colonialism and had a personal motto on his memorial: "For God and the King". I felt goose-pimples on my arms.

250

Approaching Nakuru we noticed a low white cloud in the clear blue sky. It puzzled me until we came in sight of the Lake. It was fine alkali dust raised by convection winds over the Lake. A wide white belt surrounded the shrunken blue of the water and I could not see the characteristic pink blur of the millions of flamingoes that I expected. "What the hell has happened?" I exclaimed. "The lake has shrunk and there are no birds." Twenty years previously, I photographed the Lake from the escarpment ten miles away and at that distance the surface had been a milky-pink blue. Two years before there was a full complement of water and birds.

We turned off the main road up to the little museum on Hyrax Hill and the warden met us after I parked the car beneath a jacaranda tree. I asked him immediately about the Lake. "It has been getting much smaller for the last year," he told us. "I don't know the reason. The flamingoes have left for the north, to Lake Bogoria and Lake Baringo. You can still see some here, but I believe the water is getting too salty for them."

Hyrax Hill was excavated firstly by Mary Leakey in 1937 and there are three distinct sites. One is Neolithic stone-age from about 3,000 years ago and the other two are Late Iron-age of about the 15th century. All three are important and the warden kindly showed us around himself. Graves are associated with both the Late Stone-age and Iron-age sites and their grave goods together with pottery sherds and other artifacts have provided exciting clues to the activity of people in the Rift Valley in the last three millennia

The Neolithic people, using a variety of obsidian tools such as axes and scrapers, were farmers as well as hunters and their grave goods featured cereal grinding stones and pestles. Here was clear proof that sub-Saharan eastern Africans sowed sorghums and millet before they acquired iron technology. I believe it was also reasonable that those people were definitely not Bantu, and I thought about Richard's thesis expounded so recently to me. I was excited, it was another piece of the jig-saw pattern of African prehistory.

The Late Iron-age sites were equally important, but did not provide me with any surprises. That did not matter because I always feel strong emotion when in the presence of old and mysterious places where man has lived. The people who lived on Hyrax Hill in the 15th century herded cattle, sheep and goats which they penned in kraals which were either dug out into pits or became sunken through long use. They used stone to build a small 'fort' or look-out on the summit of the hill and to construct circular hut wall foundations. Grindstones

251

show that they grew cereals. They did some hunting, because there were wild animal bones in the middens and they had definite contact with the Indian Ocean because glass beads, cowrie shells and Indian coins dating from 500 years ago were excavated. This site showed that the culture and lifestyle of these people was practically identical to that of the people between the Limpopo and Zambezi valleys of southern Africa at exactly the same time.

Associated with the Late Iron-age settlements was a permanent stone 'bau' game board which I found fascinating. 'African chequers', a fast-moving game played with counters and either marked wooden boards, scratches or hollows in suitable hard earth or, as at Hyrax Hill, with stone boards with hollowed cups, is played throughout eastern and southern Africa. The rules change from place to place and the name is different in the various Bantu languages. It is one of the interesting cultural links over this vast portion of the continent and I was delighted to see a stone board associated with Iron-age sites there. I do not remember reading a convincing reason for its widespread popularity over so many centuries, but I like to think it is another example of a culture link with the Middle-East.

I took several photographs of the Neolithic site and the Iron-age stone hut circles with Lake Nakuru in the background and was moving about in the rough grass concentrating on my camera and the view. I put my camera away and when I rejoined Jonathon and the warden I was suddenly stabbed by a powerful mental shock. The heavy gold signet ring on my left hand was missing. I stared at the white, indented circle on my finger in total disbelief. That ring had fitted me well, almost too tightly, and had never slipped off my finger before. I was desolated and although all three of us searched the thick grass and stony ground of the Neolithic site for a half hour, I knew that I would not find it.

What will an archaeologist think of a gold cygnet ring adorned with the arms of a Scottish clan of Norman origin in 500 years time? It reminded me of the indirect damage that tourists do to ancient sites. But, if I had to lose my precious ring that was a better place than most, where ancient farming and trading contacts with the Indian Ocean along the rivers to the coast has been proven.

Our safari in East Africa was coming to an end, but there was a last short expedition to enjoy. I suggested that we took Julius, my Kamba friend, and go off for the day.

Next morning his liquid eyes greeted me affectionately when we picked him up and he grinned his wide white grin as he brought a young man forward. "This is going to be a special day, Denis. We are together and you have your nephew, Jonathon, as your companion. Now, here is John, my nephew, and he is my companion."

He laughed delightedly, clasping both my hands in his. "There will be four of us together!"

We drove south through Karen, where Karen Blixen lived for seventeen years, immortalised in *Out of Africa*. On another occasion I visited her refurbished bungalow kept as a museum which clearly illustrates the British colonial era in eastern Africa. The low profile, stone construction and wide verandahs is so typical of those short years. There are bungalows in Ooty and Cochin, Nairobi and Pietermaritzburg that show the uniformity of culture that the British carried with them. But there were some differences and many people alive to-day who can testify to them, and that made me remember that material evidence of cultural uniformity in Bantu Africa does not imply a dull grey sameness.

The town of Ngong was an untidy straggle of dukas, around a small market and park for the matatu Kombi-taxis. In the street there were mostly rural people, poor and roughly dressed. Bantu Kikuyu farmers in baggy trousers and threadbare coats mingled with Nilotic Masai herders who still clothe themselves in red-coloured lengths of printed cotton and carry long staves. The principal dukas were owned by Indians. Those dukas made me think of beads and coins at Hyrax Hill, all along the coast and in the depths of South Africa beside the Limpopo.

Along the shoulders of the green Ngong hills, patched by shambas of maize and crowned by the mist-shrouded remnants of ancient forest, our chattering party was silenced in awe by the sudden blast of light and distance of the eastern Rift Valley. We stopped and got out of the car. It was cool at 8,000 feet above sea level and the air was damp and hazy. To the west the sky was a clear blue and below us a glare of yellow stretched as far as we could see: the Rift Valley was semi-desert in this part below us, sheltering in the rain shadow of the Ngong Hills.

We had not crossed any dramatic mountain range, yet in our view we could see over the escarpment into another world; an arid inhospitable wilderness. We descended on a lonely twisting road into a country of leafless thornscrub scattered across a sandy, rock-strewn land riven by dry stream beds. Gone were the shamba homesteads and patches of maize and vegetables of Bantu farmers, gone were any signs of life, in a journey that lasted twenty minutes. Nor was this a temporary aberration, for in front the semi-desert stretched beyond the horizon. This was the essence of Africa where the difference between lush grass and stony dust is often controlled by only a couple of thousand feet of altitude. The climate and therefore man's existence is dictated by vast plateaux and huge plains. I had been thinking and talking about the importance of the moist highlands around the Rift Valley to the development of mankind and the Bantu peoples, and the significance of the hundreds of miles of inhospitable wilderness between them and the Ocean, and here was the most dramatic example. The view from the Ngongs south and west that day was imprinted on my mind.

We stopped at Olorgasaillie where the Leakey family made one of their major explorations of palaeolithic, Early Stone-age, man. It is probably the clearest example of a settlement of people who lived half-a-million years ago when there had been heavier rainfall and that section of the Rift Valley had been filled by a lake. Earthquakes that shifted the landscape had helped the demise of the lake and caused the abandonment of the area. Dust and ash from volcanic eruptions had preserved the evidence of the settlements. It was hot there, probably 110°F, and very dry. The dust puffed around my flip-flops as I plodded heavily in the wake of our guide. It was also very still in that bleached bowl under a blue-white sky. Half-a-million years is a number that our minds are absolutely incapable of comprehending, yet Olorgasaillie is young in African Man's lifetime. I tried to think myself into a feeling for the Early Stone-age people who had a fixed settlement at that place on the shores of a wide lake. It would have been something like Lake Naivasha is to-day with the ancient hunter-gatherers and stone toolmakers living a good life in small clan groups. I found that I could imagine the people when I thought of Lake Naivasha, but there was no way that I could imagine half-a-million years.

Had the primitive ancestors of those people at Olorgasaillie migrated from the coast up the rivers, having mutated under the stress of becoming aquatic apes? I believed it was so. I sat in the shade wrapped in noonday heat, while Julius chattered away happily, dreaming.

Jonathon and I returned to England a few days later, but I had not finished yet. I had to go south.

SOUTH AFRICA

Punda Maria lodge in the Kruger National Park, with Miriam's faithful car, "Horatio".

CHAPTER TWENTY THREE : 'BOOGIE' AND REFUGEES.

It was about a year later that I crossed the Limpopo River, thirty thousand feet above, determined to finish my Indian Ocean odyssey by going right to the end of its western shores.

The Limpopo River provides a boundary as important in Africa as the Berlin Wall in Europe. But whereas the Berlin Wall was an artificial barrier symbolising the political and economic divide of Europe, the meandering Limpopo is a typical eastern-flowing African river that lazily moves through mopani and acacia bush beneath a blazing tropical sun. It is like the Galana in Kenya and the wilderness on either bank is equally empty. But the political and economic divide was probably as wide as that at the Berlin Wall. Jonathon's cynical, simplistic remark in the Tsavo Park of Kenya was true.

My friend, Miriam, with whom I had travelled the Malabar Coast of India the previous year, met me at Jan Smuts airport in Johannesburg, the busiest in Africa. Standing in the packed arrivals concourse, awaiting my baggage, I could understand one reason for the divide at the Limpopo. Putting aside the enormously powerful and irrational effect of politics, there were the extraordinary differences in socio-economics. South Africa cannot be properly compared with any Black African country. The differences in scale, complexity, wealth and diversity are so vast. I often feel that South Africa suffers from the same disease as the United States, the disease of material success. For all its many and gross faults, by Western standards it works. Despite the increasing power of immoral sanctions by the West, it is still strong. There is constant and well-informed political comment and dialogue. The power and volume of political protest, unimaginable elsewhere in Africa, is interpreted as confirmation of the vileness of the present White-dominated regime rather than as a picture of the only sub-Saharan African country where a semblance of Western-style democracy prevails in massively diverse ethnic circumstances. Most Black South Africans were wealthier, more articulate, more sophisticated and better educated, and more politically active, than in any other sub-Saharan African nation. Their political domination by the Whites was surely coming to an end, at last.

The main concern that aches within me whenever I contemplate Africa is not the detail of contemporary politics which seems to delight our media, fuelled by articulate and charismatic revolutionaries whose importance changes so fast and who exaggerate and distort reality in pursuit of their often dubious causes, but the sustained Western onslaught on the whole continent which is changing it for ever. If I find that Western culture and technology is alien in Africa, with downtown Nairobi as one simple example, a kind of threat to Africa, a growing spawn fuelled by the masses of Africans attracted by its cancerous materialism, then Johannesburg is its clearest symbol, a fully mature Western cultural organism, powerful and smug in its contemptuous hold on the ancient land.

I wanted to go north to the Limpopo River and traverse the tropical lowlands southwards through the wilderness of the Kruger National Park. Early Iron-age people, connected by pottery culture with Kwale and the Shimba Hills had lived in that area. So we headed

256

directly north on the motorway system bypassing Johannesburg and Pretoria

It was getting dark when we reached Pietersburg and reluctantly decided to stay in that town. Pietersburg is in the heartland of Afrikaner conservatism. New reactionary White political parties had emerged in the Northern Transvaal in recent years in opposition to the racial reforms of the Botha government and I was not sure what to expect. I certainly believed that I would feel an ambience of twenty years before and see Apartheid alive and well. We were in for amazement.

Neither of us liked the international conformity of Holiday Inns, but we thought we had better try the one in Pietersburg. It was full and the lobby teemed with jolly Black men in business suits and trendy gear, milling about with the forced bonhomie of a sales convention. "Why Pietersburg?" I muttered. The carpark was filled by shiny late-model cars and more prosperous Black people strolled talking in the grounds.

In the town centre where the streets were lined by brightly lit facades of chain stores full of every variety of consumer goods we saw an old colonial hotel which had been recently refurbished. On a rough approximation of black-and-white English Tudor decor a legend proclaimed 'The Great North Road Hotel'. A pub sign advertised the 'London Club' with a Union Jack.

"A Union Jack in Pietersburg!" I said, laughing. "That's where we have to stay."

A Black couple were checking in ahead of us and the receptionist was a large man with a wide grin and dark glasses stuck on his face.

"Welcome," he called. "If you need rooms you are just in time. We are filling fast."

African boogie music pounded in the background somewhere and a handwritten sign advertised a disco that evening. We went out for a meal, wandering in the civic centre park where large bronze statues stood amongst carefully cultivated indigenous trees and a floodlit fountain spraying a small artificial lake. An operatic voice was singing John Denver ballads in a modern concert hall next to a bright and cheerful steakhouse. White families including a clean-cut group celebrating a teenager's birthday sat amongst smart Black couples. The steak was excellent and the South African *vin de table* drinkable. American country music and African boogie played softly. Our neighbours were speaking a Bantu language.

257

"It's too much!" I laughed with Miriam. "Yesterday evening I was in Zurich, this morning we passed by that city that I dislike so much and here we are in the centre of reactionary 'White Africa'. Neo-Nazis rampage here in the heartland of Apartheid, according to the BBC." I gestured. "What happened?" A pretty blonde girl in some pseudo central European folk outfit interrupted to offer a trolley of cream-cakes. I sat back and ordered coffee and a large South African brandy.

At breakfast, the amazement continued. An elderly man with red leather face and colonial style shorts, long stockings and *veldskoens* sitting in a corner with his plump wife in a floral frock. I was glad to see something that I had expected. There were also two big husky young men with long blonde hair, droopy moustaches and sweat shirts with macho slogans and I could imagine them brandishing placards supporting Apartheid for a thousand years. But there were also a trendy Coloured guy with silk neckerchief, an elderly Black couple in sober Sunday clothes and an aristocratic Black man in black jacket and striped trousers, grey silk tie and a gold chain with official insignia. The waiter was a very cool dude in a dark brown suit, shades and an incredible brown trilby hat perched on his crinkly black hair: he was a time traveller from Chicago in the thirties! Boogie music was playing throughout the hotel. And the breakfast would not have been bettered in the London West-end.

The civic park was spread in front of the hotel and in the shining light of the hot morning sunshine I saw that one of the bronze statues was a donkey. A plaque claimed that the donkey was remembered for its irreplaceable role in the establishment of European settlers in the 1880s. I sighed as I watched the stream of cars and people getting to work in the morning rush. I had warm feelings for Pietersburg.

We entered the Kruger Park at the Punda Maria gate. punda milia is kiSwahili for zebra, an interesting link with East Africa, and the name of the place was created as a pun by the first game-ranger of the area, Captain Coetser, whose wife, Maria, habitually wore striped dresses: 'striped Maria'. The gate was manned by a cheerful young White official and two Black assistants. We were given a pack of brochures and a detailed map of the Park. It was all very efficient. Punda Maria camp was not far from the gate and was situated on the side of a rocky mountain covered with acacia and willow scrub and we were allocated rooms in a long thatched whitewashed building. A broad grassy terrace with thatch-roofed clusters of cooking equipment, barbecues and sheltered seating overlooked the valley. Flowering indigenous trees scorched the eyes with brilliant reds and yellows and bougainvillaea crawled over the restaurant.

That evening we ate grilled steak and salad on the terrace, watching the sun go down and listened to the quiet talk and easy laughter of others around us. Later, a lion paraded the valley, roaring as it went by.

Next day we drove up to the Limpopo River, to the north-east corner of South Africa. On the way, driving through a mopani forest, punctuated by the glorious pink bulks of baobabs, we saw animals: kudu, waterbuck and impala antelopes, zebras, buffaloes, giraffes, elephants, baboons and warthogs running with their tails straight up. We stopped to watch and photograph a fine mature lion with magnificent golden mane close to camp. He must have been the lonely roaring wanderer of the night.

This area was steeped in history. I had stronger feelings about the Limpopo River than I had about the Galana and Tana Rivers in Kenya, because I knew more about it. It was also one of those mysteriously important, eastern flowing rivers of Africa. It is not a river with the perennial power and huge volumes of the Congo, the Nile and Zambezi that rise in high rainfall zones of central Africa and it often fails for part of its length, declining to a series of pools within wide sand banks. It runs for many miles through arid scrub bush. It is unnavigable except for small boats and canoes. But it has played its part in the rise of humanity and the history of Black Africa. Later, after the White man penetrated this far, the Limpopo near Punda Maria became a resort of ivory traders and vagabonds who travelled back and forth between the Northern Transvaal and the Mocambique coast.

The *Australopithecine* ape-men fossils of South Africa were found at Taungs, Sterkfontein and Makapan's Poort, within striking distance of the Limpopo and these half-brothers of the *homo* line could conceivably have migrated up-river from the southern tropical seashores where 'aquatic man' evolved. Cut off from the mainstream, they got lost along the evolutionary trail whereas others evolved further around the Great Lakes of East Africa and became our direct human ancestors. Perhaps the fossil *Australopithecines* are the nearest we will ever approach to discovering earliest 'aquatic man'.

To the north and south of the Limpopo there are gallery upon gallery of magical rock-paintings created by San-Bushmen artists in the last thousands of years, before and after the Black Early Iron-age people moved south. The Early Iron-Age people, who must have

259

migrated first along the Indian Ocean shores from Kenya, left their mark on the Lowveld country east of the great Drakensberg escarpment which is broken by the Limpopo valley. Pottery of the Matola tradition, related to Kwale of Kenya, was found in 3rd century sites to the southeast of Punda Maria.

Not far from where we were that morning, iron and copper were smelted and worked, and later gold. The hills have mystic spiritual meanings right down to the present day. The prosperous, sophisticated and happy crowd at the Holiday Inn in Pietersburg were not there for a sales convention, I had discovered. They were there for an Afro-Christian religious gathering at a holy mountain that is a place of pilgrimage for people from all over South Africa. Hundreds of thousands come at Easter.

And when the strange and powerful change came over the whole of eastern-southern Africa in the 10th century, coinciding with the second wave of Indian Ocean seatraders fuelled by Islam, trade via the coastal middlemen exploded forming new feudalism and the stone-building empires of southern Africa, culminating in Great Zimbabwe at its peak in the 15th century. Mapungubwe and other stone towns along the Limpopo were founded before the Zimbabwean Empire further north.

In the 1960s it was maintained that Mapungubwe was an outpost of the Zimbabwean Empire for obvious reasons: it was roughly contemporary, there was stone walling, there were gold artifacts in elite graves and there were glass beads and Chinese ceramics proving contact with the Indian Ocean trading system. A natural assumption by some was that Zimbabwe was the source of the stone-building medieval society in south-central Africa and Mapungubwe was just one of several southern 'frontier towns'. At that time, some skeletons in graves were thought to be Khoisan Stone-age hunter-gathering pastoralists which tended to support the idea of Mapungubwe being at a southern limit of Negro Bantu colonial conquest, expanding into the lands occupied until then by those primitive people of another race. Even as late as the 1960s, academics were hesitant to date the arrival of Bantu speaking Negro people from the north; a few scattered radio-carbon dated sites suggested a concerted crossing of the Limpopo at about the time that Mapungubwe was founded. There were a great number of stone ruins, undated then, south of the Limpopo River and a natural assumption could be that this tradition spread gradually southwards from the

260

fountainhead of the medieval Zimbabwean Empire and culture. Basil Davidson was still suggesting this in 1984.

Roger Summers, an authority on Zimbabwe, wrote, as late as 1971:

> However, following on the 'developed Gokomere' industries [about 1000 AD] there comes a great change: new ceramic styles, a marked increase in imports [from the Indian Ocean], the appearance of cattle and a variety of forms of stone building. It is inevitable that this division of the Iron Age should go by the name Zimbabwe, since the site appears to have been the centre of cultural influences which spread throughout Rhodesia, westwards to Botswana and far away southwards. It is far less easy to see how this change in outlook reached Zimbabwe or whence it came.

In the 1970s and 80s, however, archaeological exploration of Iron-age sites in South Africa burgeoned and it became clear that Mapungubwe was not a 'frontier town'. Early Iron-age people, presumably Bantu-speaking Negroes, had settled widely south of the Limpopo as far as Natal in the 3rd century AD, 500 years or more before a stone town was founded at Mapungubwe.

In 1973, Peter Garlake, excavator of Zimbabwean ruins wrote:

> ....it is even possible that further investigations will show that the distinctions between the first Leopard's Kopje [K2 at Mapungubwe et al] and Zimbabwe people cannot be upheld and that they are culturally identical.

By 1977, Tom Huffman, Professor of Archaeology at Witwatersrand University in Johannesburg, was showing, from a detailed analysis of pottery supported by other reasoning, that the founders of the feudal Zimbabwean Empire and culture may have migrated there north-eastwards from the Indian Ocean coastal areas of Natal and southern Moçambique, via the Eastern Transvaal and Limpopo. (Historian Monica Wilson had tentatively suggested this from oral and written sources in the 1960s). Later research indicated that there was a definite movement of people associated with cattle away from coastal Natal and the Transvaal Lowveld onto the interior Highveld plateau of South Africa from the 6th century AD. New carbon dates at the K2 site of Mapungubwe proved that it was not contemporary with Great Zimbabwe, and was fully functioning in the

11th century, two to three centuries earlier. K2 at Mapungubwe was a substantial trading town with evidence of being a great ivory collecting depot and processing factory with considerable wealth in imported glass beads and other artifacts. It reluctantly became accepted that Mapungubwe and the associated Leopard's Kopje culture to the immediate north was a forerunner of Great Zimbabwe. The stimulus for Great Zimbabwe came from the Limpopo valley trading towns and the ocean, not from the north. (Richard Wilding has pointed to the importance of the ivory trade being a stimulus to Arab exploration southwards after the decline of the Sudanic Aksum state and the failure of that convenient source).

Further, hilltop stone towns along the Limpopo were not only established before Great Zimbabwe, but the tradition survived centuries after the collapse of that empire in the 15th century. John Campbell, a British missionary in South Africa wrote, in 1820:

> Every house was surrounded, at a convenient distance, by a good circular stone wall. Some were plastered on the outside and painted yellow. One we observed painted red and yellow, with some taste. The yard within the inclosure belonging to each house was laid with clay, made as level as a floor, and swept clean, which made it look neat and comfortable. In the centre of the town there was an extensive inclosure surrounded by a stone wall, except at the gate by which we entered.

This town was estimated to have more than 15,000 inhabitants and stood on the top of a great hill, Kaditshwene, in the Western Transvaal not far from the Limpopo. Robert Moffat, the famous missionary and Livingstone's father-in-law, described Kaditshwene in 1829 shortly after it had been destroyed by the invading Nguni warriors of Mzilikatse who went on to conquer much of Zimbabwe, founding the Ndebele nation. Thereafter Kaditshwene died.

Besides the massive continuity of culture in southern Africa, exhibited by the large stone towns still flourishing in 1820, there is oral evidence of the continuity of trade with the Indian Ocean at that time. The trading tradition with the Indian Ocean which began in the 10th century or earlier and resulted in the towns by the Limpopo, and the later Zimbabwean Empire, still existed in the early 19th century.

Campbell writing further about his visit to Kaditshwene:

He [the chief] had heard of a nation to the north-east called Mahalaseela, who use elephants as beasts of burden, beads came from them, and they lived near the Great Water. He had also heard of a people called Matteebeylai [Ndebele] to the eastward, who also lived near the Great Water, and have long hair; and of another nation to the north east, who bring beads to the Boquains, called Molloquam; pointing to the many beads on his arms, he said he got them by means of a servant whom he sent to the Boquains with an elephant's tooth.

Moffat wrote of a statement made to him in 1829:

At a great distance north or north east of the Bamangwato, a people came up rivers with boats [probably canoes on the Limpopo] who exchanged ivory and Khotlo [gold or copper].

After going as far as we could right up into the north-east corner of South Africa, Miriam and I backtracked to a picnic place on the Luvuvhu River which runs through a deep defile between rocky hills before joining the Limpopo. We drove entranced through a veritable forest of healthy pink baobabs. I don't think I have ever seen a greater concentration of these benign monsters and they gave magic to the place. We sat at painted cement tables beneath the shade of giant African figs and mahogany of the riverine forest and watched vervet monkeys gambolling about and grooming each other. There were crocodiles in the river. A family speaking with the accents of the English Midlands quietly enjoyed a pack of beers next to us.

The caretaker of the picnic place was tending the barbecue fires and his Shangaan wife dressed like a Berber of North Africa in loose printed cloths in bright scarlet and yellow was steadily sweeping the picnic ground clear of fallen leaves. I had often been delighted at the tidiness of the immaculate bare-earth compounds of African homesteads and was interested to learn some years ago that there is a practical as well as aesthetic reason for this. Snakes, rats and other vermin quite naturally do not like crossing alien bare earth. The grass lawns and flowering bushes and creepers clustered around White homes in tropical Africa make no sense to Black people.

I felt the caretaker hovering and wandered over to greet him. We exchanged pleasantries in the African way until he described his problem. He had intended to go to Punda Maria camp to collect sugar but had missed the truck that came round. He loved sugar and was missing it in his porridge and tea. By chance we had spare sugar in the car and I offered him some. Elaborately its value was judged, he rejected a hand-out. It seems a trivial incident, but I was struck by it as a symbol of changing South Africa. Ten or twenty years before, there would have been no suggestion of payment, unless I demanded it; but now a Black man would not accept the face-losing fact of a solicited gift from a White man. We were equals, in a natural easy way. We chatted on about life and the weather and when we parted I clapped my hands without any conscious thought. I don't know why I did it, it is a central African custom for a particular friendly greeting. His face lit with a joyful grin and he clapped in reply. Those customs are also south of the Limpopo.

Along the riverside, at that time of year in the dry season the flame trees and cassias were brilliant with red, orange and yellow blossom; the leaves of the mopani trees were graded from green through yellow to russet. It was a beautiful afternoon's drive back to Punda Maria under the warm sun, and we saw a small herd of elephant close to the camp, where we had seen the lion in the morning. I cooked a chicken stew and rice for dinner on the terrace and as we ate we listened to the roaring again.

Next morning we headed south to Shingwedzi, a camp on the river of that name. The Kruger Park lies vertically on the map, 220 miles from north to south and varies up to fifty miles wide. Until recently all of the land below the high Drakensberg escarpment to the west of us, which encloses the South African Highveld, and eastward to the sea was infested with tsetse fly in the summer season, making it no-go for cattle and horses.

Because they had no cattle to be affected by tsetse, the first Early Iron-age people who had migrated south along the Indian Ocean shore were able to inhabit it and settled at suitable places and followed rivers into the interior. By the early 1980s, three particular Early Iron-age sites in the area we were traversing had been explored and dated: Silver Leaves, Eiland and Harmony. Dates were ±250 to ±390 AD, and their pottery culture was defined as Matola, related to Kenyan Kwale. There are abundant minerals in the Drakensberg escarpment of the Transvaal and metal working clans established themselves later to smelt copper and iron and traded their artifacts with the people from the coast or the interior.

Not far from Punda Maria, there was an unusual conical mountain, Dzundwini, standing high above the flat mopani-clad plains. On impulse, I drove towards it and found a rough stony track

264

that ascended it. Slowly, bumping over rocks and ruts, we reached the top and stopped to admire the view. Inevitably, I was reminded of similar marvellous views in Tsavo Park that Jonathon and I had admired together and I stood staring away to the eastwards to the low Lebombo mountain range that runs from the Limpopo southwards all the way into Natal. It is a strange uniform fold in the earth, 450 miles long, varying in height from a few hundred feet in the north to a couple of thousand in the south. Throughout most of its length it forms the boundary between Moçambique or Swaziland and South Africa. We could see the Lebombo Range, about 15 miles away, and then over its ridge into the hazy distance of Moçambique, fading into the greying silver of the heat of morning at the horizon. Turning about to look into the west it was possible, with a bit of imagination, to sense the faint hazy outline of the Drakensberg escarpment against the blue sky. Africa! How I love to find wilderness away from the pockets of development, look into the baking plains of Africa and dream of the thin psychic threads that link the sparse and precious sparks of human history on the surface of this vast, still-empty continent.

The great conservator of the Kruger Park was Colonel James Stevenson-Hamilton, who devoted much of his life to this piece of Africa. I was at school with his son. He maintained throughout his career that culling and managing of game reserves was bad practice. He believed that the reason for game reserves was to keep them as true wildernesses. Any kind of management, however benevolent and 'scientific', destroyed the truthfulness of the wilderness, and if these areas were not left totally undisturbed, how then would we ever know what a wilderness was? What perfect logic! To-day, the Kruger Park was managed and every year scientific counting and long-range weather forecasting decided the cull for the next year. Each season's cull stimulated the animals in their breeding. Bore-holes and artificial dams on the seasonal rivers maintained populations at an unnatural level. Natural procreation and selection has ceased in the Kruger Park, it was more-or-less animal husbandry by man: a giant game ranch. But, thank God it was there, and there were plenty of animals with poaching at a minimum. When there are no elephants left in East Africa, maybe quite soon, they will still be there in their herds in the Kruger Park.

Miriam and I were talking of these matters and lamenting the demise of the rhino and the imminent destruction of elephants and other game in Kenya. "Do you know that there are large parts of Tsavo that have been more-or-less abandoned and cattle herders have moved in behind the poachers? If only the great game reserves of Africa could be administered by one wise master authority. Where is a new Stevenson-Hamilton...?" I was declaiming away when she clutched my arm.

"There's a child down there." She pointed to a tall solitary thorn tree by the track up Dzundwini hill. "She's gone, now. But what would a child be doing there, walking across the road."

"Probably a baboon," I said, pulling myself to my feet. "But I suppose we'd better be moving on anyway. It's got really hot." The sun was high in a cloudless sky.

We rumbled and bucketed down to the thorn tree where I stopped. There *was* a child standing in its shade, a spindly girl of about eight years with a filthy rag of cloth wound around her. Beyond there was a woman and a boy of about three. "What the hell?" I said softly, staring at them. The woman began crawling towards us on her elbows and knees, her head flopping about. "Jesus Christ! They're refugees from Moçambique!" My heart raced with adrenalin as I jumped from the car and ran to the woman. "It's all right, it's all right," I repeated foolishly. "Don't move." She stopped crawling and slumped, her head lolling weakly, her eyes fixed on mine. Miriam came with our plastic water bottle and a tin mug. "How awful," she kept saying. "We must give them water. But how much? What is best? Do you know?"

White rime surrounded their chapped lips and their eyes were filmed. The woman tried to speak but the effort made her cough drily. She pointed to the children. Miriam filled the mug and held it to the girl who pointed to the boy. He gulped at it. She offered it to the girl who drank, and only then would the woman take some. She was too weak to hold the mug and Miriam had to prop her up with one arm and hold the mug to her mouth. She could only sip slowly, pausing to cough.

I fetched sugar and powdered milk from the car and a teaspoon. "Here, mix a lot of this in." In turn, Miriam fed them sweetened water until it was all gone. We repacked the car and managed to get them into the back seat together with a pathetic bundle of possessions: some lengths of cloth, a chipped enamel bowl and plate, some ground cassava flour inedible without water, a bent old spoon. The little boy was the strongest and must have had all the attention his mother and older sister could give, but he had no energy to cry or complain. He stared at Miriam's face. The girl could walk on her legs like sticks and her shrunken face had the doomed eyes of a saint under torture; but the woman could not move without help. How long had they been there? I know that they would have died had we not come there that day.

From the top of Dzundwini looking east there had been no river in that glare of sunshine on the endless bush of Africa. The Limpopo from that point was 50 miles away and each day the distance the children could walk would have been shorter until they could not go on. I supposed that the thorn tree sticking up out of the scrub had seemed a natural beacon, somewhere to aim for, somewhere where there was shade for the terribly long days.

"Why?" Miriam was asking as I turned onto the main road. There were tears in her eyes. "Why?"

"It's that dreadful civil war," I said. "God-damn all revolutionary politicians. Damn them, damn them!" I breathed deeply. "I suppose that their man was killed or taken away, their village put to the torch by one side or another. There was no solution except to walk into South Africa. Maybe they don't realise that they've got to cross the wilderness of the Kruger Park. .... I don't know." We drove in silence for a while.

"Did you see how the mother refused water until the children had drunk?" Miriam asked after a while. "And can you imagine her agony of thirst and misery? I'm amazed that she was still rational."

"I saw," I said.

"I can't understand how they survived the lions, leopards and hyenas," she said after another while.

"Humans are not natural prey," I said. "But hyenas would have taken them. They were lucky. When the mother died, maybe in the next twenty four hours, the hyenas would have sensed it and would have come."

"We saved three lives to-day," Miriam said, in awe. "I can't believe it."

They sat in the back like statues. The boy whimpered gently every now and then, the woman coughed drily but the girl was silent all the way to Shingwedzi.

I remembered a TV documentary I had watched back home on the famine refugees of the Sudan. Those people had been Nilotic nomad herders and there had been comment and discussion on the fact that the mothers grabbed drink before allowing their children their portions. There had been uninformed criticism of this 'uncivilised' behaviour, but I had understood that it was consistent with the circumstances. In nomadic cultures, it was natural instinct and clear logic that if the mother is not strong, children cannot survive. Our little group were Bantu farmers, and the logic was different; natural death from thirst was so unusual because no settlement would ever be placed where water was not available, whatever digging and effort was necessary in drought, and the mother had acted to a different instinct.

Driving up to the gates of Shingwedzi Camp, I thought that I would never forget the eyes of the woman, fixed on mine, as she wobbled forward, crawling on her elbows. All of it was there: sustained agony and despair, the deep fear of those last days, the miracle of our appearance, the trust and hope. Especially the trust. Oh God! I had touched her soul that morning, I had met a human animal at the end of life and had seen her naked soul with all pretence and conscious complexity wiped clean.

The officials at Shingwedzi came quickly out of the administration building when I reported. At first, I thought their professional calm was callous, but discovered that it was because the incident had become commonplace.

"Just put them here in the shade," Robin, a uniformed warden with a brisk manner, told us. "I've got things moving." Two women cleaners materialised with a plastic bucket and began bathing their faces gently and a Black assistant from the self-service shop ran up with a two-litre bottle of Coke. He borrowed our mug and began drenching the children before helping the woman.

"Hey, is Coca-Cola good for them in this condition?" I protested.

"The best thing," Robin said. "It's liquid, there's lots of sugar, a bit of caffeine and the gas helps fill their constricted stomachs so they don't take too much at once. It's standard procedure." The two cleaning women crooned over them, wiping the dried mucus from around their mouths and eyes.

A pipe-smoking, bearded White man joined us. "I'm the public relations officer for this area. I see you've saved some refugees. *deurlopers* we call them in Afrikaans. I picked up half a dozen the other day not far from where you found these. Some months three to four hundred come through. Most are starving and dying of thirst like these but some have terrible gunshot wounds. One woman had her foot shot off but she had looked after herself so well that the medics had nothing to do. It's amazing what hardship human beings can tolerate."

A pick-up truck arrived and our little family were loaded on board. "What happens now?" asked Miriam.

"The army takes over. There's a special budget to look after them, and they are taken to a field clinic that has been set up. They get a general antibiotic and are put on a drip. If there are no wounds or infections they are sent down to the rehabilitation camp near Ressano Garcia on the border and fed up there. They get clothes from the South African Red Cross and other voluntary agencies, then they are handed over to the Moçambique government's welfare organisation."

"And maybe end up here again in a year's time," I said bitterly.

He shrugged. "That's the agreement with the FRELIMO government of Mocambique. I'm not a politician. We just look after the wreckage of the civil war. It's no pleasure, I can tell you."

A camouflaged army Landrover drove up and a tall suntanned young man with sergeant's stripes jumped out and talked cheerfully to the official, who turned to me. "This guy is a medic. He says your little family are going to be O.K." The sergeant smiled at me and gave me a thumb's-up sign. "Thank you from all of us," he said. "You did a good thing to-day."

We stayed some days at Shingwedzi and Satara, another camp further south, enjoying the wilderness. We watched lions courting and saw a leopard very close, resting near its kill which was being munched at by two spotted hyenas. We watched an old elephant keel over and die, suddenly, while a young *askari* bull stood by on guard. From look-out points we stared across those endless square-miles of African wilderness. In the mornings we fed bread crumbs to flocks of bright cheeky glossy starlings, doves and hornbills. In the evenings along the river, impala and water buck, elephants, Egyptian geese, various storks and herons congregated. At the Olifants River I watched seven hippos grazing in the heat of noon, and reflected that it is often erroneously said that hippos only feed at night because they can't take harsh sunlight on their sensitive skins. Miriam compiled a satisfactorily long bird list. It was a pleasant idyll. I saw those haunting eyes sometimes, and we wondered what they were thinking about as they recovered their health and were being processed by official machinery. I feared that they were despairing of their future in their terrible trauma.

After leaving the Kruger Park and heading on southwards towards Natal, we climbed the massive eastern Drakensberg escarpment that encloses the interior plateau. Geographically, the eastern side of southern Africa is extraordinarily similar to the western side of southern India. The Drakensberg mirrors the Ghatts, the Highveld mirrors the Deccan. We recognised this and reminisced about our traverse of the Malabar Coast.

But the climb up the Drakensberg escarpment on the fast and superbly engineered highway from Nelspruit to the summit at Machadodorp, from where President Paul Kruger led the last despairing efforts of the Boer commandoes against the might of the British Empire, was important for other reasons 1400 years before Kruger's last stand. As late as the 1970s, archaeologists identified a particular Iron-age pottery culture thereabouts that was subtly different to the coastal Matola pottery. It has become known as Lydenburg, from the town not far north of the road we were travelling.

There are several 'Lydenburg' sites in the Natal interior, in the headwaters of the Tugela River valley. Suddenly, another whole culture sprang into sight. They were still Early Iron-age people, farmers and hunter-gatherers, but they began to acquire cattle from nomadic herders who brought them south and may have settled amongst them, so they had to move inland to where there was no tsetse and the grazing at the interface of savannah thornbush and high grasslands was better. The change in pottery styles tends to prove that with the cattle another culture was also absorbed.

Miriam standing where we found the refugees. The wilderness stretches away for 200 miles.

CHAPTER TWENTY FOUR : EMPIRES AND A CAVE

I awoke to the thundering of wind. My face was cold and I buried myself for some moments in the blankets while I remembered where I was. Faint light outlined a low, ill-fitting semi-circular door. Chinks showed through patterned grass thatching. It confirmed that I was sleeping in a Zulu beehive hut close to the actual site of King Cetshwayo's great Kraal at Ulundi. It was named *Ondini*.

The night before I had arrived at Ulundi, the capital of the autonomous self-governing state of KwaZulu, within the Province of Natal. It had been warm and I had eaten curry and rice by firelight with my friends within a circle of beehive grass huts surrounded by a jaggedly impenetrable fence of twisted branches and trunks of thorn trees, which would have kept the lions out in the old days. The weather forecast had threatened a severe depression and cold front sweeping up from the winter deeps of the Antarctic. During the night it had arrived.

I crawled painfully out of the low doorway to face the cold gale and driving drizzle. It was not the expected picture of a glorious African dawn. In the nearby modern kitchen serving the exact replica of a Zulu kraal that was available as accommodation for official visitors to the Zulu national museum, I brewed coffee and swallowed a couple of painkillers. The previous day I had tripped and fallen into a spiked aloe bush and twisted my back, straining various muscles, trying to avoid having my face severely scratched. I hadn't succeeded in that either. Dear oh dear, it was a sorry start to an exciting expedition.

The Zulu nation was founded by Shaka, a strange and messianic offspring of the ruler of a minor clan of that name, a

271

member of the Nguni group of tribes who inhabited to-day's Natal and Transkei.

The great Nguni tribal group lived between the main Drakensberg escarpment and the sea. Their northern boundary was the territory of the Tsongas, who inhabited the fever-ridden thornbush lands from Delagoa Bay in Mocambique northwards. Their southern boundary was the end of the grasslands in the eastern Cape of Good Hope, where geography abruptly changes. Inhospitable semi-desert scrub and succulents dominate in the interior there and forests made the coastal routes impenetrable. Shipwrecked Portuguese survivors described the Nguni in the 16th and 17th centuries and their settled society of scattered clans was stable. These scattered Nguni clans, each with its own established dynastic hierarchy, lived in an Eden. But squabbles over a trade monopoly with the Portuguese started the change to imperial rule in the latter 18th century and Shaka's genius completed it by 1820.

The lands filled by Late Iron-age Nguni had been gradually settled by Early Iron-age peoples between the 3rd and 8th centuries. The particular mystery of the Nguni is that in historical time they were a cultural pocket, surrounded by people speaking different Bantu languages and practising some fundamentally different customs, particularly regarding food and marriage. For instance, the Nguni had to marry outside their clan group, whilst the neighbouring Sotho-Tswana preferred marriage within it. Nguni followed strangely Semitic food lore, particularly abhorring scaled fish. The Zulus, particularly, built grass beehive huts instead of the pole and mud huts of all other Bantu tribes. My own observation suggests that the language closest to the Nguni group is kiSwahili, far up the eastern coast. When in the Shimba Hills, talking with Jonathon, I had a strong intuitive feeling that the ancestors of the Nguni had a special relationship with the ancestors of the Nilotic Samburu of Northern Kenya. Their material culture, even their modern beadwork, is uncannily similar. Could the Nguni, modified and changed over many centuries with other genes added and culture transferred from time to time, be direct descendants of the original coastal stream migrants?

Monica Wilson in *Oxford History of South Africa* (1969) wrote:

The most conspicuous fact about Nguni history, as opposed to the history of most other groups in South Africa, is the absence of clear links in language or tradition with any other

272

group further north other than those which split from the Nguni south of the Drakensberg and travelled northwards.

I described my meeting with Samburu near the Ewaso Nyiro River of Northern Kenya in 1985 in my book *Reflected Face of Africa*:

> These people were Nilotic nomadic herders and their huts were almost identical to those of the Khoi of Southern Africa: withies were bent and fastened to form a hemispherical shell which was then covered by cattle hides or goat skins. ....
> They lived on the milk of their animals like their Nilotic cousins, the Masai, and the Bantu Zulus of far away Natal. ....
> I noticed that the beadwork on the girls was in bright, primary colours, similar to that of the Zulus and Ndebele of Southern Africa, in contrast to the pastels of the Masai and Kamba,....

The Zulu clan, into which Shaka was born probably in 1787, had lived for many generations in the beautiful Emakhosini valley surrounded by high plateau. About seventy miles eastwards of this valley is the great St.Lucia lake and estuary by the sea where there are some of the most significant Early Iron-age sites of the Matola culture in southern Africa dating from the 3rd century.

Nguni custom forbade marriage between people of the same clan and Senzangakhona, chief of the Zulus, infringed this rule by marrying Nandi, of a neighbouring clan. The reason for this doubtful marriage was that she had become pregnant, a romantic indiscretion as old as time. Shaka was born of their union. History may have been different had Nandi not been a strong and troublesome woman who made enemies of all her kinsfolk and was eventually booted out with Shaka to return to her own family. Nurtured by his fierce mother, Shaka surmounted the stigma of his origin and became a great warrior. Proven in local tribal skirmishes, he was appointed a regimental commander by Dingiswayo, chief of the Mthethwa clan, who was striving to control the growing trade with the Portuguese at Delagoa Bay by dominating a federation of clans through warfare and intrigue.

This was in the early years of the 19th century and it was a new departure from the intermittent skirmishes of personal rivalry, cattle-raiding and mild inter-clan feuding of the past. The idea of consolidating power and wealth through military domination and monopoly control of trade was not new to the Bantu people of

273

southern Africa; from the Mapungubwe complex in the 10th century to Great Zimbabwe and later it was common from the Limpopo valley northwards. But, it was an innovation in Natal and having occurred in historical time is a text-book example of how external trade can stimulate imperialism in simple Iron-age society in eastern-southern Africa. Always there had to be outstanding men and whereas the names and dynasties of Great Zimbabwe are lost, the founders of the Zulu national kingdom are known.

Shaka, under the tutelage of Dingiswayo who was locked in conflict with Zwide, an equally powerful rival chieftain, saw a dream of empire which would need a radical restructuring of Nguni society. He saw that he would have to rebuild this society from a small nucleus; endless warfare between large clan-federations based on existing culture which was not suited to military empire was a waste of time and people. Shaka had a clear vision and he was in a hurry. He gained control of the insignificant Zulu clan by eliminating the rivalry of his half-brothers and built a military machine. In a comparatively short time he fought a series of brilliant battles with powerful clan groups and gained victory after victory using new tactics and unprecedented ruthlessness. Conquered clans were transformed into his model and their armies reorganised in the new Zulu fashion. He became invincible and a terror far beyond the lands he directly ruled.

Like all great military conquerors his great feats had to include vast social and economic reforms. He created one integrated empire out of the conquered traditional clan groups; the socio-religious 'totem' groupings of young men and women who were annually initiated into tribal lore became military regiments; marriage laws were utterly changed and regiments of men and women were married en masse as rewards for military success; food production and distribution was controlled by a central bureaucracy; maize earlier acquired from the Portuguese became the national staple replacing the less productive sorghums and food surpluses were carefully stored; medicine men and women were employed as secret service agents to seek out dissidents using magic or simulated magic; miners and metal smiths were organised into mass weapons producers; new towns ('kraals') were founded; external contact and trade with Europeans was strictly controlled. Nothing was untouched by Shaka's centralised power machine.

Shaka imposed direct rule over an area that he could easily control with messengers and armies that moved on foot. Iron-age Bantu people had no wheels or horses. He ruled from Tsonga country to the Tugela River and from the Indian Ocean to the foothills of the Drakensberg, a rough square, 140 miles a side, about 20,000 square miles, more than half the size of England. And he had no horses. His armies were sent raiding far beyond to keep them sharp, reward them with plundered cattle and to cower the neighbours. Clan chiefs who refused to accept Shaka's imperial suzerainty fled with their personal armies and an extraordinary Nguni invasion spread as far north as Lake Tanganyika, disrupting many established tribal dynasties and causing migrations of maybe hundreds of thousands of people over several decades and the deaths of tens of thousands in refugee-caused famines: a pattern repeated in to-day's civil wars in Africa. This turmoil of marching armies and fleeing multitudes was called the *mfecane* by the Zulus.

New tribal nations were founded by these warrior-chieftains who fled Shaka: the Swazi of Swaziland, the Shangane of southern Mozambique and the eastern Transvaal and the Ndebele (Matabele) conquerors of the Shona peoples who built the stone towns of Great Zimbabwe. The furthest reach was gained by the *Ngoni* branch in Tanzania and Malawi, an incredible 1,500 miles directly from their Nguni homelands, probably wandering 3,000 miles before settling in the lush tropical lands of the Great Rift Valley. This particular movement in one generation proves the possibility of earlier migrations over large distances in southern Africa. The Ngoni had the advantage of obtaining information about the terrain ahead from the people they travelled through, or absorbed after conflict, but the problems were similar to those of 1700 years before. And who knows how many battles they fought and hardships they endured on the way?

In 1988, I spoke to the watchman of an hotel on Lake Malawi who told me proudly that he was an Ngoni and his great-great-great-grandfather had come north from Zululand under their great chief Zwangendaba. His family had always married within the Ngoni tribe and cared for their heritage. When thinking about the history of Mombasa and the arrival of the fierce Simba warriors who disrupted all of the Swahili towns at the end of the 16th century I cannot help but remember the *mfecane* of the 19th century. The Portuguese recorded the Simba crossing the Zambezi going north in 1570 when they sacked Tete and Sena in Mozambique. I have always thought that there was a relationship. It has been suggested that the same thing may have happened in the 9th century when overlords arrived, perhaps from the south-east, to set up a form of feudal society along

275

the Limpopo river which later grew into Great Zimbabwe. The Nguni are a strange and powerful people.

Shaka granted British settlers small-holdings around Durban Bay before he was assassinated by his half-brother, Dingane, in 1828. Dingane was a caretaker rather than an innovator and maintained the status quo. The engine of Shaka's new Zulu empire was kept running. The *mfecane* continued its knock-on effects over all southern Africa. The greatest significance of this was that the Afrikaners who had become disillusioned with British rule at the Cape of Good Hope moved into the vacuum. Many Afrikaners believed that the lands that had been depopulated by war and famine were empty by tradition. Some believed that the Bantu peoples had never permanently inhabited those lands which were there for the taking.

Dingane greeted the Afrikaners who came seeking 'empty' lands south of the Tugela River in Natal and then became fearful of the power of their guns and horses. He ordered all-out massacre and assassinated their leaders. Dingane succeeded in destroying the Afrikaner's will temporarily, but continued pressure by migrants from the Cape and the fresh leadership of Andries Pretorius resulted in the defeat of the Zulus in 1838. The Tugela River was established as the division between lands of Zulu and White settler suzerainty and the peace held until 1878.

It was the British who destroyed Zulu military power in the infamous war of 1879. Cetshwayo, king at that time, was a strong ruler. His military organisation copied Shaka's, his reign was stable and his diplomatic posture towards the White settler states ringing his country was correct. But his massive military potential worried the British colony to the south and the Afrikaner Zuid-Afrikaansche Republiek to the north. Coincidentally, imperial Britain was busy with a grand scheme to confederate southern Africa with Canada as the model and the Zulus were a major stumbling block, therefore trivial excuses were used to make impossible demands for submission to British supervision leading to incorporation.

Cetshwayo annihilated the first invading British army at Isandlwana but instead of following this up and laying the colony of Natal waste he leashed his armies within the borders of Zululand. He did not understand why the British were making war on his nation and thinking that the trivial excuses were the real reasons, however incomprehensible, he sent out peace missions which were ignored or imprisoned. To the end, Cetshwayo insisted that minor complaints could be settled amicably whilst resisting invasion with all the disciplined power of his massed regiments, the greatest Iron-age infantry military force ever, south of the Sahara. But the British Empire had been challenged, the Zulus had to be put down.

Overwhelming British force achieved this finally on 4th July 1879 on the plain of Ulundi. Cetshwayo was exiled, the nation broken up into simulations of the old clan system and puppets installed as clan rulers. Native 'locations' were established and racial segregation began.

My friend, Leonard, the archaeologist at the KwaZulu museum, came to fetch me in his battered Landrover that cold winter's morning at *Ondini*, Cetshwayo's 'kraal'. I had been sitting, drinking coffee, gazing over the plain of Ulundi, mulling over the despair that must have filled Cetshwayo's heart as he watched the British army advancing, a hundred and nine years before. The Zulus called it *impi yaso cwecweni*, 'the glittering army', because it advanced in full regimentals with shining badges and polished lances with gay pennants flying. It was the last time in British history that colours were marched into battle unfurled with bands playing.

The prime of two empires clashed that day. Cetshwayo watched his superbly drilled army, each regiment accoutred with distinguishing shields, head-dresses and fur decorations, smashed by artillery, machine guns and the massed rifle fire of the famous infantry square. It all happened there, on that great plain spreading away to the west of where I sat. Low clouds raced mistily across the Mahlabatini Heights and the cold wind moaned through the tall fence of the cattle enclosure and the thatch of the beehive huts.

I was silent as we passed along the wide tarred streets of the new Ulundi. Modernistic, concreted capital buildings of the reborn KwaZulu state, child of Apartheid, spread over the sere winter hillsides. Buses were disgorging swarms of Zulu clerks and administrators heading for box-like offices furnished with the filing-cabinets of bureaucracy. Where were the brave warriors?

Leonard had invited me to join him in some field work and I had been delighted to accept. He had with him, Gordon, a mature student from Cape Town University notching up practical experience, and the back of the Landrover was filled with camping gear and some of his Zulu crew. A heavily loaded truck followed with the rest of the workmen and their equipment. The first task was to fence the important Stone-age site of the Border Cave high in the Lebombo Mountains, at the southern end of that range that I had stared at on the morning of the Mocambique refugees a few weeks before.

We drove through the Zulu heartland, climbing to the bare grassy heights where the gale-driven purple clouds raced close above us and plunged into valleys where homesteads and villages clustered about bare cultivated land awaiting the spring sowing. We stopped at Mkuze for lunch, at the foot of the Lebombo Mountains which rise to two and three thousand feet at this southern end. Icy rain swept the forecourt of the service station where Leonard bought hamburgers and soup for his men. We huddled in the shelter of the truck and I studied my companions for the next few days. They were beefy men, quick to laugh, easy of movement, with shrewd eyes and scrappy beards or moustaches. Leonard had a relaxed camaraderie with them, but there were many quick glances at me, the stranger. A summing-up was going on, but it was unobtrusive and courteous, there were no rude stares. I had been introduced around as a man from far away who loved the history of Africa and had come to see the famous places that were the work of their museum. One of the younger men was a dandy with a quick wit who led the joking. The oldest had a dry sense of fun and a quietly confident personal authority. Our eyes met often and we achieved rapport. His name was Dubé.

After Mkuze we climbed over the Lebombo and from its summit we looked down onto the Makatini flats spreading to the Ocean. This was the land of the Tsonga people, incorporated to-day into the KwaZulu state, but we had crossed a massive cultural divide. To the west of the mountain the Nguni peoples were as obsessed with cattle as the Nilotic Samburu of Kenya and, traditionally, fish were anathema. To the east and north, along the fringe of the ocean and in the tsetse infested lowlands, the Tsonga loved fish and cattle had less importance. Also, the Tsonga kept domestic fowls which the Nguni, traditionally, did not.

Crossing the Lebombo into Tsonga country, I entered a culture zone that spread away up along the Indian Ocean littoral as far as the Shimba Hills and the hinterland of Mombasa and Malindi wherever the Swahili influence waned, and up the Great Rift valleys to the Kenya Highlands and hills of Rwanda and Uganda. What massive, massive continuity is Africa! Here at the southern end of it all I was breathless with excitement. I suddenly thought strongly of my friend, Richard, at Fort Jesus Museum, and wished that he was there with me.

I looked down eastwards to the sea and pointed ahead: "The 'coastal stream' came down here."

Leonard shared as much of my vision of African pre-history as professional caution permitted. He grinned, "Always get's to you,

278

doesn't it, Denis?" I nodded. "We'll see if we can find an Early iron-age site for you on this trip," he said. "I don't know what we'd call it, something specially romantic of course."

We descended to the eastern side to drive northwards along the foot of the range and the rain fell heavily, driven by the wind. The road was dirt but well-tended and gravelled. "It's going to be hell this evening," Leonard said grimly peering ahead where the clouds had lowered to cover the mountain tops. "It's just as well that I packed a couple of bottles of Scotch."

"Leonard, you're a star!" I said.

"You can thank my wife for that," he grinned. "She heard the weather forecast. There'll be snow down to two thousand metres to-night, they said."

"The Lebombos are below one thousand metres, aren't they?" Gordon asked anxiously, and we all laughed.

In the dull light of the dreary afternoon the landscape changed to typical acacia scrub so familiar in tropical Africa. There were a few simple kraals set amid small holdings with a goat or two and chickens sheltering under a scrap of corrugated iron. I thought again of the Shimba Hills and turned to Leonard as he began speaking: "You remember sending those prints of the Kwale pottery sites in Kenya?" He waved his hand. "I thought of this country and the Tugela valley where I was digging Early Iron-age all that time. It's the same country."

"That was telepathy." I laughed. "I wish the weather was the same. I bet those early migrants hated the winters this far south."

Leonard thought seriously for a moment. "You're right. If they moved south in only three or four generations, the weather must have been culture shock. We should think about that. Mind you, I bet it can be cool enough in those hills near Mombasa in the rainy season?"

I nodded. "It rained when I was there and I could have worn a karos of skins with pleasure. But, it would never have been as cold as to-day."

The Landrover had to strain up the track beyond the Ngwavuma River gorge as we climbed to the summit of the Lebombos again. We entered the mist whistling past us and turned down a cut-line through highveld scrub, Leonard peering ahead searching for landmarks. "This track is the border between South Africa and Swaziland," he explained as we jolted over rocks. "The army cleared it some years ago." An old hand-pump came into sight beside a piece of level ground and Leonard stopped the vehicle. "Here's our camp for the next few days," he said. The rain drove onto the windscreen.

The workmen climbed out of the truck and the back of our Landrover, clad in yellow plastic coats over their pale blue uniform overalls with KwaZulu Bureau of Natural Resources badges. They screwed their eyes up against the rain and rubbed their hands together while Leonard paced about measuring for the tent. I was glad that it was a routine for them and I could be a passenger. My strained back ached in the cold. With a minimum of fuss the camp grew although the big tent, twenty feet square, with its tall central pole was a monster to erect in the wind. Once the pole was up and guyed, the canvas flogged until subdued by the burly men hammering in foot-long spikes. Then the gear was hurriedly carried in and I was able to assist with cooking and cold-store boxes. I erected my camp-bed in a corner and spread my damp bedding ready for the night.

The truck had pulled a trailer with the fencing equipment and firewood had been piled on top. Two of the men got busy with axes, chopping logs into useful pieces and a fire was laid in the lee of the tent and we all gathered around it. Diesel fuel was poured over the wet wood and it was soon roaring. Smiles appeared on all our faces and the men began laughing and joking. We sat on logs and hands were held to the flames. I listened to the deep, lilting Zulu voices around me, understanding some of the conversation, suddenly very happy to be there.

A man loomed out of the murk and after elaborate greetings he joined us. I noticed that he spoke with a distinct accent, 'z' sounds hardened to a 'd', which proved that we had left the Zulu heartland. It was the *tekela* dialect that I had read about. "He's the local headman come to check and offer help," Leonard told me.

He was followed by half a dozen young women wanting work and they met a battery of suggestions and teasing guffaws which they accepted without offence and some giggles. Eventually they were told to return in the morning. I had not forgotten the gentle earthiness of these people, but was intrigued by its strength. Dubé was teased by the others, suggesting that he was beyond attending to such attractive young girls. He gave me a grin and said that we older ones had more experience, and so I was included in the joking.

Leonard had brought pre-cooked chickens and potatoes and these were heated on a grill after the fire had died down and the rain ceased briefly as dark fell. Afterwards, Leonard brought out his whisky and a generous dollop went into each coffee cup. Life improved even as the rain began again. Logs went onto the fire and steam rose from damp clothing. The men talked slowly with gentle chuckles, the conversation slowly going the rounds, each speaking at length until he finished his theme before the next took it up. I listened, admiring the art. That was how men sat around fires whiling away the evening over all rural Africa; it was how Europeans had behaved before electricity.

"What are they talking about?" asked Gordon. "I wish I understood."

"They were discussing Indians," explained Leonard. "They were telling stories about the 'cleverness' of Indian shopkeepers and how to outfox them by pretending to be stupid Blacks from the bush. They were uncomplimentary about Indian women because they are thin. They are now telling stories about the dangerous drivers of Kombi-taxis."

"*Matatus* and *duka-wallas*," I muttered to myself, sipping whisky.

"On about Kenya are you, Denis?" Leonard smiled.

"Of course," I said. "The similarities are so clear. But these Zulu men we are camping up with are different. They seem more self-confident and relaxed than East Africans."

Leonard got up to pass the whisky bottle around again and one of the workmen offered cigarettes. Dubé got up, slugged back his drink and went in to make up his bed. With interest, I watched him select the place next to mine and smiled to myself, feeling warm in my heart.

Later we got onto the question of common culture up and down Bantu Africa. I said that one of the things that always amazed me was the universal tradition of 'wire-cars', toy cars or carts made of wire with a long steering arm that I have seen boys playing with from the Cape to the edge of the Sahara in the Cameroon. The wire-cars reflect local culture; in South Africa they are technically correct, in Zambia and Malawi they tend to be more artistic, surrealistic even. In East Africa the variety spreads more to buses, tractors and bicycles.

"There is a PhD thesis in there somewhere," I suggested.

"And what about African checkers?" Leonard asked.

"At Hyrax Hill... you know of it?" He nodded. "At Hyrax Hill in the Rift Valley of Kenya I saw an African checkers board last year carved out of living rock which is estimated to be 15th century, if I remember rightly. They call it the *bau* game in East Africa."

281

"I excavated an exactly similar board carved from soapstone in the Tugela Valley in an 8th century site," Leonard said. "I was told that it had to be 19th century because it was supposed to be impossible earlier. I must remember to look up Hyrax Hill when I get back."

"That's really exciting," I said. "And academics who should know better forget the massive cultural continuity of Bantu Africa."

Leonard grinned. "Let's have a last nip from that bottle."

In the middle of the night the storm blew up heavily again and rain dripped onto my face while the tent canvas boomed and flogged like a windjammer's sail. Dubé snored away contentedly next to me, but I had a bad night.

In the morning we all set to tidy the ravages of the storm. The tent guys had to be tightened and leaking places seen to. The rain had stopped and a cold dry wind blew so a gay collection of blankets and sleeping bags flew all about like pennants on an Elizabethan warship. Dubé and I made up the fire and brewed coffee. Chunks of whole-meal bread and margarine were the breakfast. The young women of the night before arrived with some teen-age boys looking for the promised work and there was more *double-entendre* badinage by our men. No offence was intended and none taken. An older woman gave me steady looks of frank interest and asked about me. Dubé and the dandy made pointed remarks that I could not understand but could perceive the meaning. There were friendly guffaws.

"You're being given the treatment, Denis," Leonard explained. "But it only means that they like you."

"Oh, I know that," I replied. "I'm richly flattered; as I should be."

Some of the young people were engaged to help and Leonard went off with his gang to the Border Cave while I stayed behind to tidy up and guard, and to orient myself.

Our location was magnificent on top of the mountain, three thousand feet above sea level. We were camped on the line of the actual international border between KwaZulu within South Africa and the Kingdom of Swaziland. A few miles to the north, the border with Mozambique was met on the crest of the range and there was the peaceful meeting of three quite extraordinarily different nations.

Looking westwards over Swaziland, I was strongly reminded of the Great Rift Valley in Kenya. The Lebombos fell steeply into the plains of Swaziland below me where the Ngwavuma River flowed in wide loops across a flat valley where a great sugar estate rested in neatly squared irrigated fields of livid green. I could hear the 'g r r r -

g r r r r' and melodious horn of a diesel locomotive on the railway. On the far side of the valley, hills rose in a jumble leading to the Drakensberg that reminded me of the Mau Escarpment to the west of Lake Naivasha, which is also surrounded by plantations.

After lunch, I went with Leonard and his men down to the Border Cave. This important archaeological site is named because of its location, but it is, in fact, within Swaziland although it is cared for by the KwaZulu Bureau of Natural Resources. We left the Landrover on the border cut-line and followed a faint track downwards to the west through rock outcrops, spiny cactus and other succulents, groups of sugar-bush trees and tangles of mountain vegetation. The path became steeper and we suddenly burst onto a view that took my breath away, staring down an almost vertical cliff-face. The others plodded and slithered down with practised confidence while I moved with care at the end of the line, steadying myself with a hand to rock and tough mountain bush. I have never had a head for heights.

Worse came at a rock ledge. We had to traverse horizontally for some thirty metres and I paused to collect myself.

Leonard looked back, "All right, Denis?" he called and I waved him on. I had to do it myself, on my own, but I was glad of my grey beard to help me save face. As if to mock me, a small stream of girls and boys emerged from the cave entrance at the end of the traverse, almost skipping along, come to fetch stones to grout in the fence poles that were being erected.

Feeling quite sick, I negotiated the traverse like a crab, leaning into the rock wall, feeling my way, being careful not to look down. When it was over, I rested in the giant cave.

Border Cave had an open mouth about 30 metres across and 4-5 metres high at the centre. It was about 30 metres feet deep, shelving gently up to the back where the roof fell to join the floor. Fine dry dust of ages covered the rocky floor. The dust was scuffed by myriad goats' footprints and their droppings lay around like piles of black peas. It was because of the need to keep the goats away from precious ancient strata that we were there. Trenches had been cut through the deep detritus of ages and then covered with excavated dust again to preserve. I wandered about beginning to achieve a feeling for this habitat of very old mankind and gazing with awe over the vertical cliff to the Swaziland plain maybe 500 metres below.

Leonard came to sit with me at the edge. I knew something about the place but he told me more which was so much more powerful, sitting in the dust of ages, and that is why I had climbed down.

The Border Cave is famous and rightly so. I saw it featured in a TV documentary in England recently. Although work still goes on, there is no doubt about the continuity of human habitation for at least 60,000 years and floral remains in different strata were radio-carbon dated. Peter Beaumont of the museum in Kimberley, South Africa, who excavated there for several seasons, has proposed that habitation goes back 200,000 years, to the Early Stone-age, but radio-carbon technique doesn't work well that far back even if good materials were available. Estimating by older conventional methods of judging time by depth of deposits and their content have to be used and this leads to the arguments and controversy beloved by professionals and academics. No matter; we were sitting where old Stone-age people had lived for many tens of thousands of years.

I thought that the people who lived here so long ago were as close to the people of Olorgasaillie as the various Bantu people were related to one another. Had they migrated along the same routes, or had geography been too different then? I dug my hand into the dirt of the excavations. Some of the sand and dust that filtered through my fingers had been touched by people at the other side of the last Ice-age! Maybe there was powder from the disintegrated bones of their quarry in my palm. I was filled with awe.

The next day, in brilliant clear sunshine, I walked down the cut-line with my camera gear, so happy to be on my own up there above the world. If I did not look towards the sugar-cane plantations in the valley I was seeing as the Stone-age people saw. The air was still and it was a lovely day.

I found my way to the dreaded rock ledge and was steeling myself to cross when the teen-age working party crashed down to me, each with a heavy rock balanced on his or her head. With a sideways glance at me and while continuing their conversations they trod quickly and surely along the ledge. They would have done well as sailors on the yards of great sailing ships rounding the Horn. What confidence and perfectly coordinated balance! I waited until they had dumped their loads and returned from the cave before making my cautious voyage above the abyss, desperately clutching my camera.

Of course, the clear example of these young Zulus scuttling around on the cliff edge proved that living in that place would be no problem from that point of view, but I had been amazed that people had chosen that cave as a home for many tens of thousands of years when the hunting grounds were so far below them on the plains.

Leonard had described the environment as it was presumed to be over the ups and downs of great weather cycles in the last few hundred millennia and it was sure that the animal bones that had been excavated in the cave had to have been brought up 1,500 feet of difficult climbing from down below. The gathering of roots and herbs and the catching of small creatures would have been done on the summit by the women and children, but the hunting of meat could only happen on the plain.

After thinking about it, I came to two simple conclusions: firstly, here was proof that hunting was always a sporadic activity. Gorging of meat was a luxury procured by considerable time-consuming effort for not only had the quarry to be stalked and felled but the hunters had to descend and then, after an exhausting hunt, the meat had to be carried up. Secondly, following from the first, it showed how different was Stone-age man's sense of time. If it took a half-day to climb down, two or three days to find, kill and butcher the warthog or zebra and a day to haul it back up, then that was unimportant. What was important was that the little clan had a comfortable and aesthetically placed home. I would not mind living there.

When I returned to the top, puffing at the steep slope, I was passed by the teen-age gang, going home and chattering happily with money in their pockets. One of the girls stopped to put on lipstick taken out of a grubby bag hanging about her neck. She stared at me for a moment, contemplating.

"Where do you live?" she asked me. "In Durban?"

"No," I laughed. "Much further away. In England."

Her eyes changed as if she was looking beyond the horizon. "England." She breathed. Then she turned to me, with a bold direct look. "Take me there, with you. I would love that." We both laughed at the enormity of the idea.

In the evenings, we all sat around the fire in that peaceful place, relaxed and at ease in our company. I cooked the evening meals for the hungry men: great meat stews with beans and cracked maize kernels, 'samp' they call it in Natal. I was complimented on the cooking, so I felt that I was not a complete passenger. Leonard, Gordon and I talked of many things: about the follies of historians and archaeologists who do not feel and taste the environments and geography of the peoples they claim to understand. Gordon described his experiences as a conscript in the army and we talked of the narrowness of the military mind. Leonard told of the waste of time and resources caused by European archaeologists attempting field work in Africa without pre-knowledge of the environment they had to tackle. We talked of life and the universe under the stars, beside the fire, in the company of the slow story-telling and quiet laughter of our Zulu friends.

Before we left and after packing up on the last day the men went off to scour the area.

"What on earth are they doing?" I asked Leonard who was waiting patiently by the Landrover.

"They're looking for *muti* to take home. That headman who came by several times showed them where to get different herbs and roots for medicine which they can't find near their homes in the township."

When they came back with black plastic rubbish bags full, we all squatted around to see the collections. All of them had to be chopped and boiled to make infusions and all had been found within a couple of hundred yards of our camp. There were roots and tubers to chase away evil spirits, settle the stomach, cure venereal diseases and inflame sexual passions. A bark removed fevers of the blood. Some very ordinary sticks would 'remove all the shadows from the body'. Looking at the powerful bodies of these Zulu workmen who had lived cheerfully, eaten and slept with me for days on the top of that mountain I thought about the millions of pills prescribed every year to prop up the health of the people of Britain where the National Health Service strained despite the force of billions of pounds of money. What have we done?

When we had packed and were ready to go, Dubé came over to me and delivered a short farewell speech in complicated, flowery language that I could not follow. We clasped hands in the African fashion and my eyes were moist.

Looking out over Swaziland from the interior of Border Cave, home to modern
African Middle Stone Age people for more than 100,000 years.
One of the more important archaeological cave sites anywhere.

NOTE : Since these chapters were written twenty years ago there has been refining of the historiography of the Iron Age in southern Africa and this is reflected in my book, *A Beautiful Ivory Bangle* (2008). Much archeological and historical research has been carried out in those twenty years, but I don't believe what is told here is misleading.

The fishtraps in the Kosi lakes system. A tradition which could be seen all the way down the eastern African coast.

CHAPTER TWENTY FIVE : FISHTRAPS

We descended from the Lebombos and headed east across the Makatini Flats, Tsonga country, after saying farewell to the workmen who were returning to Ulundi in the truck. On the way, we rendezvoused with attractive Catherine, Leonard's wife. She was a teacher at a state school near Ulundi and it was the school holidays.

Leonard drove up to Ngwavuma village to collect Catherine and Gordon and I waited on the concrete bridge spanning the rushing river in the valley below where untended cattle were drinking from the edge of the turbulent brown waters, engorged after the storm. Gordon had been reading Michener's *The Drifters* and we talked of Lamu and the 'hippy' era.

"I've always been struck by the fact that the hippies had to dress in all sorts of outrageous gear and wear long hair and so on," said Gordon. "I don't see that having a kind of uniform and offending the ordinary majority is finding freedom. My generation would like 'freedom' as much as they, but I don't feel that dropping out, trying all the drugs and so on will get it for me."

"You do have the example of the hippies to help you decide," I pointed out. "They were the explorers. But I know what you mean, of course. I suppose the main thing is that the 'freedom' that we are all seeking, even if it is only in imagination, can only be found in the wilderness away from civilised, urban society. Some of the hippy generation knew this and founded rural communes, but most just drifted about in cities following the drugs and music trail. Michener describes the tragedy well."

Gordon was nodding. "Yes, I was thinking about all that up on the Lebombo these last few days, of course. We were 'freer' up there than most contrived hippy groups ever could be. I could do what I liked, after doing the job; run about naked, expand my consciousness in any direction, behave weirdly without upsetting anybody, if I just walked away from our companions. But I felt so relaxed and happy without any of that. The hippies were so visual. They wore hare-krishna gowns, coloured headbands, all that, just making themselves stand out from the crowd. They never learned the simple freedom of wilderness."

I smiled. "No different from a raucous crowd of football fans I suppose who are maybe to-day's hippies, trying to escape the dreariness of urban life. Who will take over from the football fans, I wonder?"

"Those Zulu workers were able to explore their consciousness for hours, just sitting around a campfire, talking to each other." observed Gordon. "In the wilderness, as you say."

Leonard drove a long way round to Kosi Bay, our destination at the ocean, rather than take the direct and less interesting tarred highway. Fourteen years previously, Leonard had been a companion in a group of us who had camped at Kosi Bay and then gone on to explore the Maputo Elephant Reserve in Mocambique and we reminisced about that happy holiday as we drove towards the coast past the Ndumo Game Reserve, well-known for its crocodiles and an especially wide range of bird species over the course of the changing seasons.

The land changed quite abruptly as we left the mountains. Rocky hills changed to flat sandy plain, clumps of palm trees appeared and the riverine forest of fever trees and great figs was decidedly tropical. It was warmer down on the plain leading quickly to the Ocean and the atmosphere in the Landrover had the gaiety of holiday.

We stopped for a picnic beside a beautiful small pan with clear water surrounded by springy green turf and magisterial fever trees. Leonard had a harrowing night there some years ago because of the behaviour of border security guards when he had camped there during a survey and he told the story while we lounged in the quiet sunshine. The Mocambique border was a brisk walk away. "I've not heard of any incidents recently," he reassured us. "Plenty goes on the other side, but very little here, except for the refugees who creep through."

Refugees that could not hide themselves were elephants. Since independence in Mozambique the elephants had been harassed in their reserve north of the border, especially in the last few years when the civil war intensified, so they had moved south into KwaZulu. The Tembe Reserve, closed to the public for the present, had been established beside the popular Ndumo Reserve and the giant animal refugees were kept within their forested area by an electric fence commonly used to control cattle.

"There are about three hundred of them in Tembe," Leonard told us. "And their numbers are slowly growing. Fencing elephants has always been a problem and the electrified cattle fence was an inspired experiment that has worked so far, keeping them away from settled areas." We drove alongside the new reserve for several miles and I was delighted with what I had learned. Apart from the family expedition which Leonard had joined, I had been to the Maputo Reserve three or four times in the early 1970s and had wondered at the elephants' fate.

At Kwa-Ngwanaze we stopped to buy fresh provisions. I vaguely remembered a small trading store, mission hospital and a petrol pump on my previous visit when the village was called Maputa. Leonard explained the change of name. An official reason was to prevent confusion when Lourenço Marques, the capital city of Mozambique about sixty miles to the north, was renamed Maputo after independence, but apparently locals had campaigned because they did not like the name itself as it was associated with the Portuguese slang for a prostitute, *puta*.

We visited the hospital where there was the shop of a Tsonga handicraft centre set up by the KwaZulu authority. "This hospital used to be run by the Star of the Sea Mission," Catherine told me. "It was a good one, subsidised by the South African government. After KwaZulu got autonomy, they 'nationalised' the hospitals and standards have dropped."

"Politicians never learn, do they?" I said. "The same thing happens all over the world. Apart from standards dropping, I bet it costs a great deal more in tax revenue."

But the crafts in the shop were tremendous. Traditional mats and baskets with elaborate patterns in finely woven grass and palm leaf matting in various sizes were mixed in great piles with purpose-designed tourist goods, all made to the same standard of excellence. A young woman explained that the craftsmanship was Tsonga and apart from providing employment and local revenue, it was keeping the traditions alive. I admired the fineness of the work, wandering about in the simple shed, enjoying the faintly sweet vegetable aroma of the goods. I bought some miniature woven grass bowls as presents.

The town supermarket store was another matter. It was a vast new barn, surrounded by some open-air market stalls in African style, and a milling mass of people.

Leonard grinned at my confusion: "It's not like the old Maputa you probably remember."

"It certainly is not," I said, watching the bright, well-dressed crowd. There was a mob at the side of the building from where loud electronic music and voices came.

"What's that?" I asked. "Go and look," said Catherine. I went over and craned over the heads around a big TV set that was fixed to the wall sheltering beneath a little roof. It was playing an endless series of 'boogie' and soul music videos interspersed with advertising plugs that ran for several minutes at a time, most being in the form of a short moral play; the moral naturally being that of using the goods being promoted. I watched one and it was a marvellous little story: well-produced, amusing, with a large cast in three short acts. In each act, the head of the household rejected the boring food that his wife produced every day until her friends introduced her to a branded curry-powder, when the man became electrified by the flavour. The first act told the story in a traditional great chief's kraal, the second in a modern farmer's home and the third in a sophisticated city apartment. The acting was exaggeratedly farcical, especially when the sulky man first tasted the 'new-improved' meal, and the crowd loved it. Many had obviously seen the ads many times before, and I saw the expressions of anticipation on the faces around me as each denouement approached. When the 'boogie' tape came on again, the crowd began to dance, and I joined in for a while, my neighbours laughing and the round faces of well-fed children grinning up at me. Our party had the only White faces in the entire town that afternoon.

Inside the supermarket I was in for another surprise. Apart from the ranges of everyday household goods there was a large area devoted to the hardware needs of people living in remote places: masses of bicycle parts (you could build one with what was there), different paraffin lamps and stoves, and all the parts to repair them, simple tools like pangas and hoes through to everything the carpenter or plumber needed. There was inexpensive clothing for all, the women's fashions obviously geared to local taste in violent colours: turquoise, lemon-yellow, cerise, purple. There were piles of printed *kangas* that I could have found in Kenya or Malawi and I was delighted to see evidence that I was at the cultural border of eastern Africa. Tsongas are the only South Africans who wear them.

292

Women were selecting from mountains of frozen chickens, cheap meat cuts, and packaged fish but there were also frozen fillets of beef and T-bones. There was fresh milk (something you never normally expect in the 'bush' in Africa), ice-cream and cheeses. In an alcove, there were glittering portable music centres, digital watches, calculators, stationery, school books, cassette tapes and Ritmeester cigars. Against one wall there were mountains of packed rice, beans of several types, flour, maize-meal and other cereals. There was every kind of soda drink, long racks of fresh vegetables and fruits and a vast variety of canned meats and vegetables on the crammed shelves.

I walked down the aisles examining the bonanza, thinking of trying to buy any kind of tinned meat in Mombasa and Nairobi. Ye Gods! That supermarket in a remote corner of a Black 'Homeland' in South Africa held more stocks of manufactured consumer goods in greater variety than whole cities in central Africa. And it was not some mad extravagance by the retail chain. The place was packed with shoppers and there were long cheerful lines at the check-outs. Buses and kombi-taxis waited outside. I wandered about quite bemused while Leonard and Catherine waited in line. I thought of the bread-queues and skeleton children in Marxist Mozambique, just fifty miles from where I stood, and felt sick in my stomach about the whole political mess of the continent. What a truly horrendous fate had descended on post-independence Africa. Where was it all going, what hope was there?

"Phew!" exclaimed Catherine outside, wiping her face. "It was quite busy, wasn't it."

"Unbelievable to me," I said.

"Kenya must be just like this?" asked Gordon.

"No, it isn't," I said slowly, still thinking. "Kenya is nothing like this."

Leonard gave me a little ironical smile. "You've forgotten that you are amongst the down-trodden oppressed of White-supremacist South Africa."

"Dear oh dear," I said. "So I am."

*

EXTRACT FROM MY DIARY: 13 July 1988.

Checked in with the Kosi Nature Reserve warden. Between the town and the sea is a wide area of undulating, ancient sand dunes covered with tough grass

293

and scrub bush. In valleys it is lush. We drove along sandy tracks and got a little lost where there is a new fence. Over some heavy dunes, Landie straining. (The authorities have deliberately not made up the tracks to keep casual sightseers away from this important ecological zone). Suddenly we see the Kosi lake system in the late afternoon golden light. The seaward lake is an estuary and the tide is full with the deep green of forested high sand bluffs along the shore behind the lagoon.

I see the FISHTRAPS ! - immaculate lines of closely spaced stakes in the shallow lagoon in intricate, aesthetic patterns designed to corral the fish on the outgoing tide. Wow! These fishtraps are in the style I've seen from Lamu southwards. I've seen them at Zanzibar, Mocambique Island, Inhambane and Delagoa Bay. Here they are at Kosi Bay, at the end of a great long culture chain down the eastern African coast. Leonard stopped so that we can admire them from the high dune and we talked about them and their significance.

Beyond is the blue, blue of the Indian Ocean.

Going down into the valley I caught a glimpse of the water tower at Ponta da Ouro, the small Mozambique town a few miles away on the other side of the border. There is a Mozambican radio mast and observation post on the peak of Monte Ouro, a great dune, marking the border.

Amongst the dune forest there was the guesthouse of the Bureau of Natural Resources where we stay - a pleasant two bedroom bungalow with a large living room with more beds where I shall sleep. Wide verandah on the edge of the lagoon and we sit watching the sunlight fade over the Indian Ocean.

I cooked dinner; ratatouille, mashed potatoes and lots of grilled sausages with a mushroom sauce, all fresh from the supermarket. Pleasant chat afterwards then early to bed.

Awoken at 0034 by thunder that rattled the windows and lay listening. Through the curtainless windows I saw the purple flicker of lightning and went out to the verandah to see it. But the little tropical storm was far away over the ocean and the 'thunder' came in clear shocks equally spaced. I could not understand it and went back to bed. At irregular intervals, but in regular groups, the sounds were repeated: "Wump! .. wump! .. wump!" The windows and doors rattled gently. Out on the verandah again, the lightning had ceased out at sea and I walked round the house in the magical starlight. The noises were coming from the north, from Ponta da Ouro. It was gunfire! Dear God!

Couldn't sleep and lay anticipating each next series of shocks. They sounded like mortars. Dozed off then woke again to hear faint scratching sounds which had to be automatic rifles. Then came sharper detonations:

"blam-blam! .... blam! .... blam-blam-blam!! .... Bloing!" I sat up in bed, my skin crawling. That was the sound of tank or armoured-car cannon fire. More scratching noises, then silence. I slept uneasily as dawn approached and had a vivid dream about Russian sailors in immaculate white uniforms, armed with shiny AK 47's, swarming through the bungalow and herding us off somewhere.

I walked about in the warming sunlight of early morning, watching the peacefulness of lagoon, forested bluffs and the ocean beyond the white line of foam from breakers on the golden beach. My eyes were raspy from the sleepless night, but had I dreamed it all? The caretaker was making up the fire for hot bath-water at the back and I greeted him. He was Tsonga so we spoke in pidgin-Zulu.

"I heard thunder in the night," I said.

He nodded gravely and pointed to the north. "Yes, it was from Mozambique."

"There was much shooting, for a long time. I could not sleep."

He smiled. "When you know it well, then you sleep without trouble."

"Do you hear it often?" I asked.

He shook his head: "Not often. Last night was a heavy one."

The others were congregating for coffee when I went in. "The Mozambique civil war was very close last night," I observed and they looked at me with puzzled faces.

"Didn't you hear the guns?" But they hadn't, and I had to assume that because their bedrooms faced the other way the noise had not been loud enough to penetrate healthy tiredness. I sat out on the verandah with my coffee thinking of the desperate skirmish in the night. I supposed RENAMO rebels must have attacked a government post at Ponta da Ouro and eventually an armoured vehicle had been summoned which drove them off. From where we were in peace and comfort, it was an easy walk up the beach to the unmarked and unguarded border beyond which life could be an everyday gamble. It was a most eerie feeling. How many young men were dead or mutilated this morning, not far from me, in an incident that would not be reported in newspapers anywhere? If it had happened in South Africa it would be on the BBC news.

That morning we were to carry out an informal search around a small freshwater lake, KuZilonde, lying in a valley behind the coastal dunes. Leonard brought out a detailed 1:50,000 survey map to brief us. "My word," I exclaimed. "That little lake actually crosses the border and is directly underneath the post on Monte Ouro. Is it wise?"

"After your battle in the night?" Leonard said thinking, then shook his head. "The local authority know that we are here and what I'm doing. The police would stop us if it was dangerous. Anyway, I expect the Mozambique military will be having beers and a good sleep after the excitement."

He went on to explain what he was looking for and how we would walk in extended line over the ground searching for pottery, animal bones or artifacts of any kind. Graves were always marked by pots and there would be marks on the ground where huts once stood. In similar country to the south, in the immediate hinterland of St.Lucia Lake, Early Iron-age sites from around 350 AD had been found where those early 'coastal stream' people had cleared land for cereals and fished in the shallow lake system. 'Fishtraps', I thought to myself.

We climbed in the Landrover and drove to the foot of Monte Ouro along a faint track.

*

EXTRACT FROM MY DIARY: 14 July 1988

Lovely coastal bush at foot of richly forested dune, grinding northwards expecting to be stopped by swampy ground but there is wider separation than the ordnance survey map suggested. Soon saw the tower on the top of Monte Ouro and turned west onto a low eminence and stopped. By the Landie was the first and best find - a pile of pots on a mound, probably a grave. Leonard pleased with them which had clear 19th century markings.

Spread out and combed up to the border fence, a double width of high mesh and barbed wire. Several bits of pottery, glass and rusted metal bowls found and I picked up a sherd with marking. Stood at border fence, thinking of the guns the night before. I photographed it and the tower, feeling vulnerable, but there were no soldiers anywhere in sight. On the next dune inland the grass on the Mocambique side is lawn-like and virginal whilst on the South African side there are several cattle trails and shrubs growing where old huts used to be - evidence of people. There is an old trading store still occupied just within South Africa with washing hanging on a line. Walked to the lake, a beautiful stretch of clean, clear water fringed by reeds, papyrus and some tall fig trees. Closer to it we found hippo tracks and fresh dung. Later we heard their powerful grunting. Leonard said there were crocs there too. The local peasant farmers were moved out about 20 years ago when the area was prepared for a nature reserve. It's a magical place close to the border and the ocean, but by turning around I could look at the military post up on the summit and be reminded of cannon-fire in the night.

We found some more old pottery and several intact bottles: Roses' Lime Juice made in Hong Kong [jetsam from a passing ship?], sand-blasted blue glass 'Liquid Fruit Essence, S.Bush & Co. London [possibly 100 years old], Borges Brandy [Portuguese], Sharwoods Chutney, 'Union Whiskey - Produce of .....' [possibly American or Indian] and plain ones without moulded names.

Combed back along the shore of the lake feeling so privileged to be there. Found evidence of two family settlements with sites of huts still quite clear amongst the new growth. Nearby were raised vegetable patches exactly as I had seen at Inhambane some years ago in which tomatoes, groundnuts or beans would be grown. When I remarked on this, Leonard told me that the coastal Tsonga people around Kosi traditionally build square reed huts which I also remember from Inhambane. He would show me some. Hippos grunting again, saw coucals and a fish eagle.

Climbing over a low line of ancient dune, Gordon found a burial mound with intact pottery which Leonard carefully excavated to photograph. One was a bowl with a very clear sea-shell decoration [Tsonga are sea-oriented unlike the Nguni], the other had rim decoration suggesting 19th century style. All the pottery in the area must have been traded because there is no clay nearer than the Pongola River, 30-40 miles away.

NEXT DAY, 15th July ..... We drove around to the western side of the small lake to the trading store. It was locked and closed. What a pleasant outlook from its verandah over the lake and onto the forest of the high dune. Nearby were Tsonga square reed huts, strongly built with decorated doorways, with small gardens of manioc, maize and beans around them, just like the abandoned ones on the other side of the lake. Drove on a track to the border fence where there was an unlocked gate! On the South African side there was a small reed hut and a two-man army tent and on the Mozambique side a rusting metal 'portacabin', probably from Eastern Europe. These were the security posts and both were deserted. All so 'African'! Leonard said that he had heard that Mozambique soldiers and their friends sneaked through there to buy consumer goods at the trading store and the South Africans turned a blind eye.

Found women doing laundry by the side of the lake and they later asked for a lift to the main road. They crammed themselves in with a big

297

mpahla (parcel of goods). I realised it was the week-end, that's why the store was closed. Passing through the Nature Reserve gate we found that a security guard had appeared, the first I had seen in all these border areas since leaving Ulundi. He was a tall, slim bearded Black man wearing dark glasses and a dark beret. He looked very menacing but spoke with a quiet, gentle voice. Found ourselves on a different track and reached the 'Star of the Sea' mission complex : pleasant old colonial buildings and decorative exotic trees, jacarandas and monkey-puzzles.

Leonard was pleased with the brief survey we had done of the area. Of course, we had not found an Early Iron-age site, it would have been an extraordinary piece of luck during such a cursory examination, but the seashell bowl and one of the pots were sufficiently valued for their photographs to make a useful contribution to his museum collection. They were not removed because they were on graves.

Leonard spent the rest of that day plotting his map and writing his notes. Gordon went swimming and I wandered the deserted ocean beach, dreaming of 'aquatic men' and 'coastal stream' rovers. The waves thundered in to break on the wide sandy beach in great smothers of spray and foam and the salt haze misted the high dunes in the light of the lowering sun. I sat watching the sea and thinking of the journeys I had made in the last year and feeling soft and nostalgic.

A soft drumming engine-sound caught my attention and for a second I had a thrill of fear. I could not forget the battle I had heard two nights previously. But it was a small diesel-driven coasting ship, wallowing in the heavy swell, quite close to shore to escape the fast south going ocean current of this part of eastern Africa. I watched it pass by and waved to a speck standing on the bridge. It flew the South African flag and I supposed it was carrying much-needed goods to Maputo in Delagoa Bay.

The coasting ship broke the mood and I wandered back around the lagoon. I remembered 'Bushybaby' in Lamu telling me that coasting ships were no more in East Africa. The tide was higher and I had to walk close to the mangrove-fringed shore and so I came across a fisherman's camp hidden in the shelter of the thick vegetation. There was a square reed house, lines strung between branches on which to hang fish to dry, log ends to use as chairs on the well-swept little yard and a dug-out canoe drawn up away from the tide. It was a timeless sight. I could have been standing there at any time in the last centuries. The only clue to the present was a rusty padlock on the door of the hut, and I pretended that I could not see it.

298

The next day was devoted to a holiday and Leonard and Gordon brought out snorkels and wet suits to dive on the two reefs, one off the point and one in the channel of the lagoon. There was live coral offshore, some of the southernmost tropical coral in the whole world. I thought of sitting on the jahazi dhow off Wasini Island and contemplating the great African coral reef; here I was at the furthest end. I walked around the lagoon and found two teen-age boys with the most elaborate 'wire cars', driving them about the rippled hard sand where the tide was out. The cars had ingenious sprung wheels and efficient steering from the long guiding wire. The boys were shy, as all teenagers are when caught in 'childish' games, but I complimented them on the engineering and they explained the construction of their vehicles. They went off making soft "brrrrm-brrrm" noises. A fish-eagle screamed.

It was a lovely afternoon. Later I saw samanga monkeys in the forest, much rarer than vervets, the only other southern African species.

The mouth at Kosi Bay, where the water flows into the Indian Ocean from the series of freshwater lagoons. This is a typical geographical feature of the coast from south of Durban as far as Sofala and the Pungwe River in Mozambique. At Kosi the pristine wilderness was preserved within the Nature Reserve. Elsewhere, holiday homes and retirement complexes steadily invade the natural beauty.

A Griqua man and his daughter, descendants of the indigenous Khoi-Khoi, in the Graaff Reinet district on the way to the end of Africa.

CHAPTER TWENTY SIX : THE END OF AFRICA.

The humming of the car's engine and the rumble of the wheels on the tarred road stretching directly out of sight over the flat plain was soporific and I turned up the volume of the radio. Miriam, who was dozing, stirred.

"Were my eyes resting?" she asked, sleepily. "These straight roads for mile after mile across the Karoo can be very boring."

The southwest corner of Africa almost exactly mirrors Morocco and Algeria in the northwest corner. The rain falls in the winter when it is cool at 35° latitude and often very cold at altitude. The Atlas Mountains of northwest Africa and the great folded ranges of the Cape of Good Hope rise to over six thousand feet and are often snow covered. The Karoo, across which we were driving, is a great upland plain of semi-desert: part of the endless African plateau, but because of the reversal of the rainy season the flora is quite different to that of tropical Africa. It is a Mediterranean scene of low aromatic bushes with small tough leaves that can survive the bone-dry heat of long summers and the cold of winter. Grasses are spare and hardy too, and trees are rare except in the shelter of valleys or along the coast between the mountains and the sea where impenetrable forests grew.

We were on our way in a southwesterly direction across the centre of South Africa, heading for the end of Africa. After a while we climbed into some mountains that had gradually appeared on our right hand. The map told me that they were called the *Renosterberge*, Rhinoceros Mountains, but the rhinos were long gone from there. Dark grey and purple clouds raced over the summits and fierce squalls shook the car. Rounding a jutting bulwark of mountain we ran into snow, thick flakes swirling around us. I switched on the headlights and turned up the heater.

301

Bantu farmers had never penetrated this region because the climate could not sustain their sorghum grains, yams and vegetables that they brought from the tropical lands. When White men ventured north from Cape Town into this region in the 18th century, they encountered San-Bushman hunter-gatherers in tiny scattered bands and Khoi-Khoi nomadic herders in larger clans who carefully husbanded their long-horned cattle and fat-tailed sheep on huge ranges of arid territory. These people had to keep within easy distance of water.

The White settlers of this region, who have come to be called Afrikaners, were of 17th century European peasant stock and pretty tough otherwise they could not have survived. They also relied on huge ranges to husband their stock and lived a domestic lifestyle not so very dissimilar to that of the Stone-age Khoi-Khoi. But they had the wheel and horses, and guns to hunt with, and they read their Bibles and believed in a stern European Calvinistic creed. And whereas the Khois moved in self-supporting clans across the land, taking their hemispherical hide huts and simple belongings with them on their pack-oxen, the Afrikaners settled in rough family homesteads miles apart from each other and travelled with waggons.

The Bushmen and Khoi-Khoi were of old Africa, descended from people from the mists of time, mixed with later trickling migrations southwards over thousands of years. The last of these migrations to mix their genes and culture in the southwest were those who brought cattle and sheep, sometime in the last 2,000 years. The same people probably exchanged these animals with Bantu farmers to the east of the Karoo, often through mutual cattle-raiding. In later centuries those Bantu were of the Sotho-Tswana tribal groups whose ancestors most probably came southwards from Zambia and Zimbabwe, down the centre of the continent.

The 'Coloured' people of the Cape were second-class citizens [in 1989 when this was written] within the racial categories defined in South Africa's political system, with their own separate elected parliament whose leaders share in some central policy-making and there are elected Coloured local government authorities. But the Coloured people are not homogenous, they are not a 'race'. They are an exciting mix of peoples, with a wide spectrum of genetic and cultural ancestry. In different parts of the Cape, this ancestry or that is more or less pronounced. I find them to be a most attractive people, full of ancient mysteries and underdeveloped talents and their numbers are growing in a virile society which overcame near

302

extinction in small-pox and measles epidemics in the 18th century. Some see them as the most charming of all Africa's peoples.

They are southern Africa's equivalent of the Aborigines of Australia, because the most prominent of their ancestors were the ancient Khoisan. In some parts, Coloured communities may be almost pure Khoi-Khoi, especially in the Karoo and Namaqualand, because miscegenation with White and Black mostly occurred in Cape Town and its vicinity or in the northeast where their traditional lands were invaded by the Bantu tribes. I admire their distinctive apricot coloured faces and the soft skins of their youth, which led the earliest travellers to think that they were migrants from Mongolia whose appearance they eerily resemble. But the contrast with the parlous state of contemporary Australian Aborigines' social well-being is stark.

Somewhere along the path of history in South Africa the Coloureds were able to take an upward path of expansion and evolution whereas the opposite occurred in Australia and North America. The Coloureds were not forced to live in 'Reservations' like the Aborigines or the native-American 'Indians'. Maybe this was what turned them from potential extinction to virility: instead of being segregated into psychically miserable groups away from the mainstream, they became clients to the Afrikaners and thrived.

So, there is a strange paradox: 19th century 'apartheid' in the US, Canada and Australia degraded the aboriginal races whereas in South Africa their equivalents surge ahead in numbers, ethnic creativity and political power. Attitudes in the West towards South Africa have prevented a proper understanding and study of these successful modern descendants of one of the world's Neolithic cultures that jumped into the Industrial period without a sojourn in the Iron-age.

The *Sunday Telegraph* carried a report on the present state of the Navajo Indians in the US on 7th May 1989:

> Few Navajo households have running water, electricity or a telephone. .... It is easy to forget that this is America. Many white Americans are happy to do just that, in spite of the legacy of national shame that surrounds the historic maltreatment of the Indians by successive governments of the United States. The self-esteem of the Navajo nation, already wracked with poverty, disease and social turmoil, has been further undermined by a political scandal threatening to split the tribe in two and cripple its independent government.

The Coloured people of South Africa seemed rather better off in every way than the Aborigines and native-Americans; even politically since they had an elected national legislative chamber with multi-party activity in classic Westminster style with representation and certain powers of veto in Central Government. We had entered lands where the Coloureds were in the majority.

[NOTE : After South Africa obtained a new constitution with universal franchise in 1994, the ANC government notoriously encouraged migrations of their supporting Xhosa-speaking people into the Western Cape with the aim of swamping the vote of Coloureds and Whites. In 2007 this game was still being played out, but one of the consequences was the growth of enormous shanty towns with high levels of unemployment, drug-induced violent crime and gang warfare in what had been a peaceful province, the most culturally integrated and sophisticated part of sub-Saharan Africa.]

In the chill aftermath of the snowstorm, Miriam and I neared the remote town of Graaff-Reinet, driving down a long valley towards a clump of high hills in bright winter sunshine. We quickly found the municipal tourist resort and hired a cottage from the Coloured supervisor for the equivalent of £6.00 a night. It had bedrooms, bathroom and a kitchen-livingroom and looked over the camping terrain and a river flanked by weeping-willow trees onto the orange-golden rocks of a high cliff. A pair of black eagles soared. Around our cottage aloes and other desert succulents were planted amongst chunks of crystalline boulders. In spring time, the Namaqualand daisies would be out all around in multicoloured glory. The cottage had a simple square Cape-Georgian facade with louvred green shutters for the summer. It was typical of the Cape and I was happy to have found it.

In the morning we went exploring. Graaff-Reinet was founded in 1786 by the Dutch colonial authorities, in a great loop of the Sundays River beneath the mountains that surround it, to administer the far northern frontier district of the Cape colony. The 18th and 19th century town was contained in the loop, so it had kept most of its original style and atmosphere. The church was quite spectacular, a blue-grey and white stone Scottish-gothic structure appealing to the sky in vertical lines. The Reverend Andrew Murray founded a famous Presbyterian ministry to the Dutch Reformed Church in the town, and there are a number of stylish and well-preserved early 19th century buildings. Streets are filled with houses registered as historical monuments. I admire Graaff-Reinet because it is a living museum of those early colonial days.

After some sightseeing in the several museums, we entered the Drostdy Hotel for coffee. This old hostelry had been superbly restored by the Rembrandt tobacco and liquor conglomerate. There is a particular charm and beauty to Cape colonial architecture and style whose uniqueness has been rightly admired by visitors for a century and more. The gabled Flemish styles of the 18th century and the squared simplicity of English Georgian were adapted superbly at the Cape to its Mediterranean climate. Local stone or rough-cured brick walls were always plastered and limewashed. Floors were polished stone, tile or broad planked hardwoods. Beamed ceilings were high and the windows large. The furniture was heavy and simple, well crafted by Malays brought from Dutch Indonesia. Much of the table-ware and decorations came from China. The Cape never experienced the extravagant wealth of the plantation-slave economies of Brazil, the Caribbean or the southern States of the USA, but arguably it may have developed the most gently elegant of European colonial cultures in its modest and quiet way.

We sat at a table on the lawn in the courtyard at the back of the Drostdy Hotel, surrounded by flower beds being tended by a slow, elderly gardener. A brisk and cheerful young woman served us excellent filtered coffee, buttered scones and honey. Cape laughing doves filled the air with their distinctive African calls and the sun shone warmly from a deep blue sky. We talked amiably and without much direction. It was an hour to savour and treasure.

That evening I was drawn back and after admiring prints of old watercolours and maps in the lounge and diningroom, I led the way into the bar. It was a rectangular, cosy room with a fire glowing at one end. The counter was highly polished wood and solid chairs and tables ran along the wall opposite. A dignified, middle-aged Coloured barman presided and I asked him for something typically of the Cape as an aperitif. I suppose that I expected a sherry or vermouth-style drink. But he took his time looking us over and brought down a bottle from high on his shelves.

"I want you to try this," he said. "If you don't like it, you won't pay and I'll let you make your own choice."

I nodded, and he poured a little of a rich golden-ruby drink into sherry glasses. I took a sip, still thinking I was going to taste something different in Cape sherries. But it wasn't sherry, it was a superbly mature muscatel, a truly typical Cape fortified wine, much neglected. The nearest equivalent in Europe is probably an old Madeira.

"My word," I said. "You decided absolutely correctly." He grinned his pleasure. "Now," I went on, "We must have a proper glass."

We sat by the fire, glowing from its heat and the warmth of the fine wine. While reminiscing about other days I remembered a drink that we used to have when I was much younger and had not thought about in years. "You'll drive back?" I asked Miriam. "I'm going to indulge myself."

The barman reached for his special bottle when I went up to the bar but I shook my head. "No, I don't wish to spoil that fine Muscatel with a second glass. I'll have a rougher version if you've got it and a cheap brandy. Mix them half-and-half in a big wine glass."

"You've been in the Cape before," he said grinning at me. "That's an old-fashioned mix I don't often get asked for. I've drunk it often myself when we were kids; when we could afford it. Mind you, it only cost a shilling or two, but that was a lot in those days."

"I was in Cape Town in 1951. You giving me that fine muscatel reminded me." He nodded and poured the mixture.

"*Gesondheid!*" I toasted him and sipped at it: it had a suddenly well-remembered rounded flavour; the harshness of the young brandy softened by the sweetness of the wine, the excess fruitiness of the grape overshadowed by the dryness of the brandy. It burned in the depths of my stomach and my eyes watered. He was watching me and his eyes crinkled. "Good memories, hey?" We smiled at each other.

"I was in the Navy then," I said. "We were kids then too. Four pounds ten shillings a month was our pay."

"*Ja-a-a,*" he drawled. "They were the good old days..."

"And now?"

He lifted his hands."I can't complain. My life is good."

"Have you always lived here?" I asked.

"*Nee*, I come from Worcester in the Boland and Graaff-Reinet seemed such a long way away in those days." He smiled. "Really in the *bundu*, you know? But this is a nice town when you are getting on. It's quiet."

The next morning we stopped to take photographs in one of the main streets. We walked along the pavement, looking at the rows of simple Victorian bungalows. Each had a verandah, *stoep* they call them, many with the distinctive curved corrugated iron lean-to roof of the Cape (there must have been a factory in Glasgow or

Birmingham which made them specially). All had that other trade-mark: small square windows tilted through 45° so they become 'diamond-shaped'. On the stoeps there were ferns and pot-plants, cane furniture or old wood-framed settees with hide strip mesh seats, dressed with patchwork cushions. Elaborate wooden or iron fretwork decorated the facades of some. In my imagination, I could see women in voluminous skirts and tight bodices wearing be-ribboned bonnets and men in moleskin trousers, long-cut jackets and wide felt hats, parading to church; and an ox-waggon trundling past, raising the dust.

From Graaff-Reinet we headed on southwestwards, onwards across the Karoo plains, seldom seeing another vehicle, the small towns forty to sixty miles apart.

Between the Karoo and the Indian Ocean there are high folded ranges of mountains that cut off much of the moist air from the interior and as you cross each range, the vegetation softens until great forests fill the land along the shore. In the 17th century, these forests were another barrier to the Black people's westward and Cape Afrikaner's eastward migrations and so the coastal strip was settled later than the interior. Areas of indigenous forest are still preserved within which there are a few of the unique Cape forest elephants, but most of that zone has been sadly converted to pine plantations.

We stopped for lunch at Uniondale, a sleepy town in a valley between these rugged ranges. We bought hamburgers and cartons of milk from a pretty Coloured girl with apricot skinned face and wandered to the car, wondering where to eat. Rearing above the town was a conical hill with a pimple on the top and a track leading to it.

"We'll try for that," I decided.

On top we found that the pimple was a National Monument with a plaque that told us that it was a fort built by the British to command the valley during the Anglo-Boer War. The circular building was constructed of dry stone walling, ten feet high with firing embrasures all around at a convenient height. It was open to the sky, but probably had a thatch or iron roof in those days. It stood on the pinnacle where some wind-torn scrub trees had struggled to grow beside it. Flowering heathers and heaths covered the ground all about. Miriam found some bright little flowers.

From the eminence I stared down at the little town below, its long straggling main street lined by old-fashioned shops and some of the typical Cape colonial bungalows with curved roofs over the stoeps and diamond windows. Further out on the one side were a few modern suburban bungalows and on the other side of town were a huddle of square cottages with little vegetable patches housing the Coloured community. The thin winter sun bathed the landscape, and beyond the town the bleak Karoo receded into the pale misty distance. The air was sharp and flavoured by the tingling aroma of the heath. I munched on my delicious hamburger prepared by the pretty girl, so different to the mechanical production of a city 'take-away', and thought about that terrible war that had nearly destroyed the Afrikaner eighty seven years previously.

In our ever-faster moving, media-dominated world with its superficial commentators, the Boer War is often viewed as a curiosity. But in South Africa the trauma is still sharp. The inevitable military defeat of the Boer armies, the massive and deliberate scorched-earth policy of destruction of their rural communities developed by General Lord Kitchener in the bitter and prolonged guerilla phase of the war when 300,000 British troops pursued three or four Boer commandoes, the deaths of 50,000 Afrikaner women and children and their Coloured servants in British Concentration Camps and the humiliation of British mastery after decades of struggle for liberation from colonialism are deep wounds that don't go away easily.

The endless rhetoric about Apartheid fails to recognise that Afrikaners began their own liberation struggle 150 years ago. Much of the psychology of the Afrikaner's political psyche is influenced by the stress of the Boer War and their determination never to be dominated again. That Afrikaner success in achieving political power in the 1950s became grossly perverted by the Apartheid racial doctrine and will stain Afrikaner honour for decades to come is terribly sad, but the deepest reasons for that perversion were laid down in the humiliation and degradation of their resounding defeat in the Boer War. Strife will not heal those wounds, only time can heal the hurt that the Afrikaners feel and the terrible hurt that they have since caused in the hearts of their Black and Coloured fellow-countrymen.

Looking down on the peaceful little town and the vast emptiness of the mountains and desert beyond I felt an ache for another piece of Africa that needs understanding, sympathy and support rather than imposed ideas and force from Europe and North America. Whereas Black African nations desperately need a rest from the monstrous pressures of Western technology and ideologies in order to find their own paths into the future, South Africa needs time for its peoples to heal their mutually inflicted wounds without old scars being constantly torn open by ill-informed foreign critics. Will we ever stop worrying at Africa like a pack of schoolyard bullies teasing a handicapped newcomer? I fear not: our hypocritical arrogance and our own immaturity is too great.

"It's so lovely in its stark beauty," said Miriam. "Look at the colours on that mountain; browns, greys and rusty colours."

"Yes, it is," I said, still thinking sombre thoughts. "Very lonely too... And this old fort is so sad."

The Natal *Daily News* of 23 November 1988 quoted Sir Laurens van der Post in an interview following his 82nd birthday:

> Black and white people everywhere were awakening to the realisation that there were no political solutions. It was as if they were deciding: let us live our lives into the solution. They must change. And they must live the change in their own lives. I believe that the whole of South Africa would have blown up a long time age if personal relationships had not already been so good - unlike, say, in the United States.

I have long believed that bad race relations in America, relentlessly portrayed in news, films, TV features and books, where almost all Blacks are descended from slaves, has cast an evil cloud over South Africa. The clear vision that people have of racial confrontation and mutual disrespect in America is wrongly translated to South Africa which has a different history of quite different people.

*

From the top of the Outeniqua Pass the Indian Ocean was spread across the southern horizon, a great pale blue-grey sheet in the late afternoon.

We stayed in a wooden chalet at the edge of the sea in Mossel Bay with a view across the wide bay backed by the Outeniqua Mountains, rising to 3,500 feet in the distance. An oil-drilling platform stood in the bay, but it was far enough away not to be too annoying; in fact in the dawn light its spidery structure was aesthetically pleasing.

Eric Axelson in *Portuguese in South-East Africa 1488-1600* wrote:

> The pilots steered eastwards and found no land - they had unconsciously rounded the African continent. They altered course to the north and encountered the coast off the mouth of a river, on the banks of which there were herds of cattle,

watched over by herdsmen: the river accordingly received the name of dos Vaqueiros. Unable to land, the caravels coasted eastwards, round a cliffy cape, into a bay which, since the day was 3 February [1488], Dias named after São Bras, Saint Blaize, and which Netherlanders were later to call Mossel Bay. Here the Portuguese landed and took in fresh water.

From the window of our chalet I could stare my fill at the place where the first European ships since the Romans entered the Indian Ocean and dropped anchor exactly five hundred years before. Dias' exploration led the way for Vasco da Gama, who died in Cochin. My safari around the western Indian Ocean shores was coming to its end.

We visited the newly completed maritime museum which would house the exact replica of Bartolomeo Dias' caravel, which had been built in Portugal and sailed out by enthusiasts to commemorate the quincentenary of the epic voyage. What followed from Dias' voyage, more heroic than anything undertaken by Columbus, was not the Dutch settlement of the Cape, which occurred over 160 years later, but the European invasion of the Indian Ocean and the establishment of trading colonies on the Indian sub-continent and the islands of Indonesia. That was the historical importance of Mossel Bay.

From our touring base above the beach at Mossel Bay we drove, one warm sunny day, along the motorway westwards, past country towns with names reflecting 18th and 19th century settler history: Albertinia, Riversdale, Heidelberg, Buffelsjagsrivier and Swellendam, seat of the magistracy administering the coastal border area in 1747. I felt a slow tremor of excitement starting within me. We were heading for the end of Africa, at Cape Agulhas.

*

The road headed south through green fields of winter wheat away from the mountains. We went through a market town, Bredasdorp, somnolent at noonday, and the land became flat and featureless for a while. We passed an old pick-up truck with Coloured youths clinging on the back who grinned and waved when I smiled at them. There was marshy ground and Miriam exclaimed at herons, plovers and the stately stalking of Stanley's bustards on fringing grass fields. A low bare ridge grew slowly on the right hand and a few miles further on we reached the sea, pounding whitely on a rocky shore. The road swung westwards to follow the shoreline and, at the end of the ridge that we now approached, the column of Cape Agulhas lighthouse with broad red and white bands came into view. I slowed the car.

"The end of Africa," I breathed reverently and Miriam grinned at me.

A track of crushed shell and white sand continued where the tarmac finished and that ceased eventually in the lee of a great grey boulder the size of a small cottage. We stopped and got out. The air was filled with the moist salt tang of cold sea and seaweed. A small concrete beacon was set into rock at the head of a narrow beach of shell and shingle where small waves hissed.

The beacon had survey numbers on it: it marked the southernmost point of Africa

*

We were a long way from Cape Cormorin or Malindi. I couldn't see any coconut palms in my sight which was suddenly blurred.

Agulhas, at the end of Africa.

314

African Insight

www.sondela.co.uk

Text for the first edition was completed in 1989 at Belmont, Lancashire.
Published in 1992 by Malvern Publishing Company.
Revised, edited and reformatted in 2007 and 2008.